Han Urban Services

Handbook of
Urban
Services
A Basic Guide for
Local Governments

Charles K. Coe

Routledge
Taylor & Francis Group

LONDON AND NEW YORK

First published 2009 by M.E. Sharpe

Published 2015 by Routledge
2 Park Square, Milton Park, Abingdon, Oxon OX14 4RN
711 Third Avenue, New York, NY 10017, USA

Routledge is an imprint of the Taylor & Francis Group, an informa business

Library of Congress Cataloging-in-Publication Data

Coe, Charles K.
  Handbook of urban services : a basic guide for local governments / by Charles K. Coe.
    p. cm.
  Includes bibliographical references and index.
  ISBN 978-0-7656-2293-8 (cloth : alk. paper)—ISBN 978-0-7656-2294-5 (pbk.   )
  1. Municipal services—United States—Handbooks, manuals, etc. 2. Municipal officials
and employees—United States—Handbooks, manuals, etc. 3. Metropolitan government—
United States—Handbooks, manuals, etc. 4. Metropolitan government—Officials and
employees—United States—Handbooks, manuals, etc. 5. County government—United
States—Handbooks, manuals, etc. 6. County officials and employees—United States—
Handbooks, manuals, etc. I. Title.

HD4431.C55 2009
352.16—dc22   2008033385

ISBN 13: 9780765622945 (pbk)
ISBN 13: 9780765622938 (hbk)

Contents

Preface

The spark for this book memorably started that summer day in 1969 when I began my career in city management. Armed with a newly minted master's degree in public administration, I began my work as an administrative assistant to the city manager of Grand Rapids, Michigan, which then had a population of 205,000. My graduate work had included courses in human resource management, budgeting, policy analysis, research methods, and statistics. However, the program taught me little about the urban services that cities and counties provide. The assumption then, as now, was that I would have the opportunity to learn about these functions on-the-job. Understandably, I felt somewhat apprehensive and daunted. For the first two years, I completed several specialized projects, which afforded me little opportunity to learn about services like police, fire, and public works. Judging that I needed a marketable skill, I transferred to the Budget Office, working as a budget analyst and then the budget officer. During this four-year period, I applied for numerous jobs as a manager in a small town or an assistant manager in a mid-sized town. I was, however, unable to land a job, principally because of my limited hands-on working experience, especially in the field of public works. In 1975, I turned my career in a different direction, serving as a management consultant to local governments in Georgia at the Carl Vinson Institute of Government, University of Georgia. There I had the opportunity to write numerous manuals and handbooks on such topics as risk management, cash management, purchasing, safety programs, volunteer fire departments, and contracting for professional services.

Since my work in Georgia, I have spent twenty-five years as a teacher and researcher at North Carolina State University in its MPA program. Many of my students, like their compatriots at other MPA programs, aim to become a city or county manager. They are a diverse lot. Many are fresh from undergraduate work and have no governmental experience. Others are working in large local units, usually in departmental staff positions, and complete the program on a part-time basis. Some are state employees wishing to switch to local government.

Unless they have hands-on working experience, landing a job in city management has proven problematic for many of these students. Full-time students must complete a local government internship, which though valuable, is often a specialized assignment, not exposing them to the breadth of local government functions. Like most MPA programs, we offer a course in urban politics and administration, but it does not cover urban services in detail. This book aims to help students seeking a career in local government management learn about the broad spectrum of urban services that they soon may oversee.

A second intended audience is elected officials. Each year, literally hundreds of thousands of local elected officials serve with honor, distinction, and at considerable personal sacrifice. Many come to office with excellent management skills grounded in private sector experience, but few have the requisite knowledge about urban services to make truly informed policy decisions. City and county managers fill in the gap, helping newly elected governing board members gain a knowledge base. This book will help elected officials to shorten their learning curve.

A third audience is the reporters who cover local government. The press is an indispensable partner in the effective delivery of urban services, informing the public about current issues and the accomplishments of city and county governments, and facilitating the democratic process. However, most local government reporters, like students and governing board members, have little or no knowledge of city and county services before they are assigned to a city or county beat. City and county managers thus expend considerable effort "educating" the press as well.

This book will not make its reader an expert. Indeed, each chapter refers the reader to materials that cover the particular service in far greater detail. Its purpose, instead, is to lay a sound foundation upon which the reader can pursue follow-up questions: to make the reader "dangerous," if you will. The book might be considered a CliffsNotes study guide to local government management. It simplifies complex processes and explains technical jargon, which is peculiar to each profession and often confusing to the nonspecialist.

A whale's gestation period is over two years. This book's has taken considerably longer—over ten years. During that period, numerous professionals have kindly given me feedback. Among them are Trey Mayo, Cal Horton, David Ammons, Russell Allen, Rob Bonne, Tim Woody, Del Borgsdorf, Michelle Wells, Jerry Williams, and Sylvester Daughtry. Three classes of students who have used the book also deserve my appreciation. They went into the field to observe and describe practices like filling a pothole, tapping a waterline, and cleaning a sewer. They toured waterworks, sewage plants, and fire stations and rode along with police officers. They interviewed department heads to compare the practices in this book to those in the field. Many of their experiences and observations have been incorporated into this work.

Handbook of
Urban
Services

1

Introduction

The life of a city or county manager is never dull. Successful managers must be diplomats, coaches, mediators, leaders, psychologists, and team players. They interact with the widest spectrum of the community: governing board members, their staff, happy and disgruntled citizens, other governments, developers, and neighborhood groups, to name but a few. Managers make a host of decisions daily. Some are easy "no-brainer" choices; others, though, require the wisdom of Solomon. Like elected officials, managers know too well that they cannot please everyone all of the time. The rewards, however, are great: a paved road in a dusty neighborhood; a new community center; neighborhood groups reducing crime hand in hand with police officers; volunteer firefighters responding to emergencies; potable, high-quality water; disease prevention; a thriving recreation program; sanitary restaurants; and a bonded community.

Managers face the challenge and reward of working with a wide range of professional specializations, each of which has its own jargon, norms, history, and practices. Engineers design public facilities and manage public-works services like road construction and maintenance, water and sewer treatment, and refuse collection. Planners guide development, zoning, and capital construction. Public-safety professionals prevent crime and fires and respond to crime-related, fire-related, and natural-disaster emergencies. Librarians operate libraries. Recreation specialists manage programs and facilities such as pools, community centers, and parks. To lead this diverse professional team, a successful manager must be a jack of all trades.

A brief history explains the evolving role of the urban manager. After the Civil War, the Industrial Revolution caused unprecedented population growth in cities as manufacturing plants located near urban services such as water supplies, sewers, and roads. Cities had to provide high quality service to meet the increased demand. Consequently, department heads formed professional associations, including the International Association of Chiefs of Police

(1893), the International Association of Fire Chiefs (1837), the National Association of Fire Chiefs (1893), the American Society of Municipal Engineers (1894), the Municipal Finance Officers Association (1906), and the National Recreation Association (1906). Following suit, city managers formed the International City Management Association (ICMA) in 1915.

To reduce corruption in patronage-driven cities, forty-six local government reform groups formed the National Municipal League (NML) in 1895. In 1899, the NML approved the first Model City Charter. A Model Charter recommends the governmental structure, the selection and powers of local officials, and the method of executing basic functions, including taxing and borrowing power. The first Model Charter recommended the strong-mayor form of government.

In 1908, Staunton, Virginia, appointed a city manager, thereby setting the stage for a new form of government: the council-manager form, in which the city manager, a skilled professional, carries out the policies set by the governing board and serves at the pleasure of that board. In 1915, the NML recommended the council-manager plan in its Model City Charter. Some strong-mayor cities likewise professionalized by hiring a chief administrative officer (CAO), usually appointed by the mayor, to assist the mayor in day-to-day operations. The first CAO worked for the mayor of San Francisco in 1931. The Model City Charter has been updated eight times, most recently in 2003.[1]

As the complexity of local services increased, city and county managers needed more education. The first universities to offer a master's degree in public administration (MPA) were Michigan (1913), Stanford (1919), Southern California (1921), Texas A&M (1924), and Syracuse (1924). At first, MPA course work principally concerned urban services like streets, sewer and water systems, and waste collection and disposal. Thereafter, though, courses focused less on urban services and more on generic skills such as budgeting, human-resource management, and policy analysis. In 1934, ICMA took up the task of teaching urban-management subjects through correspondence courses in public-works management, city planning, police administration, fire administration, property assessment, public-welfare administration, municipal finance, and municipal management. ICMA also published "green books" on these topics for use as study guides.

After World War II, when the degree of choice for a budding public manager became the MPA, the number of MPA programs mushroomed. More recently, students with an interest in nonprofit management and inter-sectoral collaboration are seeking an MPA. Currently, a typical MPA program primarily offers courses that teach the generic skills mentioned above, plus program evaluation, information technology, and research methods. Most MPA programs offer only a few courses in urban services; some offer none. A would-be city or county manager must learn about these functions on-the-job. Some graduates are fortunate to work as an assistant to a seasoned mentor-manager. Others, though, find that gaining experience is more problematic, particularly if they are working in a specialized position such as a budget analyst, policy analyst, departmental assistant, or planner.

This guide is an introduction, a basic primer, to sixteen core urban services. It does not cover the services in great depth but refers the reader to materials that go into greater detail. The book has been field-tested by MPA students who have used it to ask department heads questions about their departments' functions. The students have found it a valuable tool for learning about the nuts and bolts of urban services.

Each chapter follows a standard format. A brief history of the service area internationally and in the United States introduces the topic. The discussion then moves to general issues faced by managers in the core service area. Finally, the guide examines the methods urban professionals follow, drawn from a wide array of recommended practices and procedures, particularly those prescribed by professional associations.

NOTE

1. For a discussion of this update, and the history of the Model City Charter in general, see Christopher Gates and Robert Loper, "Reviewing the Model City Charter: The Making of the Eighth Edition," *PM Magazine* 85, no. 3 (2003).

FOR FURTHER READING

Ammons, David. *Municipal Benchmarks*, 2nd ed. Thousand Oaks, CA: Sage Publications, 2001.
Stenberg, Carl and Susan Austin. *Managing Local Government Services*, 2nd ed. Washington, DC: International City/County Management Association, 2007.
Wood, Len, and Joe Baker. *Tales from the Trenches*. Ranch Palos Verdes, CA: The Training Shoppe, 2003.

Part I

Public Safety and
Public Health Services

2

Police

The Volunteer Era (Roman Days to 1844)

Caesar Augustus formed the first police department, responsible for his protection, general police duties, intelligence gathering, and night security patrols. In the United States, volunteers initially performed most of the policing. Slave patrols helped Southern slaveholders recover and punish runaway slaves. An elected sheriff, assisted by volunteers, policed rural areas, as U.S. marshals (for example, Wyatt Earp) did in western towns. In New England, volunteers performed a night watch, often overseen by a paid police officer, called a constable. Boston established a night watch in 1631 with an officer and six men. By 1635, male property owners over age sixteen took turns preventing crimes and disturbances. By 1796, watchmen carried a badge, a rattle to alert citizens of problems, and a six-foot pole to nab lawbreakers. Men were often assigned to watchman duty as a punishment or in lieu of military service. Hence, many of them, less than vigilant, drank and slept on the job.

The Political Era (1844–1919)

After the Civil War, as cities industrialized, they became more crowded, diverse, and crime-ridden. Consequently, they established paid police departments. Using London's Metropolitan Police Department as a model, in 1844, New York City created a paid department managed by a police chief appointed by the mayor. In 1854, Pennsylvania created a state police department, mainly to crush coal strikes. By the 1870s, every major city had a full-time police department, many of which were controlled by a political machine like Boss Tweed's in New York. Cities were broken down into wards overseen by a ward boss, who decided who would be hired. Those hired usually had to pay off the ward boss. Moreover, the political machine sometimes used police officers to "discourage" political opposition and collect political bribes.

Walking a beat, police officers became intimately familiar with peoples' problems on their beat, acting somewhat as social workers—operating soup kitchens, providing lodging and food to the homeless, and visiting houses to check for cholera and other diseases. Police officers then used the watchman policing style. They enforced ordinances regarding health, lighting, public lewdness, and street fights but left solving serious crimes (such as murder, rape, and robbery) to private authorities, like Pinkerton agents. Later, municipal police detectives took on crime-solving but were often paid a fee or a percentage of stolen money recovered.[1]

The Professional Era (1920 to the1980s)

Crime incidence increased in the 1920s and 1930s for three reasons. First, the Volstead Act (Prohibition), enacted in 1920, caused more gang-related crimes. Second, robberies increased as cars enabled robbers to flee the scene of a crime. Finally, abject poverty, brought on by the Great Depression, spawned crime sprees during the 1930s, personified by notoriously colorful criminals like John Dillinger, Pretty Boy Floyd, Ma Barker, and Bonnie and Clyde. To combat crime, police departments professionalized, adopting standard procedures and engaging in more training, planning, research, and crime-solving.[2] Two founding fathers of police professionalism were August Vollmer and O.W. Wilson. Vollmer, the police chief in Berkeley, California, from 1909 to 1932, pioneered the use of fingerprinting, handwriting analysis, and motorcycle units. Wilson, a protégé of Vollmer, initiated one-officer motorized patrols, two-way radios, and rotating beat assignments to curb corruption and promote rapid response.

Other signature events during this period included:

- The creation of the International Association of Chiefs of Police (IACP) in 1902, which promulgated training standards, new technologies, and a code of ethics
- The publication of *Municipal Police Administration* in 1930 by the International City Management Association, which was used in civil-service promotional examinations
- The FBI's creation of the Unified Crime Report, a crime laboratory, and the National Police Academy in the 1930s
- The publication in 1950 of *Police Administration*, written by O.W. Wilson, which became the leading text in police management

In the early 1970s, states mandated basic law-enforcement training, initially about nine weeks in duration, but now lasting four or five months.

The Community Policing Era (1980s to the Present)

The urban population spread out, especially after World War II, making foot patrols ineffectual. Moreover, crime-preventing community bonds weakened: telephones reduced face-to-face conversations, families dispersed to the suburbs, and more women entered the workforce. Police officers could not reduce crime simply by random patrolling, as attested to by the well-known Kansas City study conducted in 1973 in which researchers divided the city into three geographic areas with similar demographics and crime characteristics. They doubled patrol cars in one area, kept the original number in another, and reduced them in the third, but found that neither the arrest nor crime rate changed in any area.

Since reactive policing proved ineffectual, in 1979, Herman Goldstein advocated the *problem-oriented-policing* (POP) approach to focus on *problems*, not incidents. A problem was defined as a series of related incidents. POP mobilizes the community to identify and reduce crimes,[3] then analytically solves crime problems, applying a SARA (scanning, analysis, response, and assessment) methodology. POP focuses on making public spaces safe by targeting little problems (for example, panhandlers, subway-fare beaters, drunks, littering, and defective streetlights and signs) that cause fear and despair.[4]

Following POP came the now widely accepted *community-oriented-policing* (COP) approach. As in POP, officers do not simply react to incidents but partner with the public, other public agencies, and businesses to prevent and solve crimes. In 1994, the federal government jump-started community policing by funding the Community Oriented Policing Program. By 2000, more than 85 percent of the U.S. population lived in communities that had adopted community policing.[5] Community policing has proven effective at reducing crime, but its implementation requires a substantial organizational commitment. Officers are trained to establish rapport with community members, public agencies, and businesses to fight crime jointly. Ideally, the departmental performance appraisal system recognizes community-policing outcomes like preventing crimes and empowering neighborhood groups.

MANAGEMENT

Most law-enforcement agencies are relatively small. Of the over 17,000 law-enforcement agencies in the United States, 78 percent have fewer than twenty-four officers, and over 1,000 have only one full- or part-time officer.[6]

In all states but Hawaii, the sheriff of a county is a constitutionally elected officer and, as such, can opt out of the county's budget process, submitting the budget request directly to the county commission, bypassing the county manager. Though subject to state and federal laws, a sheriff has autonomy in hiring and firing employees. Because of sheriffs' involvement in budgetary and human resource management, county managers may find themselves at loggerheads with the sheriff. The manager should thus cultivate a close professional working relationship, recognizing the sheriff's legal independence.

HUMAN-RESOURCE MANAGEMENT

Selection of Officers

In the selection process, large departments typically polygraph applicants, but administering a polygraph may be unaffordable to a small department. Two commonly used personality profiles administered are the Minnesota Multiphasic Personality Inventory and the Inwald Personality Inventory. The Americans with Disability Act requires that a person be conditionally selected *before* being psychologically tested. The department also typically checks candidates' criminal, financial, educational, and work history.

A sometimes prickly hiring and promotional question is whether to give extra weight to education. More education correlates slightly with better job performance, fewer disciplinary actions, and fewer citizens' complaints. The trend in policing nationally has been toward more education, and over 60 percent of departments provide tuition and education loan reimbursement.

Selection of the Chief

Selecting a police chief is a most important decision. The chief's values should match the organization's. For example, if the government values customer satisfaction and community policing, so should the chief. A critical question is whether to hire from without or within the department. Hiring from within may boost departmental morale, but hiring from outside may bring in someone with fresh ideas. The general rule should be: hire the *best* person, whether an outsider or insider. To attract a wide field, the organization can advertise in *Police Chief* magazine, magazines of the state League of Municipalities and Association of County Commissioners, and with the Police Executive Research Forum. CEOs should discreetly check applicants' credentials. The hiring process, whether conducted by a search firm or the local government, is most likely to falter due to inadequate review of resumes and candidate screening.[7] The candidate screening should thus be systematic, not biased by the views of a single screener. If the agency has a police officers' association, it may be given input in the selection process.

Some departments select the chief and other high-ranking officers by the assessment center method. An assessment center simulates problems normally encountered and skills needed on the job. A panel of assessors rate performance on exercises in small-group management, "in-basket" tasks, problem-solving exercises, and written and oral communications. Compared to the traditional paper-and-pencil cognitive test, an assessment center better predicts job success and selects more ethnically diverse personnel. The assessment center method has two caveats, however: (1) it is more expensive than a written test, and (2) it is ineffective if poorly administered. The process should follow the standards of the International Congress on the Assessment Center Method, including training assessors, establishing inter-rater reliability, and conducting a job analysis.

Field Training

After graduating from a police academy, newly minted officers undergo field training under the tutelage of a field training officer (FTO). The field-training experience, which builds on the police-academy training, can *profoundly* affect officers' future performance. The FTO should therefore be experienced, have an exemplary service record, and be specially trained. Some departments compensate FTOs for the extra work. FTOs reinforce organizational values, teach interpersonal skills, and orient officers to the ways of the street. An effective FTO patiently mentors slow-to-respond recruits, does not negatively stereotype an officer based on his or her academy performance, and judges performance based on objective, measurable criteria.

Non-Sworn Employees

Non-sworn employees free up sworn police officers for police-related duties. The IACP Policy on Civilian Personnel recommends that a department analyze the tasks that could be civilianized. To free up officers, departments may require citizens to engage private security personnel or off-duty police officers to perform nonpolice functions like providing an escort service, unlocking cars, and providing security at sporting events.

Stress Reduction

Policing can be a highly stressful. Among stressors are rotating shifts, a frustrating prosecutorial and judicial system, poor physical fitness, improper eating, working in a quasi-military organization, and family problems. The suicide, divorce, and injury rates among police officers greatly exceed national norms. To reduce stress, police departments often offer the following types of programs:

- Critical-incident (for example, a shooting) counseling and debriefing
- Training in interpersonal communications, stress recognition, relaxation, and anger management
- Employee assistance programs to counsel employees with problems like substance abuse, family worries, and traumatic incidents
- A physical-fitness facility
- A spouse-awareness program, which lets spouses ride along on a beat so they can be more informed about what their spouses actually do
- A departmental counselor whom officers can see confidentially about personal and professional stress-related problems.

IT Management

Technology is an indispensable tool for police departments, big and small. For instance, most departments equip police vehicles with a mobile data terminal that enables

- car-to-car communication;
- entering reports via the terminal, saving time;
- running a license-tag check before approaching suspicious stopped vehicles;
- having on-line access to reports, maps, and other documents.

Departments, particularly large ones, have a Web site that provides information such as

- crime statistics broken down by geographic area,
- mug shots of wanted criminals,
- complaint-reporting procedures,
- crime-prevention methods,
- police department phone numbers,
- job opportunities.

Departments also may have intranet capability to communicate officer-to-officer and division-to-division, share intelligence information, publish an employee newsletter, and broadcast departmental news.

Some medium- and large-sized departments use a Geographic Information System (GIS) to geographically plot crime-incident patterns, times, and modus operandi (MO). The GIS links various data (such as calls for service, crime data, and census information) to

- depict spatially subsets of crimes with similar MOs,
- identify crimes that a particular suspect has committed,
- predict where new crime "hot spots" will occur.

The crime-analysis system records crimes by time of day, type of weapon used, entry point, type of structure or residence, speech patterns, and other data elements. Large departments typically have a full-time research-and-planning unit to analyze crime trends. Smaller departments, which cannot afford a full-time analyst, typically designate an officer to analyze crimes on a part-time basis.

In 1994, New York City introduced the GIS-supported Compstat model, which has five aspects:

1. Specified crime-reduction objectives;
2. Timely and accurate intelligence;
3. Effective tactics;
4. Rapid personnel deployment;
5. Consistent follow-up and evaluation.[8]

Chiefs hold commanders responsible for analyzing and reducing crime in the geographic areas that they command. Figure 2.1 shows police commanders at a Compstat meeting.

The FBI manages the National Crime Information Center, the National Incident-Based Reporting System (NIBRS), and the Integrated Automated Fingerprint Identification System (IAFIS). Police departments can access federal crime files through their state computer system. Retrievable data include names of suspects, probationers, and parolees; prisoners in federal prisons; mug shots (taken since 2000); right-index-finger prints, and records of convicted sexual offenders and predators. Departments transmit fingerprints electronically to the IAFIS. When a match is made, the complete criminal history on the person is sent to the requesting agency.

Accreditation

In 1979, the International Association of Chiefs of Police, the Police Executive Research Forum, the National Organization of Black Law Enforcement

Figure 2.1 **Compstat Meeting**

Used by permission of City of Raleigh, North Carolina.

Executives, and the National Sheriff's Association established the Commission on Accreditation for Law Enforcement Agencies, Inc. (CALEA). CALEA accredits departments in forty-three states. A state agency does accrediting in the seven other states.

Accreditation is a five-step process: (1) application, (2) eligibility approval, (3) self-assessment, (4) on-site assessment, and (5) appearance before CALEA reviewers. There are 436 mandatory and optional standards. The mandatory standards apply to duties with substantial liability risk, such as training and police pursuit. Agencies must comply with 100 percent of these standards and with 80 percent of the optional standards. About 23 percent of full-time officers serve in accredited departments.[9]

Media Relations

The media can partner with the police department to publicize the names of wanted suspects and encourage the public to submit tips. The most commonly used crime-prevention program, Crime Stoppers, supported by the media, publicizes details about unsolved crimes. Large departments usually have a full-time public information officer (PIO) to be the chief liaison with the media. Small departments, in contrast, usually designate the chief or another high-ranking officer as the PIO. A newly designated PIO should be trained in how to interact effectively with the media, including making TV presentations, knowing when to talk "on" and "off" (if ever) the record, and managing the press corps at the scene of a major emergency.

PATROL

Patrol officers are "master generalists" who handle a wide range of calls. They normally are the first to respond to incidents, but less than 20 percent of calls for service involve a crime.[10] Police officers instead mostly respond to such incidents as traffic accidents, animal disturbances, family and friend disputes, noise complaints, disorderly conduct by intoxicated persons, and issues of the emotionally disturbed. Of the serious crimes responded to, about 75 percent are "cold," meaning they were reported after the perpetrator left the scene, making immediate apprehension unlikely. Indeed, less than 4 percent of arrests are attributable to a fast response.[11]

Traditionally, arrest statistics have been the most-used performance measure.[12] Though of some value, the number of arrests does not measure performance related to order-maintenance activities (for example, responding to a noise complaint or domestic dispute), traffic control and accident handling, and community policing.

Today many departments follow a community-policing strategy. Community-policing officers interact with community members both at regularly scheduled community meetings and on patrol. Ideally, officers establish rapport with community members who are more willing to identify neighborhood problems, report criminals' whereabouts, and assist in solving crimes in their neighborhood.[13] Two types of surveys generate community input:

1. A *community-wide survey* asks citizens how satisfied they are with police services in general.
2. A *problem-oriented survey* asks citizens to identify the causes of, and solutions to, problems in the neighborhood, such as gangs, speeding traffic, or burglaries.

Manpower Staffing and Allocation

To determine staffing size, a department may use as a guide the staffing complement of like-sized committees in the state or region. Such a comparison, however, may be misleading because it ignores a community's unique characteristics. A more appropriate comparison is between departments with similar workloads, including the number of calls for service, the amount of free patrol time, the crime rate for serious and less serious crimes, and the number of crimes solved.

On average, police activity occurs at these intervals:

- 22 percent of calls at night (12 AM to 8 AM)
- 33 percent of calls during the day (8 AM to 4 PM)
- 45 percent of calls in the evening (4 PM to 12 AM)[14]

Some departments calculate staffing needs by multiplying the number of incidents and complaints responded to by the average amount of time spent responding to particular service calls (for example, a traffic accident, domestic dispute, or auto break-in). Based on the workload calculation, manpower is assigned to each shift.[15]

There are three types of shifts: variable, fixed, and rotating. A *variable shift* assigns some officers to a fixed shift and other officers (such as community-policing officers) to a variable shift. About 65 percent of departments *rotate* shifts; about 35 percent of departments (mostly large) fix them.[16] There are two ways to rotate shifts. A *backward* shift rotation is physically the hardest to adjust to because the body's circadian-rhythm interval adjusts better to a *forward* rotation (that is, from day to evening shifts).[17] About 20 percent of officers adjust well physically to a rotating shift, whether backward or forward; about 60 percent adjust with some difficulty; and about 20 percent adjust with extreme difficulty.[18] Sustained sleep deprivation poses considerable health risk and causes faulty judgments. A fixed shift eliminates such risks and provides community-policing officers time to establish rapport with community members. On the other hand, the least experienced, least senior officers are typically assigned to the more crime-filled evening shifts that require the most experience. The negative effects of a rotating shift are mitigated by

- overlapping shifts to give time to exchange information during the shift change,
- making the meal break at least forty-five minutes,
- scheduling a sixteen-hour interval between shift rotations,
- balancing staffing to meet shifts' varying workloads.[19]

Changing the type of shift may prove controversial among officers; some naturally prefer one schedule type over another. In particular, some officers may prefer a duty schedule that more easily permits them to work on a second job to supplement their income. Whenever change is contemplated, management should give the rank and file some input into the change.

Call Response

In responding to a call for service, officers are guided by three principal policies: use-of-force, pursuit driving, and domestic violence. The use-of-force policy requires that an officer apply the least amount of force necessary to control a situation. Officers are trained to follow a use-of-force continuum, such as the following:[20]

1. *Physical Presence.* Most suspects cooperate simply by being in the presence of a police officer.
2. *Soft Hands.* Officer softly grabs a suspect.
3. *Mace or Pepper Spray.* Officer uses mace or pepper spray.
4. *Hard Hands.* Officer pushes or hits a suspect.
5. *Baton or Taser* (conducted energy device).
6. *Threat of Deadly Force.* Officer unholsters his or her weapon, threatening deadly force.
7. *Use of Deadly Force.* (Most departments prohibit a warning shot.) Used only when an officer or a bystander is clearly in great threat of bodily harm.

Officers do not, of course, necessarily start at the beginning of the use-of-force continuum. For instance, if an officer encounters a suspect with a gun, force level 6 or 7 may be appropriate.

A *pursuit-driving policy* specifies the conditions under which an officer should drive a police vehicle in pursuit of a fleeing violator. There are three types of policies. One permits officers to use their own judgment whether to pursue, considering the nature of the offense, weather, and traffic conditions. The second type bans a high-speed pursuit unless a serious crime has been committed. The third limits the speed of the officer's pursuit unless a serious crime has been committed. In any event, the on-duty supervisor should monitor the pursuit over the police radio, exercising discretion to curtail the chase.

A *domestic-violence policy* specifies when to make an arrest and/or to take other actions, such as escorting a victim to a shelter. About 65 percent of all police-service calls come from repeat locations.[21] Chief among these repeat calls are domestic-violence incidents. Departments should thus train officers how to intervene in a domestic crisis. Some departments assign a civilian to follow up on "hot spot" cases, offering counseling assistance.

Crime-Scene Management

A most important factor in whether a crime is solved is the quality of the information gathered by patrol officers in their initial report.[22] Patrol officers complete a comprehensive preliminary investigation, actively searching for witnesses and clues that may lead to solving a crime. Some departments provide patrol officers with latent-fingerprint and photographic equipment.

Crime Reporting

Most crime patterns are short-lived, lasting just weeks or days. Criminals can be apprehended by anticipating their crimes, but real-time crime analysis is necessary. Officers should thus report crimes within twenty-four hours to update the crime database and detect shifting crime patterns. Crime reporting is expedited if data are entered via a mobile data terminal in the police cruiser. The data-entry format should be compatible with other departmental reporting systems, as incompatibility causes unnecessary redundancy and delay.

COMMUNICATIONS

Dispatchers must remain calm and ask good questions, sometimes under extreme duress. They must provide sure and accurate information to officers driving to a crime scene. They should have the authority to override the computer-recommended manpower-response force. Many small departments, though, do not control central dispatch; instead, calls are routed to them via a centralized dispatch facility, operated by the county government or a large city. In addition to dispatch communications, officers communicate with cell phones and personal digital assistants (PDAs).

Dispatching

Some dispatch centers have a computer-aided-dispatch (CAD) capability. Though used since the 1960s, a CAD system now can

- continually track the location of police cars, using an automated-vehicle-location system;
- silently route messages to terminals in patrol cars;
- silently send text messages;
- append information electronically to a case file so that basic case information is recorded only once.

A CAD system differentiates when to respond, prioritizing responses according to the severity of an offense, thus queuing low-priority calls behind high-priority calls. A field supervisor can override the dispatch system if a closer unit can handle the call.

Community policing requires that officers have *free-patrol time*, not responding to service calls, in order to interact with community members. Call diversion can give officers this free-patrol time; it also decreases communications traffic. One study found that 47 percent of all calls for service were divertible and that most citizens were pleased with the alternative.[23] Call-diversion methods include:

- Handling particular incidents (such as an auto break-in or theft report) by phone rather by an officer at the scene
- Warning particular offenders (for example, citizens making loud noises, owners of barking dogs) by phone first
- Making an appointment for an officer to follow up later on cases like abandoned vehicles and youth problems
- Diverting nonemergency calls to a 311 number that queues calls behind unanswered 911 calls
- Asking citizens to report nonemergency problems via the Internet

Citizens usually understand that many of their calls do not require that a police officer respond immediately. Still, they can be very disappointed when the dispatcher significantly underestimates the response time. Dispatchers should therefore conservatively estimate when an officer will respond, alerting callers to the fact that an intervening higher-priority call may take precedence.

Automatic alarms, a large portion of the dispatch load, turn out to be false 97 percent of the time.[24] To reduce false alarms, departments can adopt the Model Alarm Ordinance, developed by the National Burglar and Fire Alarm Association, whose enforcement reduces false alarms by as much as 50 percent.[25]

INVESTIGATIONS

Being an investigator is usually a promotion from being a patrol officer. Investigators usually do not wear a uniform, and they have considerable autonomy over their work. Investigators comprise about 16 percent of sworn personnel.[26] Principal criminal-investigation policies include:

- *Safeguarding Evidence.* Specifies how to store, inventory, and dispose of evidence.

- *Informing Crime Victims.* Specifies what investigators can tell crime victims, including whether the crime has been assigned a low priority because of its unlikely solvability.
- *Paying Informants.* Specifies how much, and under what conditions, informants can be paid for information. Some departments require that an independent source verify an informant's tip before making payment.

Case Assignment

By virtue of temperament, some detectives may be more suited to investigate particular crimes. Small departments with few detectives must assign them to investigate any type of crime, while large departments may have more discretion. Detectives assigned to juvenile cases should establish rapport with families, victims, social-service agencies, schools, the juvenile prosecutor, and, especially, juveniles. Homicide detectives need expert interrogation abilities, knowledge of new technology (such as DNA and hair-fiber testing) and chain-of-custody procedures, and an ability to work intelligence sources. Drug and vice detectives must be good actors when working undercover, have good informants, and work well with other agencies. Because very few auto-theft and robbery cases are solved, these detectives need to be able to manage large caseloads and coordinate with insurance agencies, the FBI, and the banking community. Finally, sexual-offense detectives should be able to establish rapport with victims.

Case Screening

Some cases are highly unlikely to be solved. Some departments accordingly establish *solvability criteria*, estimating the likelihood of a case being solved. Among the solvability criteria are whether there is a witness, a suspect, a workable lead, or physical evidence. The district attorney may be consulted as to whether a case should be investigated. Regardless of the solvability factors, investigators usually work serious violent-crime cases, such as murder. When investigators decide not to pursue a case, they should explain why to the victim.

Crime-Scene Handling

Patrol officers, though not investigators, are a critical element in an investigation. The quality of the police officer's initial investigation affects the likelihood of solving a case.[27] These officers preserve the crime scene, obtain information from witnesses and victims, and canvass the neighborhood for witnesses.

CALEA standards require that the department adopt written guidelines specifying when a crime-scene-search officer should be summoned and how extensive the search should be. The more serious a crime, the more crime-scene resources are usually deployed. The National Institute of Justice has likewise issued standards to guide crime-scene investigation. The guidelines specify the actions to be taken by first responders, investigators, and the technicians who recognize, preserve, collect, document, and submit evidence to laboratories for analysis.[28]

Fingerprints are the most frequently collected type of physical evidence. Two methods speed up the tedious fingerprint-matching process. First, prints can be organized by attribute (such as a thumbprint with a particular feature) or type of repeat offender (for example, burglar). Second, fingerprints can be sent to IAFIS, which searches an extensive database for a match. Other physical evidence, popularized by the CSI TV shows, includes body fluids and hairs to match with blood and DNA samples. Some states have a DNA databank for use in a cold search.

Repeat-Offender Tracking

Some offenders repeat particular crimes after their release from incarceration. Some departments track their whereabouts with the assistance of parole and probation officers. The FBI's Registered Sex Offender database can locate the residence of sex offenders. After arresting a repeat offender, the prosecutor and investigators may conduct an extensive post-arrest investigation to ensure that he or she gets the longest possible sentence.

Performance Evaluation

Chiefs should develop workload measures for particular types of cases, based on the average amount of time taken to process cases and investigate repeat offenders. Key performance measures include:

- *Suspect-Detection Rate.* The percentage of cases in which a suspect was identified after the initial investigation.
- *Clearance Rate.* The percentage of cases that have been cleared by arrest.
- *Prosecution Rate.* The percentage of arrests accepted by the prosecutor.
- *Conviction Rates.* The percentage of cases that led to conviction and the percentage of cases that led to a conviction on the charge first filed.

CRIME PREVENTION

Crime prevention should involve the whole community: its citizens, businesses, social-service agencies, neighborhood groups, and schools. At the core of an effective crime-prevention program is *citizen surveillance*, whereby informed citizens team with police to prevent and solve crimes. Through informational handouts, one-on-one meetings with a police officer, and the departmental Web site, the department informs citizens how to prevent crime. The most well-known community crime-prevention program, Neighborhood Watch, teaches techniques for making homes and neighborhood more crime-resistant, including:

- Making and keeping an inventory of valuable property
- Installing deadbolt locks
- Anchoring windows to prevent their being raised if broken
- Installing alarm systems in homes

Engaged citizens report crimes and suspicious activities. A departmental Web site can post crime-incidence data in each neighborhood. Large departments may also operate a crime-reporting hotline to provide anonymity to informants. They may also offer cash rewards for tips that lead to an arrest of a felony suspect. A counterpart to Neighborhood Watch, Business Watch, publishes a newsletter, encourages businesses to display a decal indicating that they are program participants, and regularly shares crime-prevention information such as how to harden premises against crime by

- installing street lighting around the business and parking lots;
- installing surveillance cameras and building alarms;
- moving merchandise that blocks an attendant's view;
- removing shrubbery to make a storefront more public.

Youth-Crime Prevention

Youth commit a high percentage of crimes in some communities. To prevent youth crime, police departments operate programs like the McGruff Crime Dog program, a multimedia campaign sponsored by the Crime Prevention Coalition of America, which informs children how to prevent crimes by their peers. Two similar programs, "Teens, Crime and Community" and "We Can Work It Out," teach youngsters how to protect themselves and their community. In some communities, police departments assign school resource officers (SROs) to prevent crimes and maintain order in schools. The students themselves are the best source of information about possible criminal activities among their peers, and the SRO conveys a positive image of a police officer.

TRAFFIC ENFORCEMENT

A traffic-safety program may be managed by an officer or civilian. The program promotes seat-belt and child-restraint usage and increases safety awareness, especially among teenage drivers, who are at highest risk of accidents and fatalities. The program attempts to reduce speeding, because accidents at lower speeds are far less likely to cause severe injuries and fatalities. Traffic speed is controlled by radar guns, traffic signs and signals, electronic devices, and speed bumps.

Traffic enforcement is more than simply issuing a citation, however. Its primary purpose should be to reduce the number and severity of accidents. Accordingly, traffic enforcement should focus on high-accident locations where reducing speed will decrease accidents, injuries, and fatalities. Important traffic-enforcement technology includes:

- Video cameras at high-accident locations to monitor speeds and issue citations
- Electronic signs for safety and traffic-condition messages
- Video recorders in police cars to record traffic stops
- Computerized traffic-diagramming systems to reconstruct accidents

Enforcement and Prevention

Some departments compile a database of accidents by location, type of violation, type of vehicle, and type of driver. They use the data to target enforcement at high-accident sites. Of particular concern is driving while impaired (driving under the influence), which is the principal cause of accidents, injuries, and fatalities. Departments can alert the public to the dangers of drinking and driving by

- posting billboards;
- supporting the Students against Driving Drunk and Mothers against Driving Drunk programs;
- working with alcohol producers to discourage drunken driving.

The National Highway Traffic Safety Administration (NHTSA) grants funds to create and operate drunken-driving-prevention programs.

To spot possible DWI offenders, officers can use the Visual Guide of DWI

Motorists, which identifies twenty-four DWI driving behaviors (for example, straddling lane markers).[29] Officers can also administer three roadside sobriety tests developed by the NHTSA:

- The one-leg stand
- The walk and turn
- The horizontal-gaze nystagmus, in which a police officer tracks a driver's eyes with a finger or penlight to detect involuntary head jerking or eye twitching

About 90 percent of the time, these three tests detect individuals under the influence of drugs or alcohol.[30] Some departments also use a Breathalyzer to measure the alcohol content of the breath.

Both the NHTSA and the IACP recommend a set of accident-investigation procedures. Simply reporting an accident differs from investigating it. An accident report states the facts of the case, the "who, what, when, and where." An accident investigation is far more painstaking and requires taking photographs, making detailed measurements, estimating speeds, and precisely locating affected vehicles at the time of the accident.

COURT FUNCTIONS

Serving warrants is a both an art and a science. An effective warrant officer has reliable informants; is flexible about the time he or she serves warrants; sensitively handles emotionally laden cases, like taking a maltreated child away from his or her parents; and establishes rapport with the clerk of the court, with whom he or she closely works. Either police or civilians can book suspects. The booker safeguards the suspect's property, fingerprints him or her, decides whether the prisoner constitutes a high- or low-security risk, and identifies prisoners in need of mental-health services. A corrections officer fairly and consistently maintains discipline, enforces security and sanitation policies, and prevents illicit gang activities.

PROFESSIONAL STANDARDS

Generally, departments with less than 400 employees do not have a full-time internal-affairs unit; instead, they designate someone to investigate complaints as they arise.[31] The internal-affairs policy should establish departmental values, ethical standards, and investigation procedures. The department may use either its own staff to review incidents (internal review) or a civilian review board (external review). A civilian review board, comprised of appointed civilians by the governing board, is the less common practice. Most common, and recommended by the National Advisory Commission on Civil Disorders, is an internal review. Perhaps surprisingly, civilian review boards are more lenient on police officers than are internal boards.[32]

The department should apprise the public of how to file a complaint. Citizens complain more often about stern faces, domineering nonverbal expressions, lectures, and sarcasm than about more serious charges such as physical abuse and excessive use of force. Officers who have received an undue number of minor complaints may be paired with a verbally skilled officer, given communication training, or referred for counseling.

NOTES

1. James Q. Wilson, *Varieties of Police Behavior* (Cambridge, MA: Harvard University Press, 1968), 142.

2. Ibid.

3. Herman Goldstein, "Improving Policing: A Problem-Oriented Approach," *Crime and Delinquency* 25 (1979): 236–258.

4. James Q. Wilson and George Kelling, "The Police and Neighborhood Safety," *Atlantic Monthly* (March 1982): 29–38.

5. *2001 Survey on Community Policing* (Washington, DC: Bureau of Justice Statistics, U.S. Department of Justice, 2002).

6. Tim Dees, "Information and Communications Technology for Public Safety," *IQ Report* 32, no. 1 (Washington, DC: International City/County Management Association [ICMA], March 2000).

7. Keith Bushey, "Sobering Thoughts on Hiring a Police Chief," *Public Management* (March 2002) (Washington, DC: ICMA).

8. Phyllis McDonald, *Managing Police Operations: Implementing the New York Crime Model-Compstat* (New York: Wadsworth, 2002), 8–21.

9. Commission on Accreditation for Law Enforcement Agencies, Inc. Available at http://www.calea.org.

10. Thomas Sweeney, *Patrol in Local Government Police Management* (Washington, DC: ICMA, 2003), 95.

11. William Spelman and Dale Brown, *Calling the Police: Citizen Reporting of Serious Crimes* (Washington, DC: U.S. Government Printing Office, 1984).

12. Sweeney, *Local Government Police Management,* 453.

13. For a description of departments that have implemented community policing, see *Community Policing in Action* (Washington, DC: ICMA, 2003).

14. Governor's Center for Local Government Services, *Administering Police Services in Small Communities,* 5th ed. Available at http://www.newpa.com.

15. For a precise method of deploying manpower, see ibid.

16. Police Executive Research Forum, *The Impact of Shift Work on Police Officers* (Washington, DC: 1991).

17. Bryan Vila, Gregory Morrison, and Dennis Kenney, "Improving Shift Schedule and Work-Hour Policies and Practices to Increase Police Officer Performance, Health and Safety," *Police Quarterly* 5 (2002): 15.

18. Ibid.

19. Ibid.

20. For an excellent discussion on actual use-of-force nationwide, see Kenneth Adams. Geoffrey Alpert, Roger Dunham, Joel Garner, Lawrence Greefield, Mark Henriquez, Patrick Langan, Chrisopher Maxwell, and Steven Smith, *Use of Force by Police* (Washington, DC: National Institute of Justice, 1999).

21. Sweeney, *Local Government Police Management*, 102.

22. Bernard Greensberg, Carola Elliot, Lois Craft, and Steven Procter, *Felony Investigation Decision Model: An Analysis of Investigative Elements of Information* (Menlo Park, CA: Stanford Research Institute, 1975).

23. Sweeney, *Local Government Police Management*, 128.

24. Ibid., 128.

25. Ibid. For details on the Model Alarm Ordinance, see Model Burglar Alarm Ordinance. Available at http://www.alarm.org/pubsafety.

26. Frank Horvath and Robert Meesig, *A National Survey of Police Policies and Practices Twenty-Five Years after the Rand Study* (East Lansing, MI: School of Criminal Justice, Michigan State University, September 2001), 5.

27. John Eck, *Solving Crimes: The Investigation of Burglary and Robbery* (Washington, DC: Police Executive Research Forum, 1983).

28. Technical Working Group, *Crime Scene Investigation: A Guide for Law Enforcement* (Washington, DC: National Institute of Justice, 2000).

29. National Highway Traffic Safety Administration, "The Visual Detection of DWI Motorists." Available at http://www.nhtsa.dot.gov/people/injury/alcohol/dwi/dwihtml/index.htm.

30. Angelo Rao, *Transportation Services in Local Government Police Management* (Washington, DC: International City/County Management Association, 2003), 233.

31. Dennis Nowicki and Marice Punch, "Fostering Integrity and Professional Standards," in *Local Government Police Management*, 4th ed., ed. William A. Geller and Darrel W. Stephens, (Washington, DC: International City/County Management Association, 2003), 315–352.

32. David Perez, "Police Review Systems," *MIS Report* 24, no. 8 (Washington, DC: ICMA, 1993).

FOR FURTHER READING

Geller, William A., and Darrel W. Stephens, eds. *Local Government Police Management*, 4th ed. Washington, DC: International City/County Management Association, 2003.

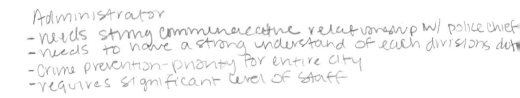

3

Fire Protection

History

Early History

The Chinese formed the first fire brigade about 6,000 years ago. Fire brigades next appeared historically in Rome about 300 BC, when wealthy Romans formed them manned by slaves. But these private companies sometimes proved to be too entrepreneurial, "encouraging" homeowners to either subscribe to their service or have their home "accidentally" torched. Caesar Augustus hence created the first public firefighting force in 24 BC. Night watches, called *Vigiles,* comprised of 600 slaves, were located in seven fire stations throughout Rome. Carriages conveyed firefighters equipped with buckets and axes. After "Nero fiddled while Rome burned," the city fireproofed better, with broad streets, thicker walls, more fire-resistant building materials, better designed roofs, and regulated building heights.

The All-Volunteer Era (Colonial Days to 1853)

In 1631, Boston adopted a fire ordinance requiring residents to keep a fire bucket in their house. Citizens sounded fire alarms with rattles, gongs, or bells or by simply yelling loud. In 1647, Peter Stuyvesant appointed fire wardens in New Amsterdam (later New York), and in 1654, Boston purchased a fire engine. Early fire departments used bucket brigades, simple ladders, and hand-pumped engines equipped with a water-cannon nozzle. Firefighters dumped water into the engine's zinc-lined tub, while others furiously pumped a levered arm. The early single-piston pump merely spurted water, but the more advanced dual-piston pump produced a steady stream.

In 1736, the amazing Benjamin Franklin created a fire department in Philadelphia, requiring volunteers to buy two leather water buckets and four cloth bags to salvage household goods. Famous volunteer firefighters included George Washington and Thomas Jefferson. Volunteers formed clubs that operated fire engines, manned by a crew of axe-and-hook specialists led by an officer. A hose company supplied water to engines, while a hook-and-ladder company actually fought the fire. Later, ladder companies were formed to rescue victims from upper floors. Departments used leather-stitched hose that broke easily under pressure.[1] Repairing the broken hose near a fire caused firefighters to be burned. In 1803, two volunteers invented a more durable hose, which was bonded with rivets.

In the early 1800s, being a volunteer firefighter had considerable cachet. Even very small towns had three and four companies, comprising up to 75 percent of the male population.[2] Each company had its own distinctive lapel pins and colors. At the scene of a fire, a steward often fortified the men with "liquid refreshment."[3] These volunteer companies, though, sometimes proved to be too competitive. Getting to the fire first became a matter of such great pride that companies sometimes impeded each other en route to the site.

The Paid Firefighter Era (1853 to the 1970s)

Such overzealousness sometimes led to unnecessary loss of life and property. Some governing boards, especially in large cities, were thus eager to form a professional, all-paid fire department but were stymied because of the great number of personnel required to operate a manual pump. In 1853, Able Shawk and Alexander Latta solved the problem, inventing a moveable steam-powered pump that threw water 240 feet through a 1¾-inch nozzle. In the same year, Cincinnati quickly formed a paid department. Cincinnati policymakers were especially primed to establish a full-time department after a major downtown building burned to the ground when ten fire companies brawled en route to the fire. Though volunteer departments remained most common, paid departments spread to mid- and large-sized communities.

Afterward, fire equipment steadily improved, including the invention of the firebox (1852), a hose elevator raising the water platform about 50 feet (1870), sprinklers (1874), the eighty-five-foot aerial ladder (1882), and the self-propelled fire engine (1890). By the 1920s, even small communities had 350-gallon-per-minute pumpers.[4] In the 1930s, a special foam was invented to fight oil and gasoline fires caused by auto accidents.

The Emergency Medical Era (1970s to the Present)

From 1977 to 2000, the number of fires fortunately plummeted from 3.2 to 1.7 million per year.[5] The precipitous decline was chiefly attributable to increased sprinkler usage, improved building codes, and better construction materials. With the decrease, the fire service was able to expand its mission to include emergency medical services. Indeed, emergency medical calls now constitute about 70 to 80 percent of a fire department's service calls.[6] Finally, in 2000, Congress passed the Firefighter Investment and Response Enhancement Act to coordinate response to major emergencies and fund training and equipment.

MANAGEMENT

The National Fire Protection Association (NFPA), founded in 1895, is the international fire-standard setting body. The standards, revised about every three to five years, cover fire protection, prevention, suppression, and safety. While advisory, the standards represent the collective judgment of the fire service. NFPA Standard 1710, which applies to a paid department, covers the organization and deployment of fire-suppression operations, emergency medical operations, and special operations. NFPA Standard 172, applicable to a volunteer department, addresses the same matters.

Human Resource Management

There are four types of fire departments:[7]

Type	% of Total Departments
Fully Volunteer	73
Mostly Volunteer (over 50% volunteers)	15
Mostly Career (over 50% paid)	5
Fully Paid	7

Most departments (93 percent) are either all or partly volunteer in nature. Though volunteers are at the core of most fire departments, recruiting and retaining them has become increasingly problematic for two principal reasons. First, training requirements have increased. Firefighters must minimally receive at least twenty-four hours of training in fighting structural fires annually. Some states require more. For example, North Carolina requires at least thirty-six hours of training annually to participate in the state's pension fund. Some volunteers, busy with their professional and personal lives, have difficulty meeting even a twenty-four-hour standard. Second, community bonds that have historically fostered volunteerism have weakened as society has become more mobile and people work longer hours. To attract and retain volunteers, some departments award benefits, including pensions for extensive service (twenty years, for example) and pay for time spent on call.

Some volunteer departments elect their officers, including the chief. Electing officers based on popularity, not merit, is inadvisable because of the stringent training requirements and complexity of the fire service.

Training

The NFPA recommends duties and responsibilities for the following fire service positions:

- Firefighter (NFPA Standard 1001)
- Fire apparatus driver/operator (NFPA Standard 1002)
- Fire rescue technician (NFPA Standard 1006)
- Fire officer (NFPA Standard 1021)
- Fire inspector and plan examiner (NFPA Standard 1031)
- Public safety communicator (NFPA Standard 1061)
- Emergency vehicle technician (NFPA Standard 1071)
- Industrial brigade member (NFPA Standard 1081)

The NFPA also proffers training standards, recommending that a department with fifty or more officers designate a full-time training officer and hire another training officer for every seventy-five additional personnel. NFPA Standard 1403 recommends that firefighters get training in a burn-building that simulates firelike conditions. Other useful training equipment and materials include:

- A miniature three-dimensional structure that simulates real conditions
- Training videos and films like those offered by *Fire Engineering* magazine
- A tabletop simulation mockup

The NFPA recommends that safety-training records be computerized, but NFPA standards are simply guidelines. Small departments in particular may find some standards unaffordable. Departments should thus take caution in adopting the National Fire Code, which adopts *all* NFPA training standards by reference.

With respect to management training, the International Association of Fire Chiefs operates a fire-chief-certification program, and the National Fire Academy runs an Executive Fire Officer Program.

Wellness Programs

Applicants to a department must pass a physical fitness test. The International Association of Fire Fighters and the International Association of Fire Chiefs cosponsor a comprehensive physical fitness test that departments may use. Thereafter, however, though firefighting operations are extremely taxing physically, many firefighters get little exercise. Indeed, heart attacks are the leading cause of firefighter fatalities. To prevent injury and illness, job candidates should be carefully screened. Pre-employment screening reduces injuries to new hires by as much as one-third.[8] After the selection, departments should require a periodic medical examination and a physical-fitness test, which must be job-related. NFPA Standard 1582 recommends how to conduct the medical examination.

To increase fitness, a department should, if possible, provide access to a fitness facility, located at a fire station, local college, local high school, or a privately run fitness center. Other recommended wellness offerings include:

- A smoking-cessation program
- A weight-reduction program
- An employee assistance program that offers counseling on marital, alcohol, and substance-abuse problems

Departmental Fire Rating

The Insurance Services Office (ISO), a nonprofit organization, serves property- and casualty-insurance agencies. Among its services, the ISO rates the fire suppression capacity of fire departments every three years with respect to their water supply, firefighting, and fire-alarm-handling capabilities. The ISO rates departments from 1 (the best) to 10 (the worst). Insurance companies use the rating to set their homeowners and fire-insurance premium rates. Table 3.1 shows how ratings are distributed among the ten classes.

A Class 10 department has no water supply. A Class 9 department, the most common type, has no piped water supply but can transport at least 300 gallons of water pumped at 50 gallons per minute (GPM) at 150 pounds per square inch pressure. A Class 8B department, likewise without piped water, must be able to spray a steady stream for two hours at 250 GPM, by shuttling water to the fire by a relay system. Other rated departments must have a piped water supply.

Fire Station Location

The location of fire stations affects engine-company response times. The ISO requires minimally that fire stations be located within five and three road miles

Table 3.1

Fire Department ISO Ratings

Rating Class	Number of Departments	% of Total
1	48	0.1
2	453	1.1
3	1,691	3.6
4	4,154	8.9
5	7,460	16.0
6	8,702	18.6
7	6,258	13.4
8	2,601	5.6
8B	441	0.9
9	13,560	29.0
10	1,328	2.8
Total	46,696	100.0

Source: ISO Mitigation Online, available at http://www.isomitigation.com/ppc/1000/ppc1002.html.

of all residential and commercial buildings, respectively. However, fire stations usually need to be located closer to properties with a high risk of loss of life and property. The greater the risk, the quicker the response needed, and the more personnel must be dispatched. A single-story residential area is usually well served by a single fire unit, but a high-rise building usually needs more engine companies.

Fire-location software programs, with a Geographic Information System (GIS) component, can pinpoint the ideal location of a fire station, accounting for speed limits, the travel distance, road conditions, traffic light and sign locations, and response times by first-, second-, and third-arriving companies. Small fire departments, however, may not need a computerized model if the site selection is obvious because of a predictable population pattern and road layout.

Locating a fire station may be problematic in a community experiencing erratic, unpredictable population changes. In that case a department may temporarily locate a fire station on a leased property. Once the growth pattern becomes certain, a permanent location can be found. Figure 3.1 shows a fire-station-location program's map of response times.

After determining the site of a fire station, fire commanders should work with the building's architect to prepare the fire-station specifications, including its complement of firefighters, its square footage, its living arrangements, and its safety features (such as infection controls and hazardous-waste disposal).

Figure 3.1   **Engine Company Response Times**

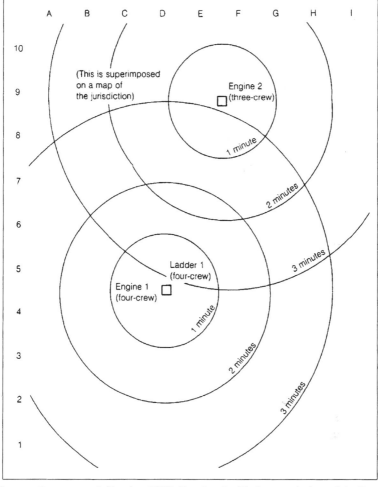

Accreditation

The International Association of Fire Chiefs (IAFC) and the International City/County Management Association (ICMA) jointly accredit fire and rescue organizations under the Commission on Fire Accreditation International (CFAI), now known as the Center for Public Safety Excellence (CPSE). A department evaluates itself with respect to 240 performance measures, 98 of which are deemed core competencies. These measures evaluate performance regarding governance, risk assessment, goal setting, finance, program management, human resource management, condition of physical assets and facilities, training and competency assurance, internal support, and external relationships. The CPSE evaluates a department's self-assessment by inspecting on-site and verifying the submitted documentation.[9] As of September 2008, 123 departments were accredited.

Planning

Risk is a measure of the likely severity and probability of an adverse event. Formerly, departments planned for fire risk only, but now they plan for hazardous-waste spills, urban search-and-rescue missions, weather emergencies (for example, hurricanes, floods, and tornadoes), medical emergencies, and acts of terrorism.

To assess the fire risk, the U.S. Fire Administration (USFA) makes available at no cost a Risk, Hazard, and Value Evaluation (RHAVE) model. RHAVE analyzes at least five years of historical data, including fire losses, type of damages, fire causes, unit availability, and response times to various exposures (residences, high-rise occupancies, high-hazard areas, and high-occupancy buildings such as hospitals). RHAVE categorizes each property as low-, moderate-, or high-risk in character. The higher the risk, the closer fire stations should be located to the property at risk.[10]

The fire department, with input from departments like police, prepares a preplan to fight fires at sites where the loss of life or property could be high, such as nursing homes, hospitals, chemical plants, manufacturing plants, and bulk-storage facilities. The information on each structure required for such planning includes:

- The construction design (including materials, utility connections, wiring, and floors)
- The layout (for example emergency exits, specifications)
- The optimal travel route to the location
- The number of engine companies to respond
- Available water supply (such as fire-hydrant locations and water main sizes)
- Shelters to locate displaced residents

On the way to a fire, some departments manually access the pre-fire plan in a large notebook, but it is preferable to review the plan via a more accessible mobile data terminal.

APPARATUS

The fire service refers to its vehicles as *apparatus*. The principal apparatus, a *pumper*, is outfitted with a pump, hoses and nozzles, a tank for water or other extinguishing agent and ladders. The *ladder truck*, equipped with an aerial ladder and a tower ladder or platform, is principally used to search for and rescue victims and to release smoke and hot gases from burning structures. The *heavy rescue* apparatus, principally used in rescue operations, usually does not carry water or a large ladder. The *quint*, a combined pumper and ladder truck, is equipped with ground ladders and an aerial device (such as a ladder, platform, or ladder with platform). Finally, a *minipumper*, a smaller version of the pumper, typically responds first to lesser emergencies like car, grass, trash, and brush fires.

A standard apparatus carries hose and water, pumps, and firefighting equipment. NFPA apparatus standards include:

- NFPA Standard 1901—Pumper
- NFPA Standard 1902—Initial attack apparatus
- NFPA Standard 1903—Mobile water supplies
- NFPA Standard 1904—Aerial ladder truck and elevating platforms

Note that the NFPA standards are *minimum* requirements. Departments should thus adapt them as needed, mindful that additional features may cost extra. The fire chief, company officer, equipment operator, firefighter, and mechanic usually collaboratively decide what additional features, if any, should be included in the standard specification. For instance, a department may require a more costly customized all-aluminum chassis, instead of the standard sheet-metal chassis, which rusts more.

Apparatus is expensive and has a long life. A small department, with one or a few vehicles, which infrequently buys apparatus, may be well served to seek assistance from a nearby large department that has more frequent buying experience. A small department may also hire a consultant to prepare the specification. An informative guide is the *Fire Apparatus Purchasing Handbook,* by William Peters.[11] To assess options, departmental personnel may also visit trade shows, meetings of apparatus associations, and manufacturing facilities.

At the pre-bid conference, prospective bidders assess whether they can comply with the specification. Disagreements between the bidders and local government may occur when the specification is unclear. The specification should require prospective vendors to supply a list of previous customers to contact about past vendor performance and also any information about their financial condition. If a vendor goes bankrupt, another company may not be available to service the warranty or provide replacement parts.

The specification should also state the number of inspection trips that departmental representatives will make to the manufacturing plant. At the manufacturing site, a departmental representative often makes a visual record of the work in progress. Typically, the representative will visit at least once before the apparatus is painted in order to detect problems, such as an improperly installed compartment or water outlet. During the final visit, the Underwriters Laboratory, observed by a departmental representative, tests the apparatus to ensure compliance with NFPA standards. At this time, the manufacturer should train personnel to use diagnostic equipment to locate electronic problems.

FIREFIGHTING[12]

There are four types of firefighting personnel. A *volunteer* receives no compensation, other than perhaps a stipend for out-of-pocket expenses (such as clothing) or time spent in training.[13] A *paid-on-call* officer is paid only for the time spent responding to a service call. A *reserve* firefighter performs non-firefighting functions like fire prevention. Finally, a permanent *full-time* firefighter is paid an annual salary and fringe benefits, subject to the Fair Labor Standards Act.

Departments organize in four ways. In a *fully volunteer* department, a dispatcher notifies responders via pagers and sirens. The *mostly volunteer* department is manned by one full-time firefighter, who drives the fire engine to the scene, where he or she is met by volunteers. The *mostly full-time* department is staffed by full-time officers, who handle routine calls, but is supplemented by volunteers, who respond to a serious incident. Finally, the *full-time* department has no volunteer assistance.

Full-time firefighters, in addition to their firefighting and emergency-medical duties, perform other duties such as teaching CPR, inspecting child safety-seat installation, conducting fire-prevention programs, and testing fire hydrants.

Fire-Response Staffing

Sometimes hotly debated is how many personnel should respond to a fire.[14] NFPA Standard 1500 recommends that at least five firefighters (one to operate the pump, two for the initial attack, and two for backup) be on the scene before the attack and use a 1.5-inch or 2-inch line that pumps 125–200 gallons per minute. Sixty-three percent of departments report having adopted NFPA Standard 1500, but actual staffing averaged 3.1 persons per pumper and 2.9 per ladder truck.[15] If the hose line is 1.5 inch or more, OSHA requires that two firefighters inside a building be backed by two firefighters outside, each equipped with a self-contained breathing apparatus (SCBA).

A volunteer cannot be counted on to respond to an incident. Experts estimate that three volunteers are needed on call for every volunteer who is able to respond to an alarm.[16] The response-time continuum is as follows:

- The fire initiates.
- Someone is aware of the fire.
- Someone notifies the department.
- Firefighters are dispatched to the scene.
- The apparatus travels to the scene.
- The hoses are connected to a water supply.
- The fire is fought and the incident terminated.

The *notification time* is the interval between the first ring of the 911 call and its transfer to the fire dispatcher (the dispatcher interval). A department should set response-time goals. The NFPA recommends these performance standards be achieved in at least 90 percent of responses from the time a call is dispatched to a department:

- 1 minute turnout time (that is, time to outfit and get on the apparatus)
- 4 minutes or sooner for the first engine company to arrive at the fire
- 8 minutes or sooner for the full deployment of a full first-alarm assignment
- 4 minutes or sooner for the arrival of an EMS first-responder unit
- 8 minutes or sooner for the arrival of an advanced life-support unit

In general, high-performance fire departments can arrive at a fire in five minutes, including the dispatch *and* travel time.[17] One measure of firefighting effectiveness is the percentage of fires responded to that are confined to the room of origin. The critical stage of a fire, the *flashover stage*, occurs when the fire spreads beyond the room of origin. Considerably more water and personnel are then required. After the flashover, typically an eight-minute period, people are rendered unconscious and suffer brain damage due to a depleted oxygen supply. Figure 3.2 shows the amount of destruction that can be expected depending on the length of a fire.

Figure 3.2   **Fire Flashover Point**

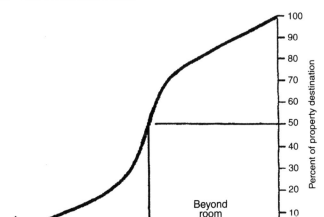

Source: Reprinted with permission from NFPA 1710-2004, *Standard for the Organization and Deployment of Fire Suppression Operations, Emergency Medical Operations and Special Operations to the Public by Career Departments* (2001). Copyright © 2004 National Fire Protection Association, Quincy, MA 02169. This reprinted material is not the official position of the NFPA on the referenced subject which is represented solely by the standard in its entirety. Available at https://www.nfpa.org/codesonline/document.asp?action=load&scope=2&path=NFPA/codes/nfpa1500.

Fireground Operations[18]

A fire goes through three stages. In the first stage, *smoldering*, the heat contacts a combustible material. A fire may proceed slowly or immediately to the second stage, *incipient*, when flames occur in the immediate area of origin. Finally, in the *flashover* stage, a superheated gas layer forms at the ceiling and banks down to the floor. All combustible objects are heated, and the fire spreads to other rooms and floors.

In 1990, the National Service Incident Management System (IMS) consortium was created, consisting of federal, state, and local government fire services. In 1993, the IMS issued *Model Procedures Guide for Structural Firefighting*, establishing standard operational protocols, which were adopted by the National Fire Academy.[19] In 2004, the Department of Homeland Security (DHS) issued the National Incident Management System (NIMS), a standard, on-scene, *all hazards* incident-management system that incorporates the best features of the IMS procedures.[20] Local units must adopt NIMS to receive DHS funds.

Fire departments often enter into mutual aid agreements with each other, ensuring that departments will back each other up in the case of particular calls for service. Engine companies systematically assist each other according to agreed-upon protocols.

The NIMS protocols call for an incident commander (IC) to set the overall objectives and strategy for the incident response. The IC develops an incident action plan. Large fires are sectored; that is, divided into smaller, more manageable command areas. Each sector is supervised by a sector officer to reduce the span of control, improve communication, and enhance safety. The commander keeps a tactical record of the current status of firefighting activities.

The attack plan specifies the optimal attack entry point, the force size, the support functions (such as ventilation, forcible entry), and the timing (when to start the attack and its duration). The IC assesses the extent of the risk (for example, threats to life, type of exposure, weather conditions, and water supply), hydrant capabilities, and apparatus requirements. Based on this analysis, the IC decides on the type of response (for example, rescue, confinement, extinguishment), taking one of two strategies:

- *Offensive Strategy.* Attack the fire inside the structure. Move people away from the area of a chemical exposure.
- *Defensive Strategy.* If conditions are too severe to make an interior attack, spray large streams on the exterior.

Whichever the strategy, the first priority is always to rescue victims either outside or inside the building who are unaware of the fire, trapped, or overcome. During the primary search, firefighters locate and rescue victims. Those who are ambulatory are evacuated to a control area. The status of each person in a building must be accounted for. Other tasks include:

- *Attack.* The OSHA 2-in/2-out standard requires at least two two-person teams at the scene. At least two firefighters are required to manage medium-sized hose (at least 100 GPM); three to manage 200+ GPM hose. The size of the line will depend on the type of structure, the distance to the fire, and the stage of the fire. A larger line is used when a fire flashes over.
- *Ventilation.* At least two firefighters ventilate a building before the attack crew enters. If ventilated too early, a fire may intensify with the added oxygen.
- *Rapid Intervention.* A minimum of two firefighters, equipped with an SCBA, search and rescue or act as a backup to the entry crew.
- *Water Supply.* One or more firefighters pull the hose to the pump, if not already laid out on the way in.

- *Pump Operator.* One firefighter delivers water, monitors water pressure, and hooks up hose to connect discharges.
- *Command.* One officer coordinates the attack outside the structure.
- *Safety Officer.* One officer ensures that safety policies and procedures are followed.

In a building fire, the primary goal is to control unburned areas, particularly stairways and hallways. Concealed spaces (such as attics, ceiling areas) are opened and fire streams applied in the appropriate volume, direction, and nozzle velocity.

Local, state, and federal regulations specify clothing and equipment to be used, as do the following NFPA clothing standards:

- NFPA 1975—Station/Work Uniforms
- NFPA 1976—Clothing for Proximity Firefighting
- NFPA 1977—Wildland Firefighting Clothing
- NFPA 1981—Open Self-Contained Breathing Apparatus
- NFPA 1999—Clothing for Emergency Medical Operations
- NFPA 1581—Cleaning Protective Clothing

During the attack, safety is of utmost importance. The incident command center tracks the location of firefighters; a simple system attaches a Velcro tag to firefighters to identify their position as they pass between locations. More sophisticated and accurate, an electronic safety system attaches an electronic tracking device to firefighters.

The safety officer has the authority to terminate operations if safety is imminently threatened (for example, a roof may collapse). Among the safety standard operating guidelines are:

- NFPA 581—Protect against exposure to AIDS, blood-borne pathogens, and hepatitis
- NFPA 1500—Create an occupational safety and health program
- NFPA 1521—Fire Department Safety Officer responsibilities
- NFPA 1401—Fire training reports
- NFPA 1403—Live conditions fire training
- NFPA 1451—Fire vehicle operations
- OSHA Regulation 29 CFR 1910.146—Entry into confined spaces

In a small department, conserving property usually occurs after the fire has been contained; however, large departments, with more staffing, may be able to attack the fire and salvage property simultaneously, especially in a one-floor residence. After the event, the occupancy is returned to its original use if it is not too severely damaged.

The U.S. Fire Administration offers a pamphlet to assist victims to recover from fires. The publication *After the Fire: Returning to Normal* (available at http://www.usfa.dhs.gov/citizens/all%5Fcitizens/atf/) addresses issues of insurance, replacement of valuable documents and records, and salvaging various items.

Critical Incident Debriefing

The National Institute for Occupational Safety and Health (NIOSH) investigates all firefighter fatalities. The NIOSH has found that five factors contribute to fatalities:

1. Lack of incident command
2. Inadequate risk assessment
3. Lack of firefighter accountability
4. Inadequate communications
5. Lack of standard operating procedures[21]

The fire department should conduct a post-incident evaluation as well, not only when a fatality occurs, but also in the event of a severe injury or a near miss. The evaluation should not be accusatory, but rather a frank, honest discussion of what happened and the remedies, if any, that should be taken. Ideally, a critical incident should be debriefed within twenty-four hours of the occurrence. A death or other traumatic incident can cause a post-traumatic stress disorder (PTSD). In such a case, the department should make professional counseling available to a victim of PTSD.

Performance Evaluation

Firefighting measures include:

- Fires limited to x percent of the area (for example, one room)
- Time to control the fire
- Number of false alarms
- Fire rate
- Response time

COMMUNICATIONS

The communications system is the link between a call for service, emergency alarms, vehicles, and traffic signals. Some departments can electronically control traffic signals en route to an emergency. The communication system should have station-to-station and apparatus-to-station capabilities. The system should also build in operational redundancy in case of a systems failure. A public utility may supply backup power; otherwise the department needs it own backup system.

In an area with numerous public safety departments, the demand for bandwidth is often extremely high. A trunked radio system alleviates such overcrowding. Usually operated on an 800MHz radio band, a trunked system permits multiple users to communicate, mediates between transmission sources, selectively encrypts messages, and enables the formation of user "talk groups."[22]

A well-designed system accommodates future technological change. For instance, the system should be able to add an automated vehicle-location system, switch from portable radios to in-car repeaters for better reception, and accommodate future demands such as more alarm traffic and dedicated trunk lines.

Departments usually adopt standard operating dispatch guidelines, including a call-prioritization protocol. For example, a house fire takes priority over a less harmful grass fire. Other protocols may include:

- Dispatcher code of conduct
- The number and type of apparatus to be dispatched to particular types of service calls
- Whom to notify in case of an emergency
- Mutual-aid backup from neighboring departments

A centralized regional dispatching facility may reduce local units' operating costs because of economies of scale. A large system typically uses GIS-supported, computer-aided-dispatch (CAD) software able to identify a caller's location and recommend the staffing and apparatus to respond to a call. The dispatcher reviews the CAD system's recommendation to make a final decision about turnout. An *enhanced 911 system* identifies the caller's number, name, and location. This system has two distinct advantages over the standard 911 system:

- False-alarm calls are significantly fewer because callers' names are identified.
- The location of non-English-speaking callers (such as the very young, disabled, and immigrants) can be pinpointed.

A 311 system takes nonemergency calls, freeing the 911 system to receive more urgent emergencies.

WATER SUPPLY

Fire departments get their water from a community water system or tanker. A water supply officer may be designated to oversee water supply and record water-system changes and hydrant locations and condition. Needed fire flow (NFF) is the amount of water required to control a fire. The NFF is expressed in gallons per minute (GPM) at 20 pounds per square inch (PSI) reserve hydrant pressure. The NFF for a one- or two-story residential property depends on its distance from other structures. Houses over 100 feet apart need 500 GPM; houses less than 100 feet apart need 1,500 GPM.

NFPA Standard 1710 requires an uninterrupted water supply of 400 GPM for thirty minutes, delivered by two water lines pumping at 300 gallons per minute. Water supply counts for 40 percent of an ISO rating. ISO specifies the number of engine companies based on the NFF in the community. The NFF must continue from two to ten hours, depending on the amount of water needed. Most pumpers are equipped with a 1,000 or 1,500 GPM pump.

In a rural area without a piped water supply, some departments supply water by means of a shuttle-tanker system. An engine company draws water from the nearest designated water source (a river, lake, or pond), setting up a mobile water relay, usually with a five-inch-diameter hose. Generally, for every 100 gallons of NFF, one tanker is needed. For a community to receive an ISO Class 8 rating, water pumped at 250 GPM must be deliverable for two hours.

The fire department works closely with the water department to decide where to locate hydrants. An ISO standard sets the maximum distance between hydrants, but departments must often set them closer; for instance, near high-rise buildings and where fire trucks have limited parking space. NFPA Standard 291 recommends that hydrants be color-coded to denote their flow, pressure, and main size. The ISO requires that hydrants be tested at least twice a year. During the test, the area around a hydrant is cleared of shrubs and brush, and the hydrant is lubricated and inspected for damage. The hydrant tester records each hydrant's water flow to determine the amount of water available should a fire occur.

Performance Evaluation

Water-supply measures include:

- The percentage of households that have at least the recommended 1,000-gallons-per-minute water supply
- The percentage of fire hydrants tested and serviced annually, and the percentage of hydrants available when responding to fires

HAZARDOUS-MATERIALS OPERATIONS

Handling hazardous-materials is highly specialized and dangerous. OSHA certifies hazardous-materials specialists at four levels:

- *Level 1—Certified* (Awareness Level). Has basic knowledge about hazardous materials.
- *Level 2—Operations.* Can handle hazardous materials.
- *Level 3—Materials Technician.* Can handle and move hazardous materials.
- *Level 4—Materials Specialist.* Can handle incidents involving highway tank trucks, rail tank cars, and compressed gases.

Another OSHA certification, Weapons of Mass Destruction Specialist, is under design. In addition, NFPA Standards 471 and 473 specify the competencies needed by Hazmat incident responders.

The department should prepare a Hazmat plan based on a risk assessment of the release of hazardous materials in manufacturing plants, chemical-processing plants, railroads, highways, airports, and other vulnerable facilities. The state typically regulates the design of containers and facilities, hazardous-materials handling and processing procedures, and incident reporting. Hazardous-materials sites should be regularly inspected.

In the event of an incident, responders evaluate the extent of the risk, don protective clothing, implement response procedures, and decontaminate the area. An excellent guide to hazardous materials regulation is *Hazardous Materials: Managing the Incident,* by Gregory Noll, Michael Hildebrand, and James Yvorra.[23] Figure 3.3 shows a hazardous material response team.

PREVENTION

Sprinkler systems (see Figure 3.4), smoke alarms, and improved construction materials have combined to dramatically decrease the frequency and severity of fires. There is still room for improvement, however. For instance, too many homes have no smoke detectors. A fire-prevention program fights citizen apathy, providing schools, businesses, civic groups, and individuals with fire-prevention information.

At the core of the prevention program are the community's construction-design regulations. Although reviewing design and construction plans is the ultimate responsibility of the city planner and city attorney, the fire-prevention head should also examine them to ensure compliance with fire- and building-code provisions regarding access, exits, sprinkler plumbing, and standpipe systems.

Figure 3.3 **Hazardous Materials Response Team**

Source: U.S. National Guard.

There are two basic types of inspections: (1) fire and building code inspections and (2) pre-fire plan inspections. As a service to homeowners, some departments also inspect household smoke alarms and extinguishers, usually upon request. Some states require local governments to follow a state fire-and-building code, others permit them to supplement the state code, and still others authorize them to adopt their own code. Whatever the case, the code is usually based on a model, such as that of the International Code Congress and the NFPA.[24] The fire-prevention code is often incorporated into the building code, including requirements that (1) fire-resistant building materials be used in construction and (2) smoke detectors be placed in large buildings and structures that pose a great hazard, such as schools and theaters.

At issue are state-required sprinklers. In particular, should states require sprinklers in nursing homes, fraternities and sororities, and large homes?

NFPA Standard 101, *Code for Safety to Life from Fire In Buildings and Structures,* recommends building-inspection procedures. In some departments, the chief inspector is a non-sworn civilian. A civilian holding a degree in fire

Figure 3.4 **Sprinkler System Design**

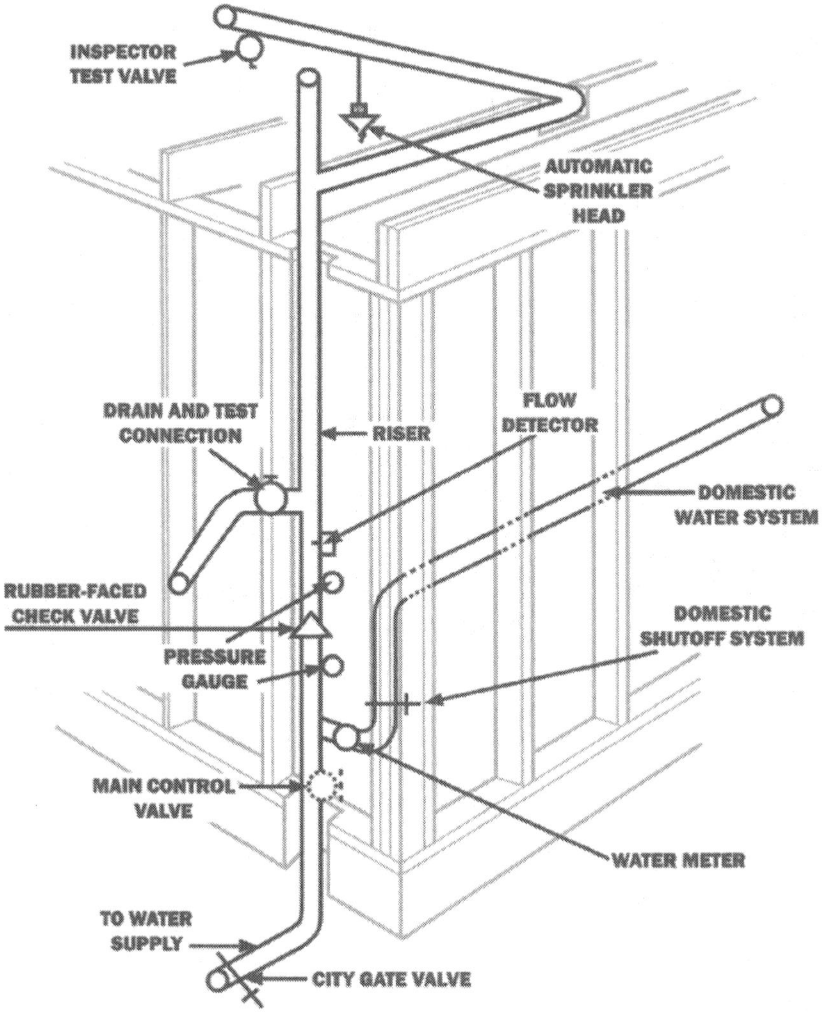

INSPECTOR TEST VALVE

AUTOMATIC SPRINKLER HEAD

DRAIN AND TEST CONNECTION

RISER

FLOW DETECTOR

DOMESTIC WATER SYSTEM

RUBBER-FACED CHECK VALVE

DOMESTIC SHUTOFF SYSTEM

PRESSURE GAUGE

MAIN CONTROL VALVE

WATER METER

TO WATER SUPPLY

CITY GATE VALVE

Reprinted with permission from Ronny J. Coleman, Fire Force One.

protection engineering is often more skilled than a less trained firefighter. The state licenses and certifies fire-code inspectors and investigators.

Inspection frequency depends on the type of structure. A *company inspection* is a routine check of standpipes, sprinkler valves, obstructed exits, and fire extinguishers. When a code violation is found, a notice is issued and a follow-up inspection made. A *technical inspection,* conducted by a specially trained

Table 3.2

NIFRS Data Elements

Basic Incidents
Incident number
Incident date and time
Location
Type
Action taken (up to three)
Aid given or received (mutual aid or automatic aid)
Times for the following: alarm, on location, control, last unit cleared
Shift working and number of alarms
Resources used (apparatus and personnel for these categories: suppression, EMS, other)
Casualties (fire and civilian)
Property use
Property owner
Person or entity involved in the incident (owner, occupant, etc.)

Fires
Property details
On-site materials or products
Ignition details, including cause
Factors contributing to ignition
Human factors contributing to ignition
Equipment involved
Fire suppression factors
Mobile property

Structure Fires
Building data (structure type, status, height, ground-floor area)
Fire origin (location, spread, damage, factors contributing to flame spread)
Detector data (presence, type, power supply, effectiveness)
Automatic extinguishment equipment (presence, type, operation, effectiveness, reason for failure)

Civilian Casualties
Casualty personal data
Cause of injury
Human factors contributing to injury
Nonhuman factors contributing to injury
Activity when injured
Location at time of injury
Primary symptom and area of the body injured

Firefighter Casualties
Firefighter personal data
Primary symptom, cause, object involved, area of the body injured, factors contributing
Location where injury occurred

Source: http://www.nfirs.fema.gov/_download/nfirspec_2006.pdf.

inspector, is an inspection of an industrial plant. Before such an inspection, the inspector reviews the building's structural makeup and location.[25] Often beginning on the roof, the inspector examines exit doors, no-smoking signs, ventilation, insulation, and wiring, recording any violations or recommendations.

Arson investigation is highly specialized. An arson investigator may be trained in a police-run arson-investigation program or in the program run by the National Fire Academy. In many states, arson investigation is the sole responsibility of the state. In which case, if arson is suspected; the evidence should be secured until a state investigator arrives. The investigator takes samples, interprets burn patterns, prepares an arson-identification report, and testifies in court if required.

Performance Evaluation

Among fire-prevention performance measures are

- the time taken to make inspections,
- the ratio of inspected to uninspected buildings,
- the percentage of buildings inspected annually,
- the percentage of detected fire and housing violations corrected within a specified time period,
- the percentage of dwellings with smoke detectors.

In 1976, the U.S. Fire Administration created the National Incident Fire Reporting System (NIFRS) to report fire incidence, fire causes, injuries, deaths, and property loss. Fire departments voluntarily report data to states, which forward it to the USFA. Forty-nine states and 46 percent of their fire departments participate in the NIFRS program.[26] Table 3.2 (on page 49) indicates the data elements reported to the USFA.

NOTES

1. For an interesting discussion of fire equipment, refer to Arthur Ingram, *A History of Firefighting and Equipment* (Secaucus, NJ: Chartwell Books, 1978).

2. Gerry Souter and Janet Souter, *The American Fire Station* (Oseola, WI: Motorbooks International, 1998), 30.

3. Ibid., 54.

4. Ingram, *History of Firefighting and Equipment.*

5. The National Fire Protection Association (NFPA), *The U.S. Fire Problem* (Quincy, MA: NFPA, 2001).

6. P. Michael Freeman, "Organizing and Deploying Resources," in *Managing Fire and Rescue Services,* ed. Dennis Compton and John Granito (Washington, DC: ICMA, 2002), 105–138.

7. Michael Karter Jr., *Fire Department Profile through 2000* (Quincy, MA: NFPA, 2001).

8. University of Tennessee Municipal Technical Advisory Service, *Physical Fitness in Public Safety*. Available at http://www.mtas.tennessee.edu/knowledgebase. nsf/PrinterFriendlyProductWeb?OpenForm&ParentUNID=652369D28D5BA0F38 5256C0900537C2D.

9. To learn more about the process, contact the Center for Public Safety Excellence, Inc., 4501 Singer Court, Suite 180, Chantilly VA 20151; (703) 691-4620 or http://publicsafetyexcellence.org.

10. For further explanation, see *Creating and Evaluating Standards of Response Coverage for Fire Departments,* 4th ed., published by the Commission on Fire Accreditation International. Available at http://www.riskinstitute.org/peri/images/file/ cfaimanual.pdf.

11. William Peters, *Fire Apparatus Purchasing Handbook* (Saddle Brook, NJ: Fire Engineering Books and Videos, 1994).

12. For a very comprehensive discussion of the fire service, see Robert Barr and John Eversole, *The Fire Chief's Handbook,* 6th ed. (Saddle Brook, NJ: Fire Engineering Books & Video, 2003).

13. CFAI, *Creating and Evaluating Standards of Response Coverage for Fire Departments,* 4th ed. (Chantilly, VA: CFAI, 2008).

14. Ibid., chapter 5, 14.

15. Evelina Moulder, *The Municipal Yearbook* (Washington, DC: ICMA, 2001), 120.

16. John Swain, "Fire and Other Emergency Services," in *Managing Local Government Services,* ed. Carl Stenberg and Susan Austin (Washington, DC: ICMA, 2007), 341–368.

17. David Ammons, *Municipal Benchmarks,* 2nd ed. (Thousand Oaks, CA: Sage Publications, 2001), 157.

18. For a detailed discussion of fireground command procedures, see Alan Bruancini, *Fire Command* (Quincy, MA: National Fire Protection Association, 1985).

19. In 1980, the National Academy adopted a similar system, Firefighting Resources of California Organized for Potential Emergencies, used widely but not adopted as a national standard.

20. For a discussion of FEMA's National Incident Management System, see http://www.fema.gov/emergency/nims/index.shtm.

21. Steve Foley, "Firefighter Occupational Safety," in *Firefighter Safety at Emergency Incidents* (Fairfax, VA: Public Entity Risk Institute, 2000).

22. For a full discussion of the advantages of trunked radio systems, see Tim Dees, "Information and Communications Technology for Public Safety," *IQ Report* 32, no. 1 (Washington, DC: ICMA, 2000).

23. Gregory G. Noll, Michael S. Hildebrand, and James G. Yvorra, *Hazardous Materials: Managing the Incident,* 3rd ed. (Stillwater, OK: Fire Protection Publications, University of Oklahoma, 2005).

24. Swain, 342.

25. For a more detailed description of inspections, see Harry Carter and Erwin Rausch, *Management in the Fire Service,* 2nd ed. (Quincy, MA: National Fire Protection Association, 1994).

26. U.S. Fire Administration, *NIFRS: Introduction to the National Fire Incident Reporting System*. Available at http://www.usfa.fema.gov.

FOR FURTHER READING

Barr, Robert, and John Eversole. *The Fire Chief's Handbook,* 6th ed. Saddle Brook, NJ: Fire Engineering Books & Video, 2003.

Bruancini, Alan. *Fire Command.* Quincy, MA: National Fire Protection Association, 1985.

Compton, Dennis, and John Granito, eds. *Managing Fire and Rescue Services.* Washington, DC: International City/County Management Association, 2002.

Ingram, Arthur. *A History of Firefighting and Equipment.* Secaucus, NJ: Chartwell Books, 1978.

4

Emergency Medical Services

HISTORY

The National Academy of Sciences (NAS) proposed the creation of an emergency medical services (EMS) system in 1966.[1] Until then, ambulance services were mostly provided by funeral homes that offered transport but no medical services. The NAS white paper advocated training, equipping, and regulating an EMS service. In 1966, Congress passed the National Highway Safety Act, requiring states to prepare an EMS program or lose their highway construction funds. The federal Department of Transportation established EMS operating standards and the qualifications for emergency medical technician (EMT) and paramedic positions. In 1973, Congress passed the Emergency Medical Services Systems Act, which funded regional systems. In 1981, Congress reduced EMS funding, but by then, EMS systems were firmly in place nationwide.

MANAGEMENT

The state regulates ambulance services, trauma care, trauma-care centers, EMS vehicle permits, EMS personnel certification, poison-control centers, and the statewide communication system. An advanced life support (ALS) system is staffed by personnel certified to give advanced medical care. A hospital sponsors the ALS, serving as its primary facility. A medical director affiliated with the hospital oversees the medical aspects of the ALS system and certifies EMS personnel. The medical director is usually part-time, spending fewer than twenty hours weekly on EMS duties.[2] Emergency responders operate under the medical license of the medical director. To be a licensed ALS, each ambulance must be licensed and regularly inspected.

EMS includes on-scene emergency care and non-emergency care. Non-emergency ambulance service transports patients to medical facilities. Medi-

53

care, Medicaid, and private insurance companies require that non-emergency ambulance service be approved by a physician. Emergency and non-emergency services are delivered through any of six organizational arrangements:[3]

- *Fire Department.* Firefighters provide the service.
- *EMS Department.* An EMS department provides the service.
- *A Private Firm.* The local government contracts with a private firm to deliver the service.
- *An Independent Agency.* A nonprofit agency—financed by donations, user fees, and government grants—delivers the service.
- *A Hospital.* A local hospital delivers the service.
- *A Hybrid.* A for-profit firm responds to non-emergencies; a fire department or EMS department handles emergencies.

Departments of whatever type must buy liability insurance and are usually subjected to an annual financial audit.

Human Resource Management

An EMS agency is staffed by paid personnel, volunteers, or a combination of the two. An all-volunteer department is typically overseen by a volunteer board of directors. EMS personnel are certified at four levels:

- First responder
- Emergency medical technician-basic (EMT-B)
- EMT-intermediate (EMT-I)
- EMT-paramedic (EMT-P)

The EMS Division of the U.S. National Highway Traffic Safety Administration has established minimum standards for the training and certification of EMS personnel who can be accredited by the National Registry of Emergency Medical Technicians or by the state. Depending upon state law, the EMT-B position requires between 80 and 160 hours of training and passing a certification exam. An EMT-B is certified to administer CPR and oxygen, splint a fracture, control a hemorrhage, perform an emergency childbirth, and immobilize spinal injuries. An EMT-I may establish an intravenous line in a peripheral vein, administer en route intravenous fluids, and obtain blood for laboratory analysis. An EMT-I and a paramedic perform approved protocols and procedures, overseen by a physician medical director. Among other procedures that a paramedic performs are manual defibrillation, chest decompression by needle thoracotomy, suction by intubation, urinary catheterization, and pulmonary ventilation. Because of the demanding skills required, a paramedic is usually full-time, not a volunteer. The number of hours that a paramedic needs for certification varies with the state. For instance, New York requires 2,000 hours of training; Washington and North Carolina, only 1,000.

A basic difference between the skill levels is in the case of "code blues," or patients without a pulse or respiration. At the basic level, responders are permitted to perform CPR, insert a nasal or oral pharyngeal airway, and defibrillate with the aid of a semi-automated defibrillator. At the intermediate level, responders additionally can intubate a patient and administer courses of drugs including epinephrine, atropine, and sodium bicarbonate. Paramedics also can induce hypothermia through IV fluids.

Some states hold full-time staff to a higher training standard than they do volunteers, recognizing that volunteers have less time to train and that recruiting volunteers is problematic in some communities. Some departments use a life-size mannequin to train. The mannequin reacts to medical interventions, including telling the trainee when she or he has killed it in the course of treatment.

EMERGENCY RESPONSE

There are two basic types of response: emergency and non-emergency. In an emergency response, among the most frequently employed lifesaving procedures are opening a blocked airway, restarting a stopped heart with a defibrillator, injecting epinephrine in response to an allergic reaction, and stopping bleeding.[4]

Dispatch

States certify EMS telecommunicators or emergency medical dispatchers as being able to assess a caller's medical condition, determine the appropriate response (for example, with or without flashing lights and siren), and relay medical instructions to responders who can call for medical instruction as well. Dispatchers follow the medical-dispatch protocols established by the National Academies of Emergency Dispatch, which accredit dispatch systems. After a call from the public, a dispatcher has the following options:

- Refer the caller to a primary health care provider/network
- Refer the caller to a social service agency
- Call for an emergency response
- Call for a non-emergency response
- Call for medical transportation
- Refer the call to law enforcement and other public safety services

Agencies take one of two service-delivery approaches. The *all-paramedic system* provides a standard level of service, regardless of the type of call. A *tiered system* distinguishes between a paramedic-level and basic-service-level response. The dispatcher follows a standard interrogation protocol to decide which type is required. Management should periodically sample dispatched calls to evaluate whether the proper response was taken. Different types of ambulances are dispatched:

- A basic-life-support (BLS) ambulance, usually staffed by two EMT-Bs.
- An advanced-life-support (ALS) ambulance, staffed with an EMT-B and a paramedic, an EMT-I and a paramedic, or two paramedics.[5]
- Some systems also employ a paramedic intercept system. A BLS ambulance may require an ALS ambulance to intercept it en route to the hospital.

Response Time

For critical events, response time is, of course, paramount. There are twelve response-time increments:

1. Time between the 911 call's being received and transferred to the EMS
2. Time between the phone ringing and an EMS dispatcher picking it up
3. Time between receiving the call and verifying the location
4. Time between verifying the location and transferring call details to the dispatcher's screen
5. Time between the call's appearance in the to-be-dispatched queue and its dispatch to a crew
6. Time between when the crew receives the call and is en route
7. Time between when the crew in en route and arrives at the scene
8. Time between when the crew arrives at the scene and reaches the patient
9. Time at the scene
10. Time between the crew's departing the scene and arriving at its destination
11. Time before the crew is available for further work

The *chute time* is the time from the receipt of the call before the vehicle gets rolling. The *hospital time* is the time to convey the patient to the hospital and be available again for dispatch. Some systems establish hospital-time maximums. Wake County, North Carolina, for example, mandates that no

Table 4.1

Cardiac-Arrest Outcomes by Response Times

Collapse to CPR (minutes)	Collapse to Defibrillation (minutes)	Probability of Survival (%)
5 or less minutes	10 or less minutes	37
5 or less minutes	More than 10 minutes	7
More than 5 minutes	10 or less minutes	20
More than 5 minutes	More than 10 minutes	0

Source: Commission of Fire Accreditation International, Inc. *Creating and Evaluating Standards of Response Coverage for Fire Departments* (Chantilly, 2003), Chapter 4, 7.

more than twenty minutes be spent by a unit at the hospital to ensure adequate service levels.

A rapid response to a cardiac arrest is literally a matter of life and death. Figure 4.1 indicates the events associated with a cardiac-arrest resuscitation attempt. The most widely accepted standard response time to treat a cardiac-arrest victim in an urban area is eight minutes and fifty-nine seconds from the time of the event in 90 percent of the times called.[6] Allowing for a one-minute interval from the time of the event to the 911 call, the time from the call dispatch to the defibrillation should therefore not exceed eight minutes.[7] A five-minute response time allows three minutes for a responder to locate the patient and administer the defibrillator shock. Even an eight-minute response, though, may not guarantee success, as shown by Table 4.1.

Emergency Care

Only about 57 percent of EMS calls require transport to a hospital.[8] Callers are not transported in the instance of a false alarm, a non-emergency, or a patient who refuses care. If treatment or transport is refused, the responder should explain to the patient the possible negative medical implications and require the patient to sign the American Medical Association's medical care refusal form. The responder should keep a patient-care record, describing the initial assessment, the treatment, and patient wishes and concerns, including the reason for refusing treatment or transport. Failure to record such information completely and accurately leaves the agency open to litigation.

An EMS responder should follow an "A–E" approach.

- **Airway:** Are the mouth, throat, trachea, and bronchi open?
- **Breathing:** Can the lungs get enough oxygen to pass into the bloodstream?

58

Figure 4.1   **Events Associated with Cardiac Arrest**

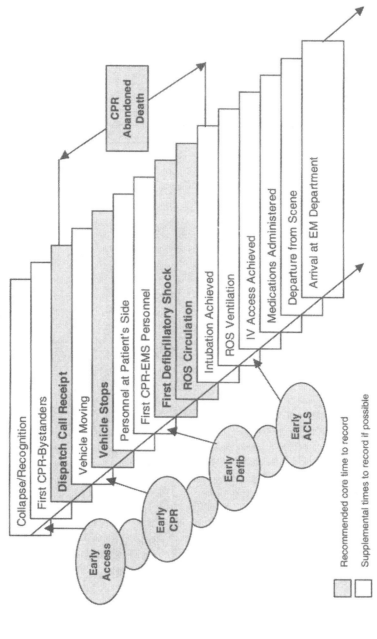

Source: Commission of Fire Accreditation International, Inc., *Creating and Evaluating Standards of Response Coverage for Fire Departments* (Chantilly, VA, 2003), Chapter 4, 6. Copyright © 2003 Commission on Fire Accreditation International, Inc. Reprinted with permission.

- Circulation: Is the blood pressure adequate for the blood to reach vital organs like the liver, kidneys, and brain?
- Disability: How is the neurological function?
- Exposure: Has any part of the body been neglected because of too much focus on one area.[9]

Responders should check to see whether they have the right patient and whether the type of medicine, dosage, and procedure (for example, orally or by injection) are correct. At the scene of a car accident or a fall, responders should check for possible spinal-cord injuries. Before administering a medication, the paramedic should determine whether the airway is open and the patient is breathing. The paramedic may then intubate the patient, inserting a tube through the nose or mouth into the trachea to facilitate breathing. The American Heart Association recommends that paramedics perform at least six to twelve intubations per year to stay in practice.

Instantaneous defibrillation is the most effective means of treating cardiac arrest. With training, nonmedical personnel can safely and effectively operate a defibrillator. Emergency medical personnel should therefore train civilians to administer defibrillation, particularly at public, highly populated locations like gyms, churches, public buildings, and shopping malls.

About three-quarters of bystanders who observe a heart attack do not perform mouth-to-mouth resuscitation, in part for fear of contracting an infectious disease like AIDS. In 2006, the National Academies of Emergency Dispatch revised their guidelines to recommend that 911 operators instruct callers to perform cardiac compression, but *not* mouth-to-mouth respiration. In 4,068 adult heart attack cases, bystanders administered conventional mouth-to-mouth resuscitation 18 percent of the time and cardiac compression only 11 percent of the time.[10] Surprisingly, those who received compression-only treatment fared twice as well.[11] Experts caution, though, that those suffering from drowning, drug overdose, or other respiratory arrests need mouth-to-mouth respiration.

For the first two cycles of CPR, responders do not ventilate the patient, performing only cardiac compression for two minutes. Research has shown that during the first minutes of a rescue, the oxygen and CO_2 levels of the patient remain within a safe level.

To provide advanced life support, some hospitals operate a critical care unit (CCU), staffed by specially trained paramedics, registered nurses, and physicians. The CCU transports the critically injured or critically ill by air (helicopter or fixed-wing aircraft) or a ground vehicle. Generally, the service area of a helicopter is restricted to a 150-mile radius. Sometimes the CCU transports patients from a small hospital, incapable of specialized care, to a large medical center.

NOTES

1. National Academy of Sciences National Research Council, *Accidental Death and Disability: The Neglected Disease of Modern Society* (Washington, DC: Division of Medical Sciences, National Academy of Sciences, 1966).

2. David Williams, "2004 JEMS 200 City Survey: A Snapshot of Facts & Trends to Create Benchmarks for Your Service," *Journal of Medical Services* 30, no. 2 (February 2005): 42–60.

3. For a discussion of the pros and cons of each approach, see Jay Fitch and Cave William, *EMS in Critical Condition: Meeting the Challenge* (Washington, DC: International City/County Management Association, 2005), 4.

4. Ibid.

5. Ibid., 6.

6. Jay Fitch, "Response Times: Myths, Measurement and Management," *Journal of Emergency Management* 30, no. 9 (September 2005).

7. Commission on Fire Accreditation International, Inc., *Creating and Evaluating Standards of Response Coverage for Fire Departments* (Chantilly, VA: 2003), chapter 4, 7.

8. Williams, "JEMS 200 City Survey."

9. Jerome Groopman, *How Doctors Think* (New York: Houghton Mifflin, 2007), 61.

10. Ken Nagao, "Cardiopulmonary Resuscitation by Bystanders with Chest Compression Only: An Observational Study," *Lancet* 9565 (2007): 920–926.

11. Ibid., 884.

FOR FURTHER READING

Fitch, Jay. *EMS in Critical Condition: Meeting the Challenge.* Washington, DC: International City/County Management Association, 2005.

Administrators need to know:
- high stress
- continuing ed is important
- trucks need to be in good working condition for quick responses
- while hired by city, operate under medical director
- low response time may mean more locations for trucks
  (cities may share service - offer locations)
- Manage volunteers

5

Emergency Management

Disasters of all kinds have plagued the United States since its earliest days. The federal government first provided financial assistance in 1803, aiding New Hampshire after an especially devastating fire. Congress subsequently passed ad hoc legislation over one hundred times to empower multiple federal agencies to assist after earthquakes, hurricanes, floods, and other natural disasters.[1] The Reconstruction Finance Corporation provided disaster loans; the Bureau of Public Roads, bridge and road repair; and the U.S. Army Corps of Engineers, flood control.

During the 1950s, the main disaster risk was that of nuclear fallout. Civil defense programs proliferated. However, Hurricanes Betsy (1965) and Camille (1969) turned the national focus to natural disaster relief. In 1968, Congress enacted the National Flood Insurance Act to offer flood-insurance protection to homeowners. In 1974, the Disaster Relief Act established a presidential disaster-declaration process to activate federal assistance to victims.

In 1979, the National Governors Association (NGA) adopted the four-phase concept of emergency management: mitigation, preparedness, response, and recovery. At that time, over one hundred federal agencies responded in some fashion to emergencies, disasters, and hazards.[2] The NGA therefore urged the federal government to centralize this haphazard approach. Accordingly, President Carter created the Federal Emergency Management Agency (FEMA) by executive order in 1979. The agencies centralized under FEMA included the National Fire Prevention and Control Administration, the Federal Insurance Administration, the National Weather Service Community Preparedness Program, the Federal Civil Defense Authority, and the Federal Disaster Assistance Administration. In 1983, FEMA adopted NGA's four-phase emergency management approach. Each local government was required to have an Emergency Operations Plan (EOP) that met state and FEMA standards.

In 1988, the Stafford Act added human-caused and technological hazards to emergency management. In 2000, the Disaster Mitigation Act required that jurisdictions develop plans to reduce the effects of disasters.

After September 11, 2001, FEMA and twenty-two other federal agencies centralized into the newly created Department of Homeland Security (DHS). To standardize the response to emergencies, DHS created by presidential order the National Incident Management System (NIMS), which state and local governments must adopt to receive a federal preparedness grant. NIMS unifies the command of multiple jurisdictions at the scene of an emergency. Nevertheless, state and local governments still have work to do. In 2006, DHS found that only 27 percent of states and 10 percent of cities were prepared to cope with a catastrophic event.[3]

In 2003, President Bush authorized by executive order the creation of a National Response Plan to provide the framework for federal interaction with state and local governments and the private sector regarding incident prevention, preparedness, response, and recovery activities.[4]

MANAGEMENT[5]

Emergency management is a coordinated effort, involving the private sector, hospitals, nonprofit agencies like the Red Cross, governments at all levels, and citizens. Local governments typically pass an ordinance that specifies

- the powers and duties of the emergency manager, who is usually appointed by the chief executive,
- a mutual-aid agreement with local units in the area,
- the penalty for noncompliance with the ordinance.[6]

Though often located in the police department, the emergency manager should be under the supervision of the CEO because the position has extensive responsibilities, especially during an extreme emergency.[7] The emergency manager acts as the liaison with other agencies (public, private, and nonprofit) and processes reimbursements from the state and federal governments.

A local government should enter into a mutual-aid agreement with other local units. The agreement delineates how each jurisdiction will share its personnel and equipment. The agreement's provisions include

- communication and incident-command protocols;
- the length of time that mutual aid will be committed;
- how to handle work-related injuries;
- what, if anything, constitutes reimbursable costs;

- training requirements;
- how to treat vehicle-repair costs.

In 2004, numerous organizations created the Emergency Management Accreditation Program (EMAP), a voluntary accreditation process for state and local emergency-management programs, based on National Fire Protection Association Standard 1600, Standard on Disaster/Emergency Management and Business Continuity Programs. EMAP requires that each government create an advisory committee. As of 2007, eight states and two municipalities were fully accredited and nine more states were conditionally accredited.[8] An emergency-management program has three principal features: emergency preparedness, response, and recovery.

PREPAREDNESS

Local governments prepare for emergencies, especially worst-case scenarios. They train responders, design their communications system to be interoperable, educate citizens to prepare for various emergencies, and enforce building-design standards. An excellent checklist of model practices, Characteristics of Effective Emergency Management Organizational Structures, is available from the Public Entity Risk Institute (www.riskinstitute.org).[9] In 2003, Homeland Security Presidential Directive 5 (HSPD-5) created the National Response Plan, which sets various threat levels as color codes (red through blue). State and local governments partner with the federal government to create and modify the plan. HSPD-5 specifies what actions to take to safeguard utilities, water systems, computer systems, transportation assets, and important industries.

Emergency Management Plan (EMP)

Local jurisdictions should prepare an EMP that assigns standard operating guidelines with regard to logistics, media relations, the line of authority, and the recovery plan. In particular, FEMA requires that an EMP include:[10]

1. *Hazard Analysis.* A risk assessment made at least every five years.
2. *Resource List.* A description of available resources.
3. *Management Mode.* The responsibilities of each responding unit, based on a clear line of authority.
4. *Communication Plan.* A public information officer (PIO) to inform the media of the emergency's status, evacuation routes, contact numbers, shelter locations, and streets that are closed.

5. *Emergency Operations Center.* A central EOC equipped with maps, a three-day supply of food and water, a generator that can provide power for at least a week, copies of the EMP, and a list of available resources.

6. *Organizing Assistance.* A plan to mobilize community resources such as the American Red Cross, the Salvation Army, and volunteer organizations in the recovery.

7. *Training.* Tabletop and mock-disaster exercises to train for likely emergencies.

8. *Intergovernmental Relations.* A plan to coordinate with federal, state, and other local units.

9. *Critical Documents.* A record of contact lists, mutual-aid contracts, bid contracts, state emergency documents, a model disaster proclamation, and FEMA contracts.

The emergency management team should engage the community—including the chamber of commerce and businesses—to identify risks of four kinds:

- *Natural Disaster.* A flood, ice storm, hurricane, wildfire, or tornado.
- *Technological Disaster.* A toxic spill, transportation accident, or failure of a bridge, dam, or pipeline.
- *Civil Disaster.* A terrorist incident, hostage-taking, or civil unrest.
- *Biological and Chemical Disaster.* An incident involving a nerve gas, lethal plant toxin, or bacterial pathogen.

The hazard analysis typically ranks the likelihood of expected loss from each type of disaster. To make a hazard analysis of natural disasters, the local unit may use the software program—Hazards in the United States (HAZUS)—prepared by FEMA and the National Institute of Building Sciences. Originally developed to predict earthquake losses, the program now also models the impact of hurricanes and flooding. The program, available free at www.fema.gov/plan/prevent/hazus/, utilizes geographic information system GIS software to compute and display a natural disaster's likely effect on prominent buildings, critical facilities, health-care programs, the transportation system, and utilities.

A comprehensive risk analysis should take stock of all hazards, including threats of a tornado, flood, hazardous material spill, major fire, major snow/ice storm, hurricane, drought, biological hazard, crashed aircraft, major power outage, volcano, civil disorder, water supply contamination, water or sewer service interruption, radiological incident, tsunami, and major bomb threat. Key stakeholders evaluate each threat with regard to three criteria:

- How likely is an incident?
- How could an incident be prevented?
- How could the effects of an incident be mitigated?

As Hurricane Katrina too tragically illustrated, the EMP should provide for the protection and evacuation of citizens with special needs, such as those in nursing homes, hospitals, and mental-health facilities. The Americans with Disabilities Act requires that the EMP provide for the disabled, including:

- Warning those with impaired sight or hearing
- Warning those who do not speak English
- Evacuating those who are not ambulatory

Training

Once created, the EMP must be continually practiced by the emergency-management team, including the incident commander, emergency managers, and first responders. Training assistance is offered by state and federal agencies, including:

- The state emergency-management agency
- FEMA, whose Emergency Management Institute offers courses in advanced HAZUS analysis, debris management, public information, incident-command systems, radiological-threat preparedness, community emergency-response teams, and homeland security[11]
- The Department of Homeland Security, which offers four incident command system (ICS) courses: Introduction to ICS, Basic ICS, Intermediate ICS, and Advanced ICS

Local units have four training options. The most common method, a *tabletop exercise,* practices on a tabletop a hypothetical scenario featuring situations likely to be faced in a particular emergency. The exercise usually includes senior staff members in an informal setting using a hazard-specific scenario and injected messages simulating field-derived information.[12] The second method, a *functional exercise,* practices in the field procedures (such as medical treatment or communications) in a scenario-driven setting. Third, a *partial-scale exercise* practices a limited response to an emergency, often combining an in-house simulation with teams deployed to the field.[13] Finally, the *full-scale exercise,* less often conducted because of its cost, completely simulates the entire disaster scenario in conditions as close as possible to an actual event. Typically, a full-scale exercise involves the participation of many stakeholders, such as other local governments, hospitals, the Red Cross, nursing homes, and businesses. Such an exercise may either be announced in advance or be a surprise. After the exercise, stakeholders evaluate what went well and what should be improved. The cost of a full-scale exercise can be funded through an Emergency Management Performance Grant from DHS.

Communications Interoperability

The communications system is critically important in an emergency. However, as the tragedies of September 11 and Hurricane Katrina demonstrated, agencies are often not able to communicate with each other in an extreme emergency. After September 11, the DHS established a national interoperability standard. Governments have since invested substantial funds to make their systems interoperable with those of other local units, the state government, hospitals, and public utilities like electric and gas companies.

Mitigation

An informed public can reduce the impact of a disaster on both people and property through knowing in advance

- where in the house to go during a hurricane,
- what supplies to keep on hand in case of a power outage,
- what evacuation route to take,
- what services governmental and nonprofit agencies will provide after an emergency.

Sound structural design likewise mitigates the impact of a disaster. The building code regulates building methods and materials. Some states, like Florida and California, mandate that local jurisdictions include building-code specifications that will mitigate the damage caused by hurricanes and earthquakes. As Hurricane Katrina attests, the structural requirements of a dike can dramatically affect the amount of damage incurred.

Sound land-use planning, including land acquisition, storm water management, easements, environmental review, and annexation policies, also mitigates damage. The land-use plan typically prohibits development in a floodplain.[14] FEMA has established a model floodplain-management policy, under the auspices of National Flood Insurance. In 1999, the Association of State Floodplain Managers created the Certified Floodplain Manager (CFM) program. Federal, state, and local floodplain managers are certified by successfully completing the FEMA home study course, *Managing Floodplain*

Development, available at www.FEMA.org. Some states (for example, New Mexico) require that the floodplain manager be a CFM in order to administer the local government's floodplain ordinance.

Another mitigation instrument is the National Flood Insurance Program (NFIP). In 1973, after Hurricane Agnes, Congress mandated that flood insurance be purchased on all federally backed loans. Communities had to pass an ordinance to join the NFIP. In 1993, after severe flooding in the Midwest, communities were told that they would be eligible for flood insurance only one time if they did not join the program. Today more than 20,000 communities in the NFIP have mitigation programs.[15]

The federal government operates numerous disaster mitigation programs including:

- *The Hazard Mitigation Grant Program.* Provides grants to state and local governments to implement long-term mitigation programs after a presidentially declared disaster.
- *The Pre-Disaster Mitigation Program.* Provides mitigation funding not dependent on a disaster declaration.
- *The National Earthquake Hazard Reduction Program.* Funds states to create public education, planning, mitigation, and loss estimation projects. Also funds local governments by providing HAZUS, the computer modeling tool.

Other less-well-funded programs include the National Hurricane Program, the Fire Prevention and Assistance Act, and the National Dam Safety Program.

EMERGENCY RESPONSE

The emergency-response program should include a warning system, an emergency operations center, an incident command system, mutual aid agreements, evacuation and shelter protocols, emergency medical protocols, and a means of handling mass fatalities.

Warning System

A warning system alerts citizens to the likelihood, duration, severity, and effect of an impending emergency. For instance, the warning may forecast expected inches of rain or snow, wind strength, utility outages, and road closings. Types of warning mechanisms include television and radio, loudspeakers, sirens, and door-to-door notification.[16]

Figure 5.1 **Emergency Operations Center**

Source: U.S. Army Core of Engineers, Albuquerque District.

The Emergency Operations Center (EOC) and Incident Command System (ICS)

The EOC is the central location where operations are coordinated. The EOC site should be safe from weather hazards, well supplied with food and drink, and have a reliable and redundant communications system and a media-briefing center if possible. Ideally, the EOC should be spacious enough to accommodate the emergency-management team as well as representatives from utilities and nonprofit agencies like the Red Cross. In small communities, a fire station or school may serve as the EOC. Figure 5.1 is a picture of an EOC.

Some emergencies, like a hurricane or flood, can be managed with an EOC. Others, like a hazardous-waste spill, fire, or terrorist event, may require that an ICS be established at the scene of an emergency. NIMS has established standard operating guidelines (SOGs) on how to structure, staff, and operate an ICS.[17] Operations are under the central direction of an incident commander (IC). The IC and the emergency-response team assess the extent of the threat, decide whether evacuation is necessary, inform the media and the public, and direct recovery operations. According to the system's SOGS, the team consists of the following:

- *Public Information Officer.* Informs the public, media, and other agencies about the status of the emergency.

- *Safety Officer.* Advises the IC on all matters related to operational safety.
- *Liaison Officer.* Is the contact person with other public, nonprofit, and private organizations.
- *Legal Counsel.* Gives legal counsel.
- *Medical Advisor.* Coordinates medical assistance.

Figure 5.2 indicates the SOGs for two levels of an urban search-and-rescue response. The emergency-management team controls the flow of information, follows preestablished guidelines for relief and rotation of personnel, adheres to SOGs when interacting with other emergency-care agencies, and regularly informs the media about the status of the emergency. The team must be aware of liability laws. For instance, a local government is typically held liable for damages incurred in removing limbs and trees on private property.

Volunteers can assist in some types of emergencies. Eighty-four percent of county officials and 74 percent of city officials reported relying on networks of volunteer groups in 2005.[18] Particularly useful are Community Emergency Response Teams (CERTs). Organized at the neighborhood level, CERTs assist with initial search, rescue, and medical operations.

Mutual Aid

The Emergency Management Assistance Compact is a national mutual-aid system, voluntarily adopted by forty-eight states. Communities pay for extra staffing during a disaster with FEMA paying for 75 percent of the cost. Communities enter into pre-incident mutual-aid agreements.

Evacuation and Shelter

The IC decides whether evacuation is necessary, evaluating the extent of risk, possible evacuation routes, time constraints, and shelter options. In some emergencies (such as a tornado) evacuation may be impracticable, so the only option may be to take shelter in a house or building, preferably in a small interior room with no or a few windows. Avoiding the effects of hazardous materials, on the other hand, requires evacuation. Other emergencies such as hurricanes can be anticipated, and evacuation may be required. The emergency plan designates evacuation routes and stipulates how to evacuate special populations like the disabled and those in nursing homes, hospitals, schools, and jails. Shelters are created at schools, churches, government buildings, colleges, and private buildings. Still, some citizens inevitably ignore the order to evacuate, preferring to stay put and take their chances.

Figure 5.2　**Resource: Urban Search & Rescue (US&R) Task Forces**

Resource: Urban Search & Rescue (US&R) Task Forces			
Search and Rescue			**Team**
Type I	**Type II**	**Type III**	**Type IV**
70 percent response	28 percent response		
NFPA 1670 Technician Level in area of specialty; support personnel at Operations Level	NFPA 1670 Technician Level in area of specialty; support personnel at Operations Level		
High angle rope rescue (including highline systems); confined space rescue (permit required); Advanced Life Support (ALS) intervention; communications; WMD/HM operations; defensive water rescue	Light frame construction and basic rope rescue operations; ALS intervention; HazMat conditions; communications; and trench and excavation rescue		
42-hour S&R operations. Self-sufficient for first 72 hours	12-hour S&R operations. Self-sufficient for first 72 hours		
Multi-disciplinary organization of Command, Search, Rescue, Medical, HazMat, Logistics, and Planning	Multi-disciplinary organization of Command, Search, Rescue, Medical, HazMat, Logistics, and Planning		
Potential mission duration of up to 10 days	Potential mission duration of up to 10 days		
Pnuematic Powered Tools, Electric Powered Tools, Hydraulic Powered Tools, Hand Tools, Electrical, Heavy Rigging, Technical Rope, Safety	Pnuematic Powered Tools, Electric Powered Tools, Hydraulic Powered Tools, Hand Tools, Electrical, Heavy Rigging, Technical Rope, Safety		
Antibiotics/Antifungals, Patient Comfort Medication, Pain Medications, Sedatives/Anesthetics/ Paralytics, Steroids, IV Fluids/ Volume, Immunizations/Immune Globulin, Canine Treatment, Basic Airway, Intubation, Eye Care Supplies, IV Access/Administration, Patient Assessment Care, Patient Immobilization/Extrication, Patient/ PPE, Skeletal Care, Wound Care, Patient Monitoring	Antibiotics/Antifungals, Patient Comfort Medication, Pain Medications, Sedatives/Anesthetics/ Paralytics, Steroids, IV Fluids/ Volume, Immunizations/Immune Globulin, Canine Treatment, Basic Airway, Intubation, Eye Care Supplies, IV Access/Administration, Patient Assessment Care, Patient Immobilization/Extrication, Patient/ PPE, Skeletal Care, Wound Care, Patient Monitoring		
Structures Specialist Equip, Technical Information Specialist Equip, HazMat Specialist Equip, Technical Search Specialist Equip, Canine Search Specialist Equip	Structures Specialist Equip, Technical Information Specialist Equip, HazMat Specialist Equip, Technical Search Specialist Equip, Canine Search Specialist Equip		
Portable Radios, Charging Units, Telecommunications, Repeaters, Accessories, Batteries, Power Sources, Small Tools, Computer	Portable Radios, Charging Units, Telecommunications, Repeaters, Accessories, Batteries, Power Sources, Small Tools, Computer		
Water/Fluids, Food, Shelter, Sanitation, Safety, Administrative Support, Personal Bag, Task Force Support, Cache Transportation/ Support, Base of Operations, Equipment Maintenance	Water/Fluids, Food, Shelter, Sanitation, Safety, Administrative Support, Personal Bag, Task Force Support, Cache Transportation/ Support, Base of Operations, Equipment Maintenance		
Federal asset. There are 28 FEMA US&R Task Forces, totally self-sufficient for the first 72 hours of a deployment, spread throughout the continental United States trained and equipped by FEMA to conduct physical search-and-rescue in collapsed buildings, provide emergency medical care to trapped victims, assess and control gas, electrical services and hazardous materials, and evaluate and stabilize damaged structures.			

Source: Department of Homeland Security, National Incident Management System, Appendix B, 121. Available at http://www.fema.gov/emergency/nims/index.shtm.

Emergency Medical Service

For disasters like an airplane crash, tornado, or terrorist attack that can result in serious injuries and fatalities, EMS personnel are a critical part of the response team. The emergency medical response is coordinated with hospitals, fire and police departments, the EMS department, and volunteers. If an event causes mass fatalities, the medical examiner/coroner identifies victims and determines the cause of death.

RECOVERY

After the emergency, interrupted services (such as electricity, gas, and water) should be restored as soon as possible. The local government may request assistance from the federal government, the state, and private relief agencies. The greatest source of financial assistance is the President's Disaster Relief Fund. The governor must ask the president to declare a disaster; after such a declaration, affected homeowners and businesses can receive federal loan assistance.

In the recovery, the EPA regulates what kind of debris can be taken to disposal sites and how it can be disposed. The EOP specifies how to handle donated goods and services. For example, food might be sent to a local food bank, clothing to Goodwill Industries and the Salvation Army, and cash donations to the Red Cross. Such volunteer organizations are at the forefront of the recovery. The National Volunteer Organizations Active in Disaster (NVOAD) includes thirty-four national, fifty-two state, and territorial and local organizations.

After the recovery, the local government should formally acknowledge their appreciation for the work of assisting organizations and volunteers. Also post hoc, the incident-command team and other key stakeholders should critique the response to the emergency, evaluating the preparedness, response, and recovery. In some events, responders and victims that suffer from post-traumatic stress disorder should be given counseling assistance.

NOTES

1. Federal Emergency Management Agency (FEMA), "FEMA History." Available at http://www.fema.gov/about/history.shtm.

2. Ibid.

3. Eric Lipton, "Despite Steps, Disaster Planning Still Shows Gaps," *New York Times* (August 26, 2006).

4. For a detailed explanation of the NRP, see George Haddow, Jane Bullock, and Damon Coppola, *Introduction to Emergency Management,* 3rd ed. (Oxford, UK: Butterworth-Heinemann, 2008), 119–139.

5. For a more complete discussion of Emergency Management, see James Banovetz and John Swain, "Emergency Management," in *Managing Small Cities and Counties: A Guide,* ed. James M. Banovetz, Drew A. Dolan, and John W. Swain (Washington, DC: International City/County Management Association, 1994), 177–194.

6. For more information on what to include in the ordinance, see David McEntire, "Disaster Preparedness," *IQ Report* 35, no. 11 (Washington, DC: International City/County Management Association, 2003).

7. Bob Hart, "Emergency Management," in *Managing Local Government Services: A Practical Guide,* ed. Carl Stenberg and Susan Lipman Austin, 285 (Washington, DC: International City/County Management Association, 2007), 285–312.

8. For a list of states and an online assessment tool, see Emergency Management Accreditation Program's Web site at http://www.emaponline.org.

9. Public Entity Risk Institute, *Characteristics of Effective Emergency Management Organizational Structures* (Fairfax, VA: n.d.).

10. Larry Collins and Thomas Schneid, *Disaster Management and Preparedness* (Boca Raton, FL: Lewis Publishers, 2001).

11. For more information on the courses, see FEMA's Emergency Management Institute's Web site at http://training.fema.gov.

12. Haddow et al., *Introduction to Emergency Management,* 201.

13. Ibid.

14. For a technical discussion of storm water management, see American Public Works Association (APWA), *Urban Storm Water Management* (Chicago: APWA, 1981).

15. Haddow et al., *Introduction to Emergency Management,* 80.

16. For a detailed description of warning systems, see ibid., 8.

17. Refer to Department of Homeland Security, "National Incident Management System." Available at http://www.fema.gov/emergency/nims/index.shtm.

18. Kiki Caruson and Susan MacManus, "Mandates and Management Challenges in the Trenches: An Intergovernmental Perspective on Homeland Security," *Public Administration Review* 66, no. 4 (2006): 531.

FOR FURTHER READING

Collins, Larry, and Thomas Schneid. *Disaster Management and Preparedness.* Boca Raton, FL: Lewis Publishers, 2001.

Haddow, George, Jane Bulloch, and Damon Coppola. *Emergency Management,* 3rd ed. Oxford, UK: Butterworth-Heinemann, 2008.

Waugh, William Jr., and Kathleen Tierney. *Emergency Management,* 2nd ed. Washington, DC: International City/County Management Association, 2007.

6

Animal Control

HISTORY

Over 60 percent of households own at least one pet. The pet population in shelters peaked in the 1970s, when over 20 million animals entered a shelter annually.[1] To reduce the load on shelters, more local governments required that animals be licensed and spayed or neutered. In 1971, Los Angeles opened the first public spay/neuter clinic.[2] In the mid-1980s, many local governments passed dangerous-dog ordinances to identify and control dangerous dogs and hold owners accountable for their pets' behavior. Currently, nearly 2 percent of the population, the great majority of whom are children and the elderly, are bitten by dogs annually. Some local governments ban ownership of specific breeds, but most enforce a "dog-bite prevention" ordinance that requires containment of potentially dangerous animals and/or conduct a program to teach dog owners how to prevent biting through humane treatment, sterilization, supervision, and safe confinement.

MANAGEMENT

Animal control may be performed through either

- a separate department,
- the police department,
- the health department, or
- the local humane society under contract with the local government.

Some operations are overseen by an advisory commission—typically comprised of a veterinarian and representatives from the local health department, the police, a humane organization, and the general public, preferably including an individual with legal expertise. The commission recommends regulations to the local governing board, reviews contracts and budgets, conducts public hearings on changes to the animal-control ordinance, and hears complaints about the conduct of animal-care personnel.

Normally the cost of the animal-control program is partially offset by a license fee. One study found that 72 percent of cities charge a fee that offsets about 25 percent of operating costs.[3] To encourage sterilization, about 80 percent of local governments charge a higher fee to register an unsterilized animal than a sterilized one, and two states mandate that animals be sterilized.[4]

Animal-control departments operate the shelter facility, restrain and handle animals, investigate complaints of cruelty, prevent diseases, educate the public, and resolve conflicts. Among the agencies that train animal control personnel are the Humane Society of the United States (HSUS), the National Animal Control Association, and the state animal-control association.

Field service personnel respond to citizen complaints, impound unregistered animals, issue citations, inspect commercial animal establishments, rescue animals in danger, and educate the public about responsible animal care. Their vehicle should be designed to transport animals, including a protective cage and place for rescue equipment.

Public outreach is an important aspect of animal-control. Informational materials can be distributed to the public at the shelter, public meetings, and heavily frequented places (such as shopping centers and post offices). Brochures should cover basic pet care, spaying and neutering programs, animal vaccination and registration, and animal-control tips.

OPERATIONS

Local governments normally pass an animal-control ordinance that requires pet owners to

- register their pets,
- use a pooper scooper to clean up excrement,
- restrain pets on a leash,
- quarantine a pet if it bites someone.

Dogs and cats are licensed and issued an identification tag worn on their collar at all times. To be licensed, the pet must have received a rabies vaccination. Veterinarians in the area may be authorized to license pets. A pet with an identification tag is more likely to be recovered if its owner should lose it. As an incentive to register pets, the department may return a licensed pet it recovers to its owner, avoiding the impoundment fee.

Animal-Control Problems

There are four principal animal control problems: rabies, free-roaming dogs, dangerous dogs, and free-roaming cats.

Rabies

Rabies is transmitted by bites, scratches, cuts, or mucous membranes. Though only forty people have died from rabies since 1980, about 39,000 annually undergo postexposure treatment because of uncertainty about the vaccination status of the biting animal.[5] Because cats are the main carrier of rabies, twenty-five states have mandated that they be vaccinated.[6] Some local governments also require that a dog or cat be vaccinated for rabies. To encourage vaccination, a local health department may perform the procedure for a nominal fee.

Vaccinated animals that bite someone are quarantined usually for ten days either on the owner's premises, at a veterinary hospital, or in an animal shelter. An unvaccinated animal bitten or scratched by a rabid wild animal must be quarantined at a veterinary hospital or an animal shelter, usually for at least six months, or be euthanized.[7]

Free-Roaming Dogs

Local governments usually require that a dog be fenced within its owner's property. Many homeowners have installed invisible, electronic fences in lieu of conventional boundary fences. Another common requirement is that dogs be on a leash when off the owner's property. The ordinance may even specify the length of leash. A local unit may further require a dog's owner to pick up its waste, requiring that owners carry a pooper-scooper to pick up droppings. They may also provide disposal bags at public places like parks and post notice of the fine for not disposing of waste.

Dangerous Dogs

A dog is deemed dangerous if it has bitten a person or another animal. States' laws may further define dangerous. For instance, North Carolina's definition includes three criteria:

- A bite that broke a victim's bones
- A bite that left a disfiguring wound
- The dog terrorized someone off its property[8]

"One-free bite" state laws do not hold the owner responsible unless he or she knows the dog's potential for violence. Still, owning breeds like pit bulls and rottweilers usually qualifies as adequate notice.[9] Some local governments specify that such breeds are dangerous because they are likely to bite. Animal owners should protect the public from dangerous dogs, securely fencing them in and acquiring liability insurance. Citizens, physicians, and veterinarians should report all animal bites to the local animal-control center.

Free-Roaming Cats

Cat ownership surpassed dog ownership in the mid-1980s.[10] For some communities, stray cats and colonies of feral cats (cats without owners) have become a major problem because cats are the most common carrier of rabies. To limit free-roaming cats, most local governments require cat registration or licensing. In 1999, Rhode Island required that cat owners outfit their cats with some form of identification, such as a collar and tag, ear tag, rabies tag, or embroidered collar.[11] Some communities require that all cats be sprayed or neutered to roam freely. Owners of unsterilized cats must pay a fine to reclaim them. Some local governments operate a trap, neuter, and release (TNR) program to control feral cats. Trapped cats are vaccinated, spayed or neutered, and then released. Animal-control staff clip the cat's ear to identify it as being in the TNR program.

Mandatory Sterilization of Adopted Animals

Though most local units require sterilization of cats and dogs that have been adopted from shelters, owners do not always obey their adoption contract to have their pet sterilized. Some local units therefore operate a "sterilization-at-adoption" program, requiring pets to be sterilized before the adoption takes place. The cost of the sterilization is incorporated into the adoption fee. Because only 20 percent of pets are acquired from animal shelters, some local units offer spay/neuter services at a minimal cost.

The Shelter

A shelter, designed to prevent disease, functions somewhat like a user-friendly police station. Animals are caged to prevent disease and reduce their stress. The facility should have good drainage, proper ventilation, temperature control, proper lighting, and suitable equipment. The American Humane Association, American Society for the Prevention of Cruelty to Animals, and HSUS have issued guidelines for the design and operation of a facility that include:[12]

- Receiving animals without charging a surrender fee
- Holding stray animals for at least five days to give owners time to reclaim them
- Maintaining a clean, safe, and healthy environment and providing food, water, and protection
- Separating different types of animals
- To accommodate customers, operating at least two nights per week until at least 7 PM.

Ideally, the facility will have built-in disease prevention safeguards, including separate ventilation systems for each enclosed kennel to reduce the spread of illness, kennels facing in opposite directions from each other to reduce the stress that aggressive animals place on other animals, housing that resembles homelike conditions, and viewing areas for prospective adopters.

Some facilities watch animals' behavior and characterize it for prospective adopters. On the outside of each cage door is an information sheet listing the animal's name, behavior characteristics, breed, approximate age, gender, date of entry into the shelter, how it came to the shelter (for example, a stray), and special characteristics and needs of the animal such as being good with children or being extremely high energy. Aggressive animals or ones with a virus symptom should be placed in a separate holding area. Some facilities use volunteers to clean the kennels in the morning and at night.

Shelters should seek responsible, lifelong homes for animals that will make good family pets. Animal-control personnel should advise a prospective pet owner about how to be a good caregiver. Some facilities even have a counselor who interviews prospective adopters asking questions about their lifestyle, time available for a pet, how much they exercise, past experience with pets, and financial ability to care for a pet. Shelters should track the percentage of animals that are adopted.

Euthanasia, the destruction of animals, must be performed by trained personnel. The recommended method is intravenous injection of sodium pentobarbital. Animal carcasses are cremated or sent to a landfill for disposal.

NOTES

1. Geoffrey L. Handy, *Animal Control Management: A Guide for Local Governments* (Washington, DC: International City/County Management Association, 2001), 13.

2. *Information on Selected Spay/Neuter Clinics and Programs* (Washington, DC: The Humane Society of the United States, 1991).

3. *Municipal Animal Control in Colorado* (Denver, CO: Colorado Municipal League, 1990), 33.

4. Handy, *Animal Control Management,* 24.

5. Center for Disease Control, "Human Rabies Prevention—United States, 1999," *Morbidity and Mortality Weekly Report* 48 (January 8, 1999), 2.

6. Christy Heitger-Casbon, "The Wrath of Rabies," *Cat Fancy* (2001), 32.

7. Handy, *Animal Control Management*, 27.

8. Josh Shaffer, "Dog-Bite Law Tough on Victims," *Raleigh News and Observer* (January 20, 2008).

9. Ibid.

10. Handy, *Animal Control Management*, 8.

11. Ibid., 9.

12. Handy, *Animal Control Management,* 48–49.

FOR FURTHER READING

Handy, Geoffrey L. *Animal Control Management: A Guide for Local Government.* Washington, DC: International City/County Management Association, 2001.

7
Public Health and Mental Health

HISTORY

Public-Health History

The precursor to public-health departments, the Marine Hospital Service, established in 1798, provided medical services to merchant seamen in American ports. Financed by a monthly deduction from the wages of seamen, medical care was provided by contracts with existing hospitals. In 1862, President Lincoln created the Bureau of Chemistry, later to become the Food and Drug Administration. In 1866, New York City set up a Board of Health. In 1887, the National Institutes of Health opened a one-room laboratory on Staten Island to research the causes of disease. Congress passed the Pure Food and Drug Act in 1906 to monitor the quality of foods and the safety of medicine, and in 1912, at Theodore Roosevelt's urging, it created the Children's Bureau to protect the health and welfare of children and prevent their being exploited in the workplace. In 1912, the Public Health Service was established; Figure 7.1 shows one of its nurses teaching a mother how to prepare a feeding formula for her infant in 1920. In 1935, Congress passed the Social Security Act. The Communicable Disease Center, later the Center for Disease Control and Prevention, was created in 1946. In 1962, Congress passed the Migrant Health Act to afford health care to agricultural workers. The Surgeon General's 1964 report on smoking led to a substantial decrease in the incidence of smoking, and in 1965, clearly a watershed year for public health, Congress created four seminal public-health programs:

- *Medicare*: Health care for the elderly.
- *Medicaid*: Health care for the low-income and disabled citizens.
- *Older Americans Act*: Nutritional and social assistance to the elderly.
- *Head Start*: Nutritional and educational assistance to needy children.

Figure 7.1   **Public-Health-Care Nurse**

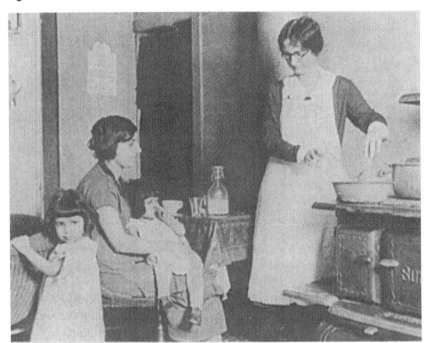

Source: National Library of Medicine, National Institutes of Health.

AIDS was identified in 1981; the HIV virus, in 1984. Also in 1984, the National Organ Transplant Act was enacted. In 1985, a blood test to detect HIV was licensed. In 1997, the State Children's Health Insurance Program was enacted to provide medical service to low-income children.

Mental-Health History

During the 1600s, Native American shamans, known as medicine men, called upon their powers to treat the mentally ill. Some colonists accused the mentally ill of practicing witchcraft and possessing demonic powers. Cotton Mather first offered a more enlightened physical explanation of mental illness in 1724. In 1812, Benjamin Rush published *Medical Inquiries and Observations Upon Diseases of the Mind,* advocating humane treatment of the mentally ill. By 1843, twenty-four hospitals, with 2,561 beds, had been built in the United States to treat the mentally ill.

After the death of his brother in 1900, Clifford Beers attempted suicide. He was then placed in a private Connecticut mental institution where he was mentally and physically abused. After his release, in 1908, he wrote the seminal book *The Mind That Found Itself,* which was the impetus for widespread mental-health-care reform, and in the same year, Beers founded the Connecticut Society for Mental Hygiene, which became the National Committee for Mental Hygiene.

In 1910, Emil Kraepelin clinically described Alzheimer's disease. In 1918, the American Psychoanalytic Association ruled that physicians must complete medical school and receive psychoanalytic training. During the 1920s, Harry Sullivan therapeutically assisted schizophrenic patients to return to the community. In the 1930s, psychiatrists treated schizophrenia with insulin injections that induced shock and a temporary coma. In 1952, the first antipsychotic drug was used to treat patients with schizophrenia and other major mental illnesses. The 1970s witnessed the beginning of the *deinstitutionalization* movement, moving patients from hospitals to the community. In the 1990s, doctors used brain imaging to learn about the development of mental illnesses, and in 1997, researchers identified the genetic links to bipolar disorder, implying that the illness may be inherited.

PUBLIC HEALTH

At the national level, the Public Health Service is responsible for public health. At the local level county governments commonly provide public-health services, but other providers may include

- a city health department,
- a district health department serving multiple local jurisdictions,
- a public-health authority,
- the state health department, under contract with one or more local jurisdiction.

The health department is typically overseen by a Board of Health, which acts an advocate for public-health issues and recommends the budget for adoption by the Board of County Commissioners. Ideally, a public-health department has two managers:

- The *clinical director,* a health-care professional, who oversees the medical aspects of the program.
- The *administrative manager,* an experienced administrator, who manages day-to-day operations.

The public-health division operates health-care clinics, controls infectious diseases, runs family-planning and mental-health-care programs, tests for HIV and sexually transmitted diseases, operates tobacco- and alcohol-cessation programs, controls vermin and mosquitoes, and runs dental clinics. The division also screens for diseases like diabetes and breast cancer, advertising the free screening service in local doctors' offices, churches, community centers, and other public spaces.

The environmental-health division inspects the sanitary conditions in restaurants, hotels, hospitals, schools, and other public places. Two state agencies enforce state public-health laws and rules. The *Department of Health* monitors and enforces health policies, provides training and technical assistance, and allocates federal and state money to agencies statewide. The *Department of Agriculture* regulates the inspection of food establishments.

Infectious-Disease Control

The department immunizes children against diseases like measles, rubella, diphtheria, tetanus, and polio, having the "police power" to control the spread of infectious diseases. A physician or laboratory must report symptoms or positive lab tests of specified communicable infectious diseases. When a problematic disease is detected, public-health staff can interview those infected to determine with whom they have been in contact. Staff treat the disease to prevent it from spreading. Isolation, a common practice in hospitals, separates or confines infected persons to protect those not infected. Quarantine, far more rare, is the compulsory physical separation of non-sick persons who have been exposed to a disease. The term comes from the Latin *quarante* denoting the forty days used traditionally by medieval Italian cities to keep trading ships anchored in the harbor to prevent the spread of bubonic plague. Infected people are isolated during the period of communicability. In a more extreme case, the department can quarantine someone for the length of the disease's incubation period. The health department also has emergency power to close a school to prevent the spread of a disease. If a disease spreads, the department must take more serious steps, diagnosing its cause, conducting an epidemiologic and microbiologic investigation, and implementing controls.

The department runs educational programs to reduce the incidence of chronically severe health problems like heart disease, cancer, liver disease, obesity, and arthritis. Partnering with schools and businesses, a department may offer smoking-cessation, weight-control, and alcoholism-prevention programs. *The American Journal of Public Health,* published by the American Public Health Association, is an excellent source of public-health-education materials.

Among public-health performance measures for disease control are

- cases per 100,000 in population (hepatitis, mumps, sexually transmitted diseases, diphtheria, and so forth),
- percent of children vaccinated,
- percent of adults immunized (flu, hepatitis B).

Environmental Health

The environmental-health division inspects restaurants and monitors sewage and water systems. Among restaurant-inspection measures are

- inspection visits per food-service establishment (annually),
- number of inspections per citation,
- time to make a follow-up reinspection.

MENTAL HEALTH

The county government or an area mental-health authority may provide all mental-health services itself or contract some services out to nonprofit social-service agencies. Among those that may be contracted out are

- residential treatment (group homes, supported apartments),
- substance-abuse day treatment,
- adult vocational programs (for example, a sheltered workshop).

To ensure compliance, the state requires that facilities such as group homes be licensed and accredited.

The mental-health department treats mental illness, developmental disabilities, and alcohol and drug abuse. The mentally ill are treated on an outpatient, inpatient, or emergency basis. Some of the mentally ill receive job placement and supported-living services as well. The agency also assists children and adults with developmental disabilities, offering short-term relief (for example, up to thirty days) to those who care for the mentally ill in their homes.

The substance-abuse program prevents and controls alcohol and drug abuse with drug-education programs, residential and outpatient detoxification services, and substance-abuse programs ordered by the courts.

Among mental-health performance measures are

- the number of clients receiving mental illness treatment,
- the number of clients receiving treatment for developmental disabilities,

- the number of clients receiving treatment for substance abuse,
- the number of clients using day-activity services,
- the number of clients enrolled in vocational programs,
- the amount of time a client must wait to be seen,
- the number of state beds utilized (on a per month, quarterly, and/or annual basis).

ONLINE RESOURCES

Mental Health America. Formerly known as the National Mental Health Association. Available at http://www.nmha.org.
National Alliance on Mental Illness (NAMI). Available at http://www.nami.org.

FOR FURTHER READING

Pickett, George, and John Hanlon. *Public Health: Administration and Practice,* 9th ed. St. Louis: Times Mirror/Mosby College, 1990.

Part II

Public Works and Planning Services

8

Planning and Inspections

HISTORY[1]

The Preplanning Era (Colonial Days to 1880)

Colonial cities typically consisted of residences, streets, open public spaces, and a few businesses, churches, and government buildings. The cities were usually laid out in grids. Savannah, Georgia, based on the grid plan, is a prime example of colonial-era planning. Washington, DC, a notable planning achievement, mixed a grid pattern with radiating diagonal avenues that met circular roundabouts. As settlers moved west, towns like Chicago continued with the grid plan.

The end of the Civil War signaled the beginning of the Industrial Revolution. Manufacturing plants were built in central cities to be near power sources. Workers crammed into nearby tenement buildings, requiring a more systematic planning approach.

The Planning-and-Zoning Era (1880–1970)

Imitating Germany's long-established use of zoning, San Francisco in 1880 adopted a zoning ordinance to control the spread of Chinese laundries. In 1907, Hartford adopted a citywide zoning plan. Daniel Burnham, the father of city planning, prepared a regional plan for the Chicago metropolitan area in 1909, while that same year Los Angeles enacted an ordinance to zone developed and undeveloped land. In 1913, New Jersey required local planning boards to review subdivision plats. New York City broadened zoning in 1916, segregating inner-city tenement housing from manufacturing plants.

After the invention of the car, development rapidly spread to suburbs. An auto-oriented shopping center was built on the outskirts of Kansas City in 1922. In 1924, the U.S. Department of Commerce issued a model standard state zoning enabling act,[2] which encouraged states to adopt acts authorizing local units to pass zoning laws. Cincinnati set up a comprehensive plan in 1925 to establish long-range community development goals. The U.S. Supreme Court upheld zoning's constitutionality in the *Euclid v. Ambler Realty* decision of 1926. By 1936, all but one state had formed a state planning board.[3]

After World War II, suburbanization further increased, ignited by a baby boom and the home buying of returning veterans, who received low-interest Veterans Administration loans. They were able to buy reasonably priced starter homes, epitomized by the Levittown housing tracts. In 1956, the federal government began construction of the interstate highway system. Some manufacturing plants then moved from the central city to locations with easier access to this road system and the suburban labor supply. Meanwhile, in order to attract industries, cities built industrial parks, complete with water, sewers, and roads.

Left behind in the exodus from central cities were many low-income citizens living in deteriorating housing. To redevelop central cities, Congress enacted the Urban Renewal Program in 1954. Deemed "urban removal" by its detractors, the Urban Renewal Program did not adequately provide housing for displaced citizens. In 1974, Congress enacted the Community Development Block Grant to fund water, sewers, and housing in low-income areas.

The Environmental and Growth-Management Era (1970 to the Present)

As national concern for the environment increased, Congress enacted the National Environmental Policy Act (NEPA) in 1970. NEPA requires state and local governments to prepare an environmental impact statement (EIS) for a federally financed project with a significant environmental impact. Following the federal government's lead, twenty-three states passed NEPA-like legislation requiring an EIS for state-funded projects.

The majority of Americans live near a coast. Accordingly, Congress enacted the Coastal Zone Management Act in 1972 to protect environmentally sensitive coastal areas from overdevelopment, improve water quality, and mitigate the impact of storms.

In the 1970s, the growth-management movement began. For example, Petaluma, California, limited residential construction to 500 permits per year in 1971. In the mid-1990s *smart growth* became a buzzword. Smart-growth advocates, concerned about urban sprawl and traffic congestion, recommended that areas be more densely developed using redevelopment of existing developments (in-fill), land-use controls, and tax policies. Planned-use development, a smart-growth tool, gave developers the flexibility to combine different land uses (residential and commercial) with different densities (single family, condominium, and so forth). Through smart-growth actions, more densely populated areas are less dependent on autos, residents can walk more, open space can be pooled for parks, and environmentally sensitive areas are preserved.

MANAGEMENT

Human-Resource Management

Most planners have a graduate or undergraduate degree in city and regional planning from an accredited planning program.[4] In a small community, a single planner usually prepares plans and studies, administers regulations, and acts as staff to commissions and boards. Medium-sized and large planning departments usually have specialized positions, such as an environmental planner, long-range planner, Geographic Information System (GIS) specialist, historic-preservation planner, graphic artist, zoning officer, and a code-enforcement/permitting officer. Planners work with a wide range of community groups, sometimes in an adversarial setting, making good people skills an essential job requirement.

The Planning Commission

Large jurisdictions usually have a multistaged planning and zoning process. A planning board or commission reviews a proposal, which, if approved, is sent to the governing board. If denied, the petitioner can request that a board of adjustment, a quasi-judicial entity, grant a variance. In contrast, the governing board in a small jurisdiction typically reviews proposals without assistance from a board of adjustment.

A planning commission has *eminent domain* power to seize land and property for public use; however, the Fifth Amendment to the U.S. Constitution prohibits taking private property without paying just compensation. If a property-taking is found to be unconstitutional, the local unit can be held liable for damages incurred by the property owner. A taking is clearly legal, though, if it prevents a use or development from being a public nuisance (such as a building in a floodway).

Information-Technology Management

GIS software digitally stores planning information. To store mapping data, a technician moves a digitizer along the contour lines of a topographical map.

Assessed values, census data, zoning data, and the like are stored as numbers or letters. A department may hire a firm to fly over the public facilities, recording the location of streets, storm drains, water and sewer manholes, fire hydrants, streetlights, and the like. At the regional level, GIS software using satellite images records data like the hydrology, topography, vegetation, and temperatures. These data are used to create planning maps, engineering drawings, and Federal Emergency Management Agency plans. The data are presented both in tabular form and spatially. For instance, the location of fire hydrants can be combined with water-system data such as the size of water laterals and hydrant water pressures. The initial cost of GIS software and data recording is high, especially for small local units, who thus may decide to share the cost with other local jurisdictions.

PLANNING

The basic planning documents are the comprehensive (or master) plan, the zoning ordinance and map, subdivision regulations, and the capital improvement program (CIP).

The Comprehensive Plan

The comprehensive plan is a statement of the governing board's policies concerning land use, transportation, housing, and economic development. As such, it constitutes an overarching statement of a community's development goals and policies. Its preparation should be informed by the input of the public at meetings and public hearings and in citizen surveys. Large governments draw up a series of neighborhood plans that are incorporated into the comprehensive plan. A comprehensive plan typically includes:

- A statement of development objectives
- A demographic long-range (for example, ten to twenty years) forecast
- A major thoroughfare plan
- A forecast of future infrastructure (including utilities, libraries, water and sewer, landfills, and schools)
- An assessment of housing-stock conditions
- A land-use plan to guide the enforcement of the zoning ordinance[5]

Figure 8.1 shows the various elements of a comprehensive plan. The governing body adopts the comprehensive plan, adjusting it as community conditions (physical, economic, and political) change. If not adjusted, a comprehensive plan quickly loses its usefulness.

Figure 8.1   **Elements of a Comprehensive Plan**

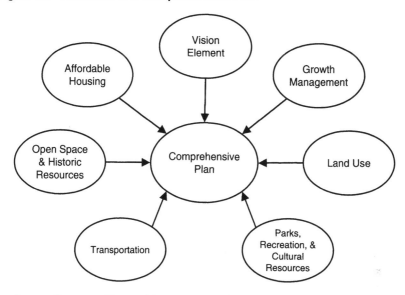

Source: Courtesy of Town of Cary, North Carolina Planning Department.

ZONING

Zoning puts the comprehensive plan into effect. State law may dictate some zoning procedures. Instituting zoning in a rural county can be inimical to those who wish to retain autonomy over their property. To counter such resistance, the county commission may institute zoning piecemeal, beginning in urbanized areas but leaving rural areas unzoned.

State law usually requires that one or more public hearings be held when adopting a zoning ordinance. To amend the zoning ordinance, the local unit must notify affected property owners of the hearing on an impending amendment. In a large local unit, the zoning regulations are typically enforced by a zoning enforcement officer. In small units, the building inspector, city or county manager, or police chief may enforce the regulations.

The Zoning Ordinance

The zoning ordinance specifies standards and procedures that are graphically illustrated in a zoning map or series of maps. The ordinance divides the land area into land-use districts or zones that vary by dimensions, density, and setback requirements, and it sets standards for landscaping, property access, off-street parking, signage, public improvements, and structure sizes (such as maximums for height, stories, and floor area). The ordinance is codified in a book of zoning regulations.

The community is divided into three types of zoning districts: *residential, commercial,* and *industrial.* Also zoned are specialized uses like office buildings, planned-unit developments, mobile-home parks, and agriculture. The zoning districts are usually classified for *general* or *conditional* (special) use.

The required lot size varies with the type of zoning district and land use. For example, a single-family residential district may be required to have a minimum lot size of 10,000 square feet. The ordinance may also limit a lot's width, depth, front and side dimensions, and building height. The ordinance may also specify *performance standards,* protecting homeowners from annoying odors, glare, dust, vibration, and noises.

After a zoning ordinance's enactment, some structures and land uses may not meet its regulations. For instance, a building may not conform to the height and setback requirements, or a lot may not conform to the width, frontage, or area requirements. The ordinance may permit such *nonconforming* uses, but usually does not permit a nonconforming use to continue after an expansion, restoration, or abandonment. Rather than permitting a nonconforming use, the ordinance may require *amortization.* Applicable mostly to nonconforming signs and such outdoor uses as a junkyard, amortization requires that the property owner bring the use into *full compliance* after a stipulated period, allowing the owner time to recover all or part of the cost of such compliance.

A building inspector examines properties to determine whether they conform to the zoning ordinance. The ordinance should establish an appeals procedure administered by a zoning board of appeals, the planning board, or the governing body.

Special Exception

A special exception enables land to be used somewhat inconsistently with the property's zoned use.[6] For example, a bed-and-breakfast may be granted a special exception to operate in a low-density residential district. The zoning hearing board, often called the board of adjustment, usually decides whether to permit such exceptions.

The governing board, though, not the zoning hearing board, makes a *conditional use* special exception because it affects the whole community (for example, a landfill or airport decision). In contrast, the zoning hearing board can grant a *variance,* which does not alter the essential character of a neighborhood, to relieve a hardship inherent in a piece of land. Types of variances include:

- *Dimensional Variance:* When the property does not quite comply with yard or setback requirements (most common type of variance).
- *De Minimis Variance:* For a minor deviation, such as a lot being a few feet short of a one-acre requirement.
- *Use Variation:* When the property would otherwise be valueless or when it is near another property to which a variance has been granted.

"Spot" Zoning

Spot zoning occurs when a small area of land or section in an existing neighborhood is placed in a different zone from that of neighboring property. In some areas of the country, courts have found spot zoning illegal on the grounds that it is incompatible with the existing land-use zoning plan. For instance, some courts have ruled against spot zoning a commercial use in residential areas. Whether an exception is granted often turns on public interest. Some spot zoning unfairly favors a particular developer, but a spot zoning may make sense if nearby property owners receive offsetting benefits. For instance, spot zoning a shopping center in a residential neighborhood may be acceptable to residential property owners who lack convenient shopping facilities. Similarly, a park or school may be permitted in a residential area if it serves a useful purpose to the neighborhood.

Permit Issuance

Zoning-enforcement officials routinely permit *by right* those uses that are clearly defined by the ordinance. On the other hand, projects with potential for being a nuisance require more scrutiny and thus should get a *conditional-use* permit. The zoning ordinance should state the requirements for granting a conditional-use permit.

Performance Measurement

The following are among zoning-performance measures for site plans:

- Median number of days from submission to decision
- Percent of staff recommendations approved by board
- Percent of applications processed within x amount of time

SUBDIVISION AND LAND-DEVELOPMENT REGULATION

A subdivision splits a land tract into smaller parcels, lots, or building sites for sale or development. Most states follow the Standard City Enabling Act,

Figure 8.2 **Proposed Subdivision Plan**

Source: Courtesy of Town of Cary, North Carolina Planning Department.

delegating subdivision regulation to a locally appointed planning commission or board.[7] Jurisdictions typically regulate subdivisions according to their size. A small subdivision (usually five lots or less) is often approved by planning staff if it meets the dimensional requirements of the subdivision ordinance. Larger subdivisions, in contrast, are subjected to more exacting board review.

Jurisdictions also regulate the development of mobile-home parks, multifamily apartments, shopping centers, office complexes, and multifamily residential construction. The governing board adopts standards for each development type, which must be reasonable and quantifiable if possible. Figure 8.2 is an example of a proposed subdivision plan.

Ordinance Provisions[8]

The subdivision ordinance enforces provisions in the comprehensive plan, the CIP, the zoning ordinance, utility-extension policies, road-improvement policies, annexation policies, and environmental-impact procedures. The zoning ordinance is usually incorporated by reference into the subdivision ordinance. Typical subdivision ordinance provisions include:

- The position (official) responsible for the ordinance's enforcement
- Subdivision plan-submission requirements
- Fee schedule for subdivision review
- Waiver procedures
- Procedures to dedicate land for parks, recreation, and road purposes
- Design standards
- Street standards

Some local units prepare a summarized version of the ordinance, including a flowchart of the review process, for use by interested developers and homeowners.[9]

State law usually requires that a landowner wishing to divide property into two or more parts of land for sale or lease prepare a *subdivision plat,* which shows streets, lot lines, and easements (right of way) for utilities. Before a lot can be sold or a building permit issued, the improvements (such as streets and water, sewer and drainage facilities) must be in place. The subdivision ordinance may further stipulate that a developer dedicate land or make a payment for a public purpose such as a road, park, school, or community facility.

Preliminary and Final Plat Approval

The ordinance may require that a pre-application conference be held wherein the developer submits a *sketch plan.* Early consultation over the sketch plan can minimize future errors and clarify a project's intent. Relatively little detail is required at this point. The sketch plan is a simple proposal, consisting of a location map, property-line map, and the general layout of the proposed subdivision.

Some local units distinguish between a major and minor subdivision. A minor subdivision is reviewed at both the sketch-plan and final stages. A major subdivision, in contrast, is reviewed at three stages: sketch plan, preliminary, and final.[10] At the preliminary stage, the developer submits a plat that shows the site's topography, nature, design, and scope. A *technical review committee* (TRC) reviews the preliminary plat. This stage is a big hurdle for a developer, for approval virtually guarantees final-plan approval as well. The examination is hence very exacting. The TRC usually requires at least minor modifications, and more significant redesign may be called for. Questions addressed by the preliminary plat include those discussed below.

Environment

The project should be consistent with the area's natural environment, particularly its sensitive areas such as wetlands, ponds, endangered-species habitats, old waste-disposal sites, and steep land, as well as with historically, architecturally, and archeologically important sites.

Stormwater

Subdivision regulations specify how to control flooding, sedimentation, and erosion and to protect water-supply watersheds. Ideally, the developer is able to model the estimated amount and speed of runoff from the development. Many states require that a project exceeding a certain size (usually one acre) be reviewed by the state regulatory agency.

Watershed-Development Standards

The local unit may adopt special standards regulating development in a watershed, such as requiring a higher lot size for septic-tank usage or clustering development to reduce roof and pavement runoff.

Landscape

The subdivision ordinance typically requires that a new project have trees, a buffer strip between adjacent land uses, lots that take advantage of natural features, and driveway cuts and a right-of-way that minimize land clearing.

Street Design

The project's streets should be consistent with the government's thoroughfare plan. The streets in the subdivision should

- facilitate local access,
- have a dedicated right-of-way on one street side to install underground utilities,
- discourage through traffic and high speeds,
- limit the points at which pedestrians and vehicles can meet,
- include pedestrian walkways, where feasible,
- locate high-traffic roads outside the subdivision,
- make streets compatible with the natural features.[11]

Transportation Impact Analysis (TIA)

Large projects in particular may need a TIA that estimates road capacity and provides for reducing road congestion and establishing safe turning and deceleration lanes.

A *Stubout*

A stubout is a street with a temporary dead end, which will eventually become a through street. Homeowners wishing privacy would naturally rather have a cul-de-sac. Moreover, developers sometimes resent having to build a somewhat longer street than is developable. Nevertheless, a stubout is needed to connect to a larger arterial or collector street planned to bisect the location in the future. Sometimes, a subdivision-ordinance standard creates undue hardship from which a developer can request relief. For instance, relief may be granted for minor changes in street-grade, curve-radii, right-of-way-width, or cul-de-sac-length provisions. Such relief is reflected in the preliminary and final plans.

Most subdivision ordinances require that the final plan be submitted and approved within a specified time period (for example, one or two years).[12] However, large-scale developments, built over several years, may be approved in stages, according to an agreed-upon schedule. The review board must approve any modification to the schedule.

The final plat (known as the record map) is the subdivision map recorded with the register of deeds. Most states require the plat be prepared by a registered engineer or surveyor and that it include four certificates:

1. A certificate of approval signed by the chair of the approval agency
2. A certificate of registration signed by the register of deeds
3. A certificate of accuracy and mapping signed by the surveyor
4. A certificate of ownership

Most subdivision ordinances require that the plat be recorded within a month or two after its approval to prevent the land from being prematurely subdivided.[13] A subdivision fee is charged to pay for the cost of plat review and approval.

A subdivision ordinance is often amended. After an amendment, a *vested-rights provision* in the subdivision ordinance allows the developer time (such as two years) to complete a subdivision under the pre-amendment conditions. However, the vested right can be terminated if the plat is changed or if portions of it prove to be inaccurate, fraudulent, or in conflict with either the public good or federal or state law.

Subdivision and Land-Development Financing

For some projects, the local jurisdiction may require subdividers to contribute to the development.[14] Local governments can exact three types of contributions:

- *Land.* The developer dedicates part of the land for a street, utility line, park, school, greenway, pedestrian access to a lake, or the like.
- *Fee in Lieu of Dedication.* The developer pays a fee commensurate with the value of the property he or she would otherwise have dedicated.
- *Impact Fee.* The developer pays a fee commensurate with cost of the infrastructure (schools, parks, water and sewer, and fire stations) needed to serve the people in the subdivision.

State law usually regulates how to set the impact fee, based on an empirical analysis of community benefits and costs.[15]

Performance Measurement

Performance measures for subdivision-regulation include:

- Median number of days from submission of a plan to a decision
- Percent of staff recommendations approved

INSPECTIONS

Building inspectors regularly evaluate construction to ensure adherence to a building code. Some states require that local units adhere to a statewide building code. Generally, state and local governments adopt the International Congress Code (ICC).[16] In 1994, the three model-code organizations—the Building Officials and Code Administrators, the International Conference of Building Officials, and the Southern Building Code Congress International— created the ICC, which is a uniform set of eleven construction codes (such as plumbing, mechanical, electrical). The principal advantage of the standard ICC is that developers do not have to research the code requirements of each local government within which they work.[17]

The building inspections department prepares a building-inspection manual based on the code to guide developers during construction. The building inspector ensures compliance with the approved site plan during construction and at the final inspection with respect to

- location and number of plants and trees;
- installation of utility connections, drainage cuts, and borings;
- drainage of gutters and sidewalks;
- meeting specifications for exterior lighting and dumpster enclosures;
- removal of debris from construction sites.

TRANSPORTATION PLANNING

Transportation modes include pedestrian travel, bicycling, public transit, and automobiles. As a condition of federal transportation funding for roads, states must establish metropolitan planning organizations (MPOs), consisting of the mayors and county chairs in an MPO district, which prioritize projects with input from their respective governing boards and CEOs. The MPO typically prepares the following:

- A comprehensive long-range highway and transit plan
- A three-to-five-year transportation improvement program
- A one-year activities program
- An energy-conservation plan
- An environmental project review

Local jurisdictions coordinate with states as well. States build and maintain roads that run through local jurisdictions. Local and state transportation planners coordinate to ensure that these state roads are constructed and maintained according to local policies and standards.

The goal in designing a road is to move traffic expeditiously while being sensitive to the problems of air pollution, congestion, and accidents. Among the ways to reduce traffic congestion are rapid-transit systems, carpooling, and HOV lanes. To route roads, the transportation planner conducts an *origin-and-destination* study, modeling where drivers originate their trip, their likely destination, and the amount and type of traffic flow. There are four types of models:[18]

1. *Trips Generated.* Estimates the number of trips based on household income, number of vehicles owned, and population density.
2. *Trips Distributed.* Estimates the distribution of trips geographically among possible destinations.
3. *Modal-Split.* If more than one transportation mode is possible (for example, a bus or subway), apportions trips among these alternative modes.
4. *Alternative Routes.* Predicts trips' distribution among alternative routes from the same origin to the same destination.

To estimate speed, density, and the traffic-flow rate, planners can reference the *Highway Capacity Manual,* published by the Transportation Research Board, which provides parameters to estimate the number of autos that a particular road can efficiently and safely accommodate. After reaching the maximum capacity/service level, the model distributes additional trips to other roads.

ENVIRONMENTAL LAND-USE PLANNING

The federal government and states regulate water and wastewater treatment, watersheds, air pollution, and hazardous-waste disposal. A local government either codifies federal and state regulations into its zoning ordinance and subdivision regulations or enacts a separate environmental ordinance. In either case, the ordinance regulates land use (for example, of wetlands, watercourses, and woodlands) and processes (such as erosion, sedimentation, runoff, and flooding).

The state and federal governments require that some projects be subjected to a *land-suitability analysis* (LSA) and/or an *environmental-impact assessment* (EIA). An LSA evaluates the suitability of environmentally sensitive sites like sanitary landfills. An EIA estimates the environmental impact of a particular project. Both analyses can be technically complex, so a local jurisdiction may employ a consultant to prepare either. A typical EIA includes:[19]

1. A description of current conditions
2. A description of the development alternatives
3. An estimate of the likely impact of the alternatives
4. The reasons why the preferred alternative was chosen
5. An estimate of the environmental impact of that alternative
6. A plan to minimize the negative impacts of the preferred alternative

Depending on a project's nature, planners choose among five methodologies to estimate the environmental impact:[20]

1. *Ad Hoc.* An estimate of the primary environmental impacts, ignoring secondary effects.
2. *Checklists.* Prepackaged questions to assess the impact.
3. *Matrices.* Proposed actions on a horizontal axis compared to the likely impact of the actions ranked on the vertical axis.
4. *Networks.* A complete tracking of a single action through a series of complex research-based iterations.
5. *Cartographic Maps.* Interpretive maps of processes, evaluated with regard to their land- use suitability.

OTHER PLANNING

Economic-Development Planning

In the early 1960s, the federal government funded economic development, principally through three now-terminated grants from the following bodies:

- Economic Development Administration
- Urban Development Action
- Community Development Block

Planners prepare an economic-development plan that assesses the present and future economic base, identifies industries to target for expansion and/or new location, and analyzes the costs and benefits of particular projects. The plan also estimates future personal-income, job, population and economic growth, and real-estate-market conditions.

Housing Planning

The housing plan projects the number of housing units that will be needed, based on state and regional workforce projections. The governing body may also adopt an affordable-housing policy to provide housing for low- and moderate-income citizens.

Historic-Preservation Planning

Local units may designate historic districts over which they exercise control, such as requiring that new structures or improvements in the district be consistent with its architectural style and scale.

NOTES

1. For an extensive historical review of planning, refer to Frank So, ed., *The Practice of Planning,* 2nd ed. (Washington, DC: International City/County Management Association, 1988).

2. John Levy, *Contemporary Urban Planning,* 7th ed. (Upper Saddle River, NJ: Pearson Prentice-Hall, 2003), 41.

3. Ibid., 53.

4. James Banovetz, Drew Dolan, and John Swain, eds., *Managing Small Cities and Counties,* 2nd ed. (Washington, DC: International City/County Management Association, 1994), 65.

5. For more discussion, see ibid., 68.

6. Governor's Center for Local Government Services, "Special Exceptions, Conditional Uses and Variances." Available at http://www.newpa.com.

7. So, *Practice of Planning,* 203.

8. Governor's Center for Local Government Services, "Subdivision and Land Development in Pennsylvania." Available at http://www.newpa.com.

9. So, *Practice of Planning,* 201.

10. Ibid.

11. Ibid., 210.

12. Ibid., 231.

13. Ibid., 233.

14. Ibid., 215.

15. Exactions are regulated by state law. For a more complete discussion, see So, *Practice of Planning,* 215–224.

16. Laura Lang, "Putting the I-Codes to Work for You," *Public Management* (May 2003), 16.

17. Ibid., 18.

18. Levy, *Contemporary Urban Planning,* 201.

19. So, *The Practice of Planning,* 129.

20. Ibid.

For Further Reading

Governor's Center for Local Government Services. Special Exceptions, Conditional Uses and Variances, 8th ed. Planning Series No. 7. Department of Community and Economic Development, Commonwealth of Pennsylvania, August 2001. Available at http://www.newpa.com; click on "Department of Community & Economic Development," then on "Publications" under "Local Government Services."

Governor's Center for Local Government Services. Subdivision and Land Development, 5th ed. Planning Series No. 8. Department of Community and Economic Development, Commonwealth of Pennsylvania, June 2003. Available at http://www.newpa.com; click on "Department of Community & Economic Development," then on "Publications" under "Local Government Services."

Levy, John. *Contemporary Urban Planning,* 7th ed. Upper Saddle River, NJ: Prentice-Hall, 2003.

So, Frank, ed. *The Practice of Planning,* 2nd ed. Washington, DC: International City/County Management Association, 1988.

9

Water Treatment and Distribution

HISTORY[1]

The Prefiltration Era (Colonial Days to 1887)

Since time immemorial, cities have located near a water source. In 312 BC, Roman engineers, adapting Etruscan technology, built a spring-fed conduit, the Aqua Appia. The Roman system, eventually including 247 reservoirs and four aqueducts, stretched over 316 miles to deliver 220 million gallons of water daily. With no water meters, water ran continuously, so that a typical Roman household used as much water daily as we do monthly.

In 1754, Bethlehem, Pennsylvania, built the first water system in the United States. In 1771, Philadelphia was the first large city to construct a water system, which leaked considerably because the pipes were wooden. Thus in 1819, the city installed iron pipes to minimize the leaking. In 1842, New York City built the Croton Aqueduct System, which transported water by gravity from a reservoir forty miles to the north. Coal-fired steam power was next used in addition to gravity to transport water. Using steam power, Chicago built a system that pumped water two miles from Lake Michigan in 1869.

The Filtration Era (1887 to the Present)

Venice first filtered water in the ninth century. In 1827, London installed slow-sand filters. However, few cities in the United States filtered water, mistakenly believing that bad "vapors," not waterborne pathogens, caused diseases. Consequently, diseases like cholera and typhoid were common as cities became more densely populated after the Civil War. In the 1880s, dysentery, the most common waterborne disease, was the third largest cause of death. Cisterns were a particularly fertile breeding place for disease-carrying mosquitoes.

In 1887, the Massachusetts Board of Health proved the germ theory of disease, proposed by Louis Pasteur in 1857. Consequently, by the 1890s, most cities had installed slow-sand filters to purify water. The filter did not, however, adequately remove suspended dirt and clay particles from highly turbid rivers. Moreover, the dirt and clay clogged the sand filter, increasing the filtration load. In 1887, Kansas City Missouri added alum, to produce *floc*, a gelatinous substance that bonds with silt to remove solids. In 1902, Little Falls, New Jersey, built a *rapid-sand plant* that pretreated water with iron, alum, sulfate, and other coagulants. Next, mechanical filters were invented to purify turbid water.

Dissolved minerals like magnesium and calcium harden water, causing pipes, boilers, and water heaters to scale. In 1905, Oberlin, Ohio, built a water-softening plant to reduce hardening. Jersey City added chlorine in 1908 to destroy disease-causing microorganisms, improve taste, and reduce odors; but wastewater from chemical plants still caused taste, odor, and algae problems. Therefore, water was *aerated*, exposing the water to the atmosphere to remove odors and restore depleted oxygen. Grand Rapids, Michigan, introduced fluoride in 1945 to reduce tooth decay.

Though used in 1850, water meters were not commonplace until the 1900s, because heavy-use customers resisted their installation, preferring to pay a lower cost, fixed fee based on the number of rooms and faucets in their buildings, regardless of their consumption.

Historically, water treatment was the exclusive purview of state and local governments until 1974, when Congress enacted the Safe Drinking Water Act to protect drinking water and regulate groundwater quality. The Environmental Protection Agency (EPA) regulates the amount of contaminants (such as barium nitrate, fluoride, chloramine, copper, and lead) in water and mandates that water operators be certified. Forty-five states enforce EPA regulations with state personnel; EPA personnel enforce its policies in the other states.

MANAGEMENT

States require that local water operators be certified at either three or four levels, depending on the state. To be a supervisor, an operator must be certified at the highest level. Moving between certification levels usually takes at least a year, but an operator with a college science degree may advance more quickly. Operators must also be state-licensed within two years after being hired. An operator must then pass a licensing exam and annually earn continuing-education units. To recruit and retain operators, some local governments pay the costs of prep raring for and taking exams.

Figure 9.1   **Forecasted Water Supply and Demand, Raleigh, North Carolina**

Max Day Demand and Treatment Capacity

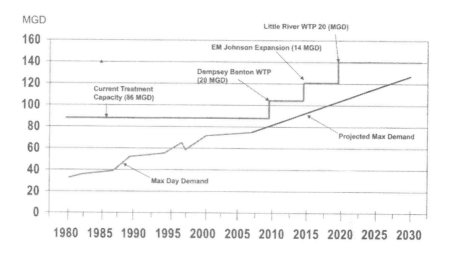

Source: City of Raleigh, N.C. Public Utilities Department

Water Supply

Each water plant has a state permit specifying the plant's treatment capacity in millions of gallons per day. To estimate the current and future plant capacity, planners calculate:

1. The percentage of capacity currently used at peak-treatment periods
2. The percentage of capacity permitted, but not yet used for buildings under construction
3. The amount of water needed for future usage (for example, over the next twenty years)

To estimate future usage, the following factors are analyzed:

- The history of residential, commercial and industrial usage.
- Estimated loss of water due to fire flow and leaks. A study of eight urban water systems found lost water ranged from 1 percent to 37 percent of capacity.[2]
- Projected population growth and commercial and industrial development.

Figure 9.1 shows the forecasted maximum daily demand and supply for Raleigh, North Carolina, until 2030.

In some cases, local governments make water-supply decisions jointly. For instance, several local governments participate in the Colorado River consortia to estimate future treatment demands.

Water-Rate Setting

There are three types of customers (residential, commercial, and industrial) and four principal types of rate structures. A *declining-block* (decreasing or sliding scale) rate structure charges the highest rate to residential customers, the next highest to commercial, and the lowest to industrial customers. Residential customers pay the highest rate because they contribute most to peak demand in the early morning and evening hours. Contributing less to the peak demand, commercial and industrial customers pay lower rates. A *uniform* rate imposes a minimum monthly charge and a flat charge per 1,000 gallons to residential, commercial, and industrial customers. A uniform rate is simplest for the customer to understand. Commercial and industrial customers, paying a higher rate than with a declining-block rate, are given an incentive to conserve water. An *inclining-block* (ascending) rate, the inverse of a declining-block rate, charges commercial and industrial customers a higher rate, respectively, to further motivate water conservation. Finally, a *seasonal* rate imposes a higher rate during a resort town's tourist season, because the system must be built to accommodate the peak seasonal demand.

Most utilities have at least one residential and one nonresidential class.[3] Some localities, though, divide residential customers into two classes (for example, multifamily and single family). Industrial customers may likewise be separated into small- and large-usage classes. Many utilities apply a fixed charge to recover the fixed costs of meter-reading, bill-processing, and a portion of capital costs.[4]

The Governmental Accounting Standards Board, which sets generally accepted accounting principles (GAAP), requires that water and sewer rates generate sufficient revenue to offset all expenses. Water systems have direct and indirect costs. Indirect costs are for services provided to the water department by the general fund (such as purchasing, legal, human resources, auditing, accounting, and the like). GAAP permits the general fund to charge the water fund for such costs, using two methods:

- *In Lieu of Taxes.* Charge the water department for the estimated amount of property taxes that the department would pay if it were a for-profit system.
- *Cost-Allocation Plan.* Charge the water system based on the indirect cost method established in federal circular, *OMB Circular A-87 Cost Allocation Principles for State and Local Governments.*

Local governments usually charge customers in unincorporated areas outside a city a higher rate than city residents pay, for two principal reasons:

- They are more costly to serve because water pipes and facilities (for example, pump stations) must be extended outside the city limits.
- They enjoy the benefits of city services like roads, parks, and public safety but do not pay city taxes.

Finally, in addition to charging recurring fees, most water and sewer systems charge new customers a "tap-on" or "connection" fee to recover a portion of past capital costs and installation expenses.

Water Conservation — *some incentives based*

Some governments are chronically short of water; others experience episodic shortages due to droughts. In either instance, local units may take the following water-conservation measures:

- Sell water barrels to residents to catch rain from downspouts to water their gardens
- Design water bills to allow customers to compare their water consumption seasonally and historically over several years
- Ask customers to take shorter showers and run water less while shaving and brushing teeth
- Mandate that customers water their lawns on a reduced schedule (such as every other day) or not at all
- Charge customers a considerably higher rate (for example, 3.5 times more) when their consumption exceeds a specified amount
- Minimize water waste (use recycling fountains, for example)
- Give rebates to customers who install ultra–low-flow toilets and high-efficiency washing machines
- Provide a financial incentive to retrofit plumbing with low-cost faucet aerators, showerheads, and toilet dams
- Construct a water-reuse system that recycles treated wastewater for uses such as golf courses
- Supply bulk reuse water for contractors and other major water users
- Require and/or provide a dual water-system infrastructure (that is, separate potable and reuse water lines) to enable water reuse
- Implement a certification program for the vehicle-wash industry that requires water recycling
- Operate a water-conservation-education program

In some areas of the country, considerable demand is placed on water systems by lawn irrigation systems. Raleigh, North Carolina, for instance, experienced a severe drought in 2007 and 2008. To conserve water, the city eventually banned the use of such systems, dropping maximum daily usage by over 80 percent.

Water pumped, but not billed, is *unaccounted-for* water, which can be caused by leaks, main breaks, flushing water hydrants, cleaning streets, and unauthorized water taps. Unaccounted-for water is the difference between the water pumped (as metered at the treatment facility) and the unaccounted for use. Unaccounted-for water is usually expressed as a percentage of water production. The American Water Works Association (AWWA) recommends that unaccounted for water loss be less than 10 percent of the water pumped.[5] To reduce unaccounted-for water, the department should operate a leak-detection-and-repair program.

WATER TREATMENT

[handwritten: In the last few chapters, Coe explains the costliness of safety, this just adds to the costs (since 9/11)]

A water plant operates under a state permit that specifies its operating standards, which are encoded in an operation-and-maintenance manual. Before September 11, 2001, standards paid scant attention to possible acts of terrorism. Now the EPA requires a water system serving more than 3,300 customers to assess its vulnerability to an act of terrorism and prepare an emergency-response plan. Most states also mandate that local units prepare a water-supply plan and meet watershed-protection regulations.

[handwritten in left margin: very expensive process]

States generally require that a professional engineer prepare the specifications for a water-plant expansion or construction. The local government submits to the state an affirmation, signed by the engineer and affixed with the engineer's professional engineering seal, which avers that the construction was done according to the state-approved specifications.

Water is treated over the ten stages shown in Figure 9.2. A water-treatment plant is pictured in Figure 9.3.

Preliminary Treatment

The load on the treatment processes is reduced by first removing some impurities from the water in the preliminary treatment (also known as pretreatment) stage, which includes chemical pretreatment, screening, presedimentation, and microstraining.

Chemical Pretreatment

Algae cause bad taste and foul odors and clog filters. Operators usually treat water for algae daily. The type of treatment depends on the type

Figure 9.2 **Water-Treatment Process**

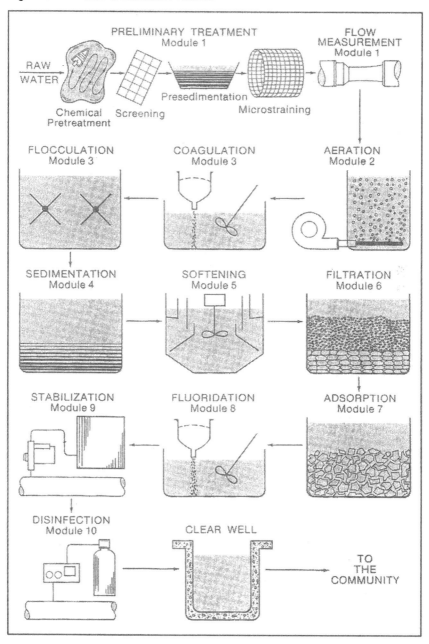

Source: American Water Works Association, *Introduction to Water Treatment,* vol. 2 (Denver: AWWA, 1984), 2. Reprinted with permission.

Figure 9.3 **Water Treatment Plant**

Source: Used by permission from the town of Cary, NC.

of algae. One treatment option uses chemicals like powdered carbon or copper sulfate.

Screening

At a surface-water-intake facility, bar and wire-mesh screens filter out floating debris such as sand, silt, and fish. If not cleaned regularly, the screens clog, causing a foul odor. The most debris is screened in the autumn, when trees lose their foliage. A lake-intake operation typically has multiple inlets to optimize water flow when the lake level varies.

Presedimentation

Some water plants draw water straight from a river without treatment; others use a presedimentation process, especially if a river has high turbidity (muddy sediment). Presedimentation reduces heavy gravel-sized sand and silt particles, which jam equipment and damage submerged moving parts like pump impellers, drive shafts, and bearings. The three types of presedimentation methods are (1) impoundments, (2) sand traps, and (3) mechanical sand-and-grit removal devices. An effective presedimentation system typically removes 60 percent or more of settleable material.[6]

Microstraining

A microstrainer is a very fine screen that removes algae, other aquatic organisms, and small debris that clog treatment-plant filters. The most common mechanism is a rotating drum, lined with finely woven material such stainless-steel wire. Algae and other aquatic material that adhere to the fabric material are backwashed into a debris trough and disposed of in a pond or tank.

Flow Measurement

Flow measurement typically occurs after preliminary treatment. Operators measure the flow of the water to

- control the flow rate,
- adjust chemical-feed rates,
- determine pump efficiencies and power requirements,
- calculate detention times,
- monitor water usage,
- calculate unit costs for treatment.

Aeration

Aeration mingles water and air by exposing water drops or thin water sheets to the air or by letting small air bubbles rise through the water. Undesirable dissolved gases enter the water from the air or by a chemical or biological reaction with the water. Aeration causes a *scrubbing* action, turbulently mixing water and air, which physically removes the gases into the surrounding air. Aeration also causes *oxidation*, combining oxygen with undesirable metals (usually iron or manganese) in the water to remove dissolved materials. Once oxidized, these substances become suspended in the water as finely divided material, which is then removed by filtration.

Coagulation/Flocculation

Coagulation/flocculation removes solids that do not settle because they are small and carry a negative electrical repelling force that suspends them unless exposed to a coagulant. In the *coagulation* process one or more chemical coagulants are rapidly mixed with water to form particles, called floc. *Flocculation* gently mixes the water and coagulants to form larger, heavier, more settleable floc that are easier to remove later in the sedimentation and filtration stages. Coagulants and coagulant aids are usually diluted at the treatment plant before being added to untreated water. Once dissolved or diluted, the coagulants are metered, fed into the raw water, and rapid- or flash-mixed by mechanical mixers, pumps, conduits, or baffled chambers.

Chemicals should be stored in a dry area at a moderate, fairly uniform temperature on pallets positioned to permit gravity-feeding to the hopper. Chemicals must be carefully handled because they are toxic and acidic. Operators should wear a respirator, protective clothing, and goggles and handle heavy containers mechanically, not manually, with a forklift, hoist, or monorail. The conveyer piping and storage tanks that handle chemicals should be noncorrosive.

Sedimentation

Sand, grit, floc, pollutants, and other settleable solids suspend in water due to velocity and turbulence. The sedimentation process removes these solids to decrease the filtration load. Sedimentation occurs in a sedimentation basin, tank, or clarifier through which water slowly flows, decreasing the turbulence and settling the solids to the bottom of the basin. *Plain sedimentation* settles heavy sediments by gravity, without adding chemicals. *Chemical sedimentation* settles heavier sediments by chemical treatment. A settlement basin typically detains materials for two to six hours, but water currents and other hydraulics may cause the water to short-circuit the basin, thus avoiding disinfection. To ensure the proper detention time, departments can add a dye tracer disinfectant to the water. If only 10 percent or less of the tracer dye gets to the customer, the system meets the federal standard.

As the solids settle, a sludge layer forms at the bottom; this must be removed or solids will resuspend, causing bad tastes and odors. Though many small facilities remove sludge manually, automatic sludge removal is preferable. The basin should be drained and inspected at least annually to wash sludge deposits into the disposal system. Frequent draining is labor-intensive and costly, and basins that require monthly or bimonthly draining should be retrofitted with an automated vacuum system that continuously removes sludge.

Spreading sludge on land reduces the cost of sludge removal. Alum is mixed with the sludge to create a spread commonly dried on a belt press. The Clean Water Act defines sludge as an industrial waste whose discharge and/or land application must be permitted by the state.

Softening

When water contains a significant amount of calcium and magnesium, it is hard. Pipes clog and soap dissolves less easily in hard water, and a lime scale builds up on laundry machines. The amount of hardness depends on the soil makeup. The two most common water-softening methods are lime/soda ash and ion-exchange.

Lime/Soda Ash

Lime is added to remove carbonates and magnesium; soda ash to remove other non-carbonates. Departments normally keep a sixty-day supply of lime and soda ash on hand. The chemicals longest remaining in stock should be used first because chemicals lose effectiveness over time. The solids-contact basin should be periodically drained and cleaned. Because chemicals such as quick-lime dust, soda ash, and calcium can be very harmful, operators should

- wear goggles and a dust mask,
- store calcium in a dry place,
- never mix dry calcium with dry alum,
- equip lime-slakers with temperature-override devices,
- immediately flush chemicals from eyes,
- immediately consult a physician if chemicals are ingested,
- ventilate the carbonation basin.

Process-control problems may include excess calcium carbonate, magnesium-hydroxide scale, carryover of sludge solids, unstable water, and interference with other treatment processes.[7]

Ion-Exchange

In a process used extensively by small water systems, water passes through a filterlike bed of ion-exchange resin material to eliminate hardness. The ion-exchange process is simpler, cheaper and safer than the lime/soda ash process. Process control problems may include resin breakdown, unstable water, water fouling by turbidity, organic color, and bacterial slime.[8]

Filtration

Water filters naturally as it percolates through layers of soil. Naturally filtered groundwater may not need more treatment than softening and disinfection. In contrast, contaminated surface water is further filtered for health reasons and because of its offensive color. Filtration lowers the amount of *turbidity*, which interferes with disinfection and causes bad odors, bad taste and bacterial growth. Turbidity is the principal water-quality measure. The higher the turbidity, the greater is the risk of gastrointestinal diseases. A calibrated nephelometer measures the amount of turbidity in Nephelometric Turbidity Units (NTU). The federal allowable contaminant limit is 0.3 NTU, but AWWA recommends, and some states require, a limit of 0.1 NTU. The 0.1 NTU limit on each filter's effluent gives the operator time to react to any problems within the treatment system.[9]

Depending on raw-water quality, two filter systems are used: gravity and pressure. A *gravity filter* moves the water through a filter medium (such as sand, anthracite coal, or granular activated carbon) by gravity. The three types of gravity filters are slow-sand, rapid-sand, and high-rate. The slow-sand filter, introduced in the United States in 1872, has been mostly replaced by the more economical rapid-sand filter, which filters forty times faster. Faster yet, the high-rate filter, using two or three filter media, operates up to four times faster than the rapid-sand filter. In each method, the type of filter medium depends on the type of chemical treatment, the raw-water quality, and the desired treatment level.

There are two basic types of filtration plants: conventional and direct. A *conventional-filtration* plant uses sedimentation to remove most suspended material. In contrast, a *direct-filtration* plant does not include sedimentation. Though less expensive to construct, a direct-filtration plant requires more monitoring and consequently is state-regulated.

There are three less common filter methods. First, *diatomaceous-earth filtration* feeds diatomaceous earth to a filter unit. The plant has a relatively low construction cost, but high operational and sludge-removal costs. Second, *biological filtration* uses microbes to break down substances. Finally, private developers may operate a *package-treatment plant* that includes a coagulation/flocculation unit, a settling-floc separation tank, and a gravity-pressure filter. Subject to stringent state and federal effluent standards, these plants should be closely monitored by local governments.

Unless thoroughly backwashed, filters will require excessive repair and maintenance costs. *Backwashing* means reversing and increasing the water's flow to flush out accumulated debris and particles. In effect, the clogged particles are blasted off the filter. States may regulate the frequency of backwashing. In North Carolina, for example, filters must be backwashed at least every 96 hours. The AWWA recommends backwashing after 15–56 hours of operation, depending on the type of plan. The cleanliness or cloudiness (turbidity) of the water coming out of the filter is the best way to determine when to backwash. Backwashing is done until the water runs clear. Backwash water is very dirty; the best and easiest way to eliminate it is through a backwash line connected to the nearest sanitary sewer.[10] When discharging backwash water, care should be taken to not overload the system, which could cause backups in homes and disrupt the sewer plant. If a sanitary sewer cannot be used, backwash can be routed to a lagoon or settling basin or combined with sedimentation sludge and disposed of.

Adsorption

Adsorption removes dissolved organic materials that cause unsuitable tastes, odors, and color in drinking water. Of the more than 700 different organic materials found in drinking water, two types are of primary concern:

- Disinfection byproducts (trihalomethanes) produced when humic materials (organic soils) react with chlorine
- Chemicals from cleaning compounds, insecticides, and herbicides

Adsorption is based on the *adhesion principle*. Organic materials and chemicals stick to the surface of an adsorbent through complex physical forces and chemical actions. The most commonly used chemicals are powder activated carbon (PAC) and granular activated carbon (GAC). Used mainly to control tastes and odors, finely powdered PAC and GAC must be carefully handled and applied.[11]

Fluoridation

Fluoridation reduces tooth decay. Surface water contains practically no fluoride. In contrast, groundwater usually has enough natural fluoride that fluoridation is unnecessary. In some instances, though, the fluoride level in groundwater may be too high. The level must then be reduced or teeth will discolor and pit. The type of fluoridation method depends on water quality and type of chemical (sodium fluoride, hydrofluosilicic acid, or sodium silicofluoride). In some states, the dental profession financially assists local governments to install a fluoridation system.

Operators should routinely inspect and clean the dry-fluoride feeder; clean the saturation tank up to three times annually, depending on the amount of scale built up; routinely maintain pumps according to the manufacturers' recommendations; safely store fluoride chemicals; immediately clean spills; and measure the fluoride level daily to avoid corrosion.

Stabilization

Water that corrodes or scales pipelines and plumbing fixtures is said to be *unstable*. Unstable water dissolves toxic metals, particularly lead and cadmium, which can pose a health threat. Lead is found in the service lines of older homes; cadmium is a byproduct of galvanized piping. Corrosive water also attacks metal pipes; causes color, taste, and odor problems; and reduces the life of valves, unprotected metal, and asbestos-cement pipe.

Unstable water also scales metal in two ways: (1) *uniform scaling* attacks metal surfaces uniformly and (2) *localized scaling* unevenly attacks metal surfaces, causing them to fail more quickly. The stabilization process treats unstable water, reducing or eliminating the corrosion and scaling by:

- Adjusting the pH and alkalinity
- Applying a protective coating to the pipe surface
- Using corrosion inhibitors and sequestering agents

The National Sanitary Foundation approves stabilization chemicals. Operators typically keep at least a thirty-day supply on hand. When handling chemicals, operators should wear gloves, a long-sleeved shirt with a buttoned collar, tight-fitting safety glasses with side shields, and a close-fitting respirator. They should immediately shower and apply a protective cream if exposed to chemicals. Other operator duties include:

- Investigating customer complaints to detect the location of corrosion and scaling
- Testing water samples and continuously monitoring the pH level
- Inspecting pipe specimens
- Recordkeeping

Disinfection

The final treatment step (see Figure 9.2), disinfection, frees water of waterborne diseases, such as amoebic dysentery, typhoid, gastroenteritis, and infectious hepatitis. Water is commonly disinfected with chemicals, but other disinfection methods include heat and radiation treatment. The most common disinfectant chemical is chlorine. Others include bromine, iodine, and ozone. Chlorine is shipped in 100–150 pound- or 1-ton containers in the form of a liquid or gas, a sodium-hypochlorite solution, or dry calcium hypochlorite. The gas solution is pressure-fed into the water in a contact chamber for a minimum of twenty minutes before the water is pumped into the distribution system.

An error in handling or storing chlorine-pressure vessels can cause a serious injury, even a fatality. OSHA therefore strictly regulates its usage, requiring operators to wear a mask when handling it. Possible operating problems can include a chlorine leak, a stiff container valve, hypochlorinator problems, noxious gases and odors, and sudden changes in residual formation.[12]

Performance Measurement

Among the water-treatment performance measures are:

Health

- Number of times health standards are not met over x period of time
- Number of waterborne-disease incidents over x period of time

Aesthetics

- Number of incidents where aesthetic standards (color, turbidity, taste) are not met
- Number of valid complaints per 1,000 customers

Water Quality

- Number of incidents where standards for hardness and pH (cleaning effectiveness) for iron and manganese (staining) are not met

Water Flow

- Number of water-restricted days on households and business by water use and type of restriction
- Number of valid water-flow complaints
- Percent of hydrants that meet the static water-pressure standard of 40 PSI
- Percent of unaccounted-for water, not to exceed x percent
- Percent of customers receiving at least x GPM fire-flow protection

WATER DISTRIBUTION

To maintain and repair infrastructure, the department should map the location and the size of pipes, pumps, tanks, valves, hydrants, and other facilities. A system-wide map, though highly desirable, may not be available, as EPA did not require mapping until the 1970s. A professional engineer prepares "as built" drawings, documenting water pipes' sizes and widths. The state approves construction plans before a local government can award a contract. A water-distribution system can be designed as a grid, a loop, or in branches. The most efficient design is a *grid*, which eliminates expensive-to-maintain dead-end lines.

When gravity cannot supply water at the required pressure, *prime movers* (electronic motors and engines) are installed to drive pumps. The pumps should be installed, inspected, operated, and maintained according to the

Figure 9.4 **Water Pumps**

Source: Used by permission from the town of Cary, NC.

manufacturers' guidelines. Large water systems can electronically monitor flow rates, pressures, and levels and can automatically change valve settings and turn pumps on and off. Figure 9.4 shows water pumps.

Maintenance and Repair

Crews maintain and repair wells, meters, water mains, fire hydrants, and water tanks.

Wells and Meters

States mandate how often wells should be tested. The testing frequency is based on the water quality. Whatever the frequency, well testing is expensive, especially for a small-sized system. Therefore, wells should be connected to the central water-treatment facility to avoid inspections if possible.

Meters are installed in outdoor meter pits (also known as meter wells) or inside the building served. Tested for accuracy upon installation, meters should thereafter be regularly maintained and systematically replaced. Master meters at the treatment plant measure the highest water volumes. These meters should be tested annually, as should customers' meters.[13] As a meter ages, it becomes encrusted with minerals or debris and runs more slowly. Customers with slow-running meters thus pay less for water than others with more accurate meters. Residential meters should thus be checked, cleaned, and calibrated every seven to ten years.[14]

Though reading meters was formerly a manual process, most water systems now read them electronically. Some systems, though, even read meters with a telemetry system that automatically records water usage and prepares the water bill.

Water Mains

Newly installed and repaired water mains are flushed and disinfected. Flushing (fully opening a hydrant) should be done only by trained personnel. The water-distribution manager should consult with the water-treatment-plant manager to ensure that adequate water pressure will be available when mains are flushed. Ideally, the whole system should be flushed annually; however, a water system may flush less frequently due to budgetary constraints. Mains are preferably flushed at night, when water pressure is greatest, in order to minimize the effect on customers' water pressure. When a customer complains about dirty water, the water line should be flushed as soon as possible.

Sediment accumulates at the end of a water line (a dead end). States therefore require that a hydrant and valve be located at a dead end to regularly flush the sediment. Records should be kept of flushed hydrants, the water conditions during flushing, and the date of the flushing. Using these data, the water manager annually estimates the amount of water that was not billed due to flushing.

A department should also operate a leak-detection program. Leakage can result from poorly constructed pipelines, poorly maintained valves, mechanical damage, and inadequate corrosion protection. Leaks cause water loss and reduced water pressure. To prevent leaks, a pipe should be thoroughly inspected at the time of its installation. Thereafter, a distribution system can experience two types of leaks: an emergency leak requires immediate repair; less easy to detect, a nonemergency leak is usually located with sonic-detection equipment that identifies the sound of water escaping a pipe. Types of listening devices include:

- Pinpoint listening devices that make contact with valves and hydrants
- Geophones that listen directly on the ground
- Devices that listen to two points simultaneously to pinpoint the exact location

The leak-detection program should focus on areas

- where system pressure is high,
- with a history of excessive leaks and breaks,
- where loads on pipe exceed design loads,
- near stream crossings.

A leak may either be repaired or the pipe replaced depending on the frequency of leaks in a given pipe and the cost of repair versus replacement. Repair clamps, or collars, are typically used to repair small leaks.

Fire Hydrants

Inspected upon delivery for possible damage, fire hydrants should be installed according to manufacturers' instructions. The AWWA recommends that all hydrants be inspected at least annually.[15] Hydrant inspection steps include:

- Check for main valve leaks and standing water.
- Loosen the cap and open the hydrant a few turns to allow air to vent, then tighten the cap and open the hydrant fully.
- With hydrant fully on, check for leaks and replace O-rings if needed.
- Partially close the hydrant until the drains open, and flush the drains for a few seconds under pressure.

Hydrants found in need of repair should be referred to repair crews. AWWA recommends that hydrant tops and nozzle caps be marked green to indicate a 1,000 GPM capacity, orange (500–1,000 GPM capacity), or red (less than 500 GPM capacity).

Water Tanks

Reserve water can be stored in reservoirs, elevated tanks, or standpipes to meet peak water demand. Peak water demand can be caused by a fire, peak-time usage, erratic pressure changes (called *water hammer*), and pump failures. Water storage enables a local government to build a smaller, less expensive water-treatment plant yet still accommodate peak water demand.

Water tanks should be regularly drained, cleaned, disinfected, painted, and inspected for corrosion. Without systematic cleaning, chemicals build up inside the tank, degrading water quality. If contracted out to the private sector, the bid specification should precisely state the performance requirements for cleaning and painting tanks.

Service Installation

A water main's size is determined by its carrying capacity. States generally require that mains meet minimum water carrying standards (for example, not less that twenty pounds per square inch) during peak demand periods. Main sizes must meet residential, commercial, industrial, and fire-flow requirements. AWWA recommends at least a six-inch water line,[16] but some towns still use four-inch and two-inch lines. In any event, a fire hydrant should never be installed on a line less than six inches.

Ductile iron pipe is most commonly used because plastic pipe ruptures more easily. When delivered, pipes should be mechanically unloaded, inspected to ensure that specifications are met, and not placed on gasoline-contaminated soil, which will eat through a PVC pipe's polyethylene seal.

Pipe Installation

Water mains are installed in the street right-of-way, on private property via an easement, or on the state right-of-way, which requires an encroachment agreement and permit. Before the excavation, a detailed installation plan should be prepared, the utilities notified, and the excavation site marked with warning signs. Generally, the trench width should not be one to two feet greater than the pipe's diameter.[17] Poor soil should be excavated and replaced with more suitable soil. OSHA regulations specify how to shore and shield the trench. AWWA recommends that a water main be laid at least three feet above a crossing sewer line.[18] After installation, the trench should be partially backfilled to test for leakage and pressure-holding ability.

Tapping

When the distribution system expands, pipes are installed (tapped) to connect the existing lines to a new lateral (usually bigger than two inches in diameter) or to a customer-service line. Tapping has two definitions:

1. Cutting threads on the inside of a drilled or cut hole
2. Connecting any type of line to an existing main[19]

A *dry tap* is made in an empty main; a *wet tap* is made in a main under water pressure. The wet tap is preferable because foreign-substance bacteria may infiltrate after a dry tap. Chlorine is added to kill the bacteria, but too large a quantity of chlorine can harm those receiving kidney dialysis treatment.

Typically, a two-inch or smaller line is tapped into a customer-service line extending from a home or small business. Most states limit the number of connections that can be made per one hundred feet on a two-inch-diameter line. Departments typically connect large pipes (three inches or larger in diameter) by emptying the main and installing a fitting.

Valve Installation

Valves stop, start, and regulate water flow. They also drain water lines, isolate water-main sections, control water hammer, prevent backflow, and bleed off air. Valves are operated manually, electrically, hydraulically, or pneumatically, depending on their use. States generally specify the distance that valves can be located from feeder mains and between fire hydrants. Valves should be stored in a fully closed position and routinely maintained.[20] Limited use often causes valves to malfunction, so they should be regularly tested.

Service-Line Installation

A service line is a small (¾-inch to 2-inch) pipe running from the distribution main to a customer's plumbing system. Copper is the best material for such a pipe because it inhibits bacteria growth.[21] Crews install service lines by placing a shutoff valve (curbstop) near the customer's property line. Normally, local governments make customers responsible for the cost of maintaining their service line.

Distribution Line Repair

Distribution lines can break because of excessive traffic weight running over a line, extremely cold temperatures, pipe corrosion, and defective pipes. If a main breaks, utility crews should repair it immediately. The water department should follow an emergency response plan that includes public safety personnel if a hazard is posed to life or property. Utility workers should notify affected customers that their water will be turned off temporarily. Valves must be first shut off in the area to isolate the break. Once the leak is detected, the repair crew digs up the pipe. The trench should be parallel to the pipe on both sides and deep enough to work around the pipe.[22]

Cross-Connection Control

A cross connection is a structural arrangement (such as a pipe, hose connection, or water outlet) where potable water in the distribution system can be exposed to unwanted contaminants. Such contaminants can pose a health risk. Usually unintentional, cross connections can occur anywhere that pipes supply water.[23] If a cross connection exists, there is the possibility of *backflow,* which is the reverse flow of contaminants. Water utilities may want to operate a cross-connection prevention-and-control program. Such a program inspects the system for potential cross connections, installs backflow prevention devices where needed, and informs consumers how to prevent cross connections.

Performance Measurement

Among the water-distribution measures are:

Service

- Percent of new water connections made within x amount of time
- Percent of customer complaints investigated within x amount of time
- Percent of service orders completed within x amount of time

Repair

- Percent of service interruptions limited to x amount of time
- Percent of emergency responses made within x amount of time

Maintenance

- Percent of valves and mains preventively maintained annually
- Percent of water meters repaired within x amount of time
- Percent of obsolete water meters replaced annually

WATER-QUALITY ANALYSIS

Operators sample water to determine whether it meets EPA water-quality standards. The National Drinking Water Regulations specify the sampling frequency. Analysts choose sampling locations that are statistically representative of the whole water system. A surface-water system serving 25,000 to 100,000 customers must take samples at a minimum of two sampling locations. Samplers use a clean, wide-mouthed sampling bottle; run water for two to five minutes to flush away stagnant water; preserve the sample; and run compliance tests. If a compliance test proves positive, the operator tests further for fecal matter.

Water managers take great pride in their water quality. For instance, at the annual AWWA conference, spouses of water treatment managers taste water for its quality in a process similar to a wine-tasting competition. The samples are not identified by unit of government. A much coveted recognition is to win the annual water-tasting competition.

NOTES

1. The history draws on Ellis L. Armstrong, ed., *History of Public Works in the United States, 1776–1976* (Washington, DC: The American Public Works Association, 1976).

2. Patrick Mann and Janice Beecher, "Cost Impact of Safe Drinking Water Act Compliance for Commission-Regulated Water Utilities," NFFI Report 89–6 (Columbus, OH: National Regulatory Research Institute, May 1989).

3. Jeff Hughes, "The Painful Art of Setting Water and Sewer Rates," *Popular Government* 70, no. 3 (Spring/Summer 2005): 11.

4. Ibid., 8.

5. American Water Works Association (AWWA), *Water Quality and Treatment Handbook,* 5th ed. (Denver: AWWA, 1995), 70.

6. Ibid., 43.

7. Ibid., 349–351.

8. Ibid., 370–371.

9. Zane Satterfield, "Filter Backwashing," *Tech Brief* 5, no. 3 (2005): 1.

10. Ibid., 2.

11. AWWA, *Water Quality and Treatment,* 392–397.

12. Ibid., 219–223.

13. Zane Satterfield and Vipin Bhardwaj, "Water Meters," *Tech Brief* 4, no. 2 (2004): 2.

14. Ibid., 4.

15. Larry Rader, *How to Begin a Fire Hydrant Operation and Maintenance Program* (Morganton, WV: National Drinking Water Clearinghouse, n.d.).

16. AWWA, *Water Quality and Treatment Handbook,* 4th ed. (Denver: AWWA, 1984), 6.

17. AWWA, *Water Distribution* (Denver: AWWA, 1986), 34.

18. Ibid., 38.

19. Ibid., 93.

20. For further discussion, see ibid., 128–142.

21. Ibid., 174.

22. Vipin Bhardwaj, "Repairing Distribution Line Breaks," *Tech Brief* 4, no. 1 (2004): 2.

23. Vipin Bhardwaj, "Cross Connection and Backflow Prevention," *Tech Brief* 3, no. 4 (2004): 1.

FOR FURTHER READING

American Water Works Association. *Water Distribution,* 5th ed. Denver: AWWA, 1995.

———. *Water Quality and Treatment Handbook,* 4th ed. Denver: AWWA, 1989.

———. *Water Quality and Treatment Handbook,* 5th ed. Denver: AWWA, 1995.

10

Wastewater and Storm-Water Management

The Pre-Treatment Era (Grecian Days to 1884)

More than 2,800 years ago, the fabled King Minos of Crete had a water closet installed, complete with a wooden seat. Around the fourth century BC, Romans created the Forum, draining the marshes at the foot of the Palatine Hill. In the second century BC, the Romans built the Cloaca Maxima, a still-used, gigantic terra-cotta sewer. In 1594, Sir John Harrington built a "privy in perfection" for his godmother, Queen Elizabeth. Until the middle of the nineteenth century, though, open gutters or covered trenches drained rain runoff and kitchen slop. Indeed, the putrid stink of sewage in the Thames River in 1858 ("The Year of the Great Stink") forced the closing of Parliament.

In the United States, outhouses were used, though the ever-ingenious Thomas Jefferson designed an indoor privy at Monticello, which hauled chamber pots away by a pulley system. By the late 1700s, wooden lines, built with private capital, drained wastewater from some houses. Until the late 1800s, though, citizens did discharge fecal matter by sewers. Mistakenly believing in the "miasma theory," the scientific community thought that disease was caused by the vapors from decayed organic matter. Thus, drains were not installed, as they were thought to produce dangerous fumes. Instead, privy vaults, backhouses, and cesspools held human waste. Garbage, thrown into the streets, was eaten by roving dogs, rats, and pigs. Disease-bearing organisms leached into the soil, contaminating the water supply and causing diseases like cholera, typhoid, malaria, typhus, and yellow fever.

Sewage was disposed of in an elongated cesspool with an overflow at the end until 1840, when Edwin Chadwick constructed a narrow sewer out of smooth ceramic pipe through which sewage flowed by gravity to a common sewer miles away. In 1880, Memphis built the first sanitary sewer system in the United States, sending sewage from a lateral line to a collector line to a large trunk sewer and finally to the Mississippi River. Nevertheless, the "solution to pollution" remained "dilution," as experts mistakenly believed that wastewater self-purified.

The Treatment Era (1884 to the Present)

Spurred by the knowledge that germs, not vapors, caused disease, cities built wastewater treatment plants. The wastewater was given *primary treatment*: screening grit and other large suspended materials with a cage screen (1884) and a grit chamber (1904). The screened materials were disposed of at a dump or incinerated. In 1915, Sacramento installed a mechanical screening device. In 1908, Reading, Pennsylvania, installed a *trickling filter,* sprinkling untreated effluent over a bed of coarse rocks covered with biological growth. In 1916, San Marcos, Texas, installed an *activated sludge* treatment system. Mechanical aerators pumped air into a mixture of raw sewage and heavy concentrations of aerobic microorganisms to stimulate bacterial reduction. The processed sludge was given to farmers for fertilizer, sent to a landfill, or dumped in the ocean. Activated sludge too diluted to dry on sand beds was incinerated or vacuum filtered. Today, activated sludge is usually digested in a heated tank, dewatered by centrifuge or vacuum filters, and then disposed of.

After World War II, sewage systems bore a heavier load. They had to treat more

- *phosphates* from washing machines, dishwashers, and showers;
- *toxic chemicals, oil*, and *grease* from manufacturing plants;
- *fats, oils*, and *grease* from households and fast-food restaurants.

Consequently, Congress enacted the Clean Water Act in 1972, which funded wastewater-treatment-plant construction, prohibited point-source pollutants, and established the National Pollutant Discharge Elimination System (NPDES) treatment standards. By 1987, most treatment plants had met these standards, so Congress largely replaced the grants with a revolving-loan program administered by states.

Wastewater is about 99 percent water by weight, but it is not just sewage. It also includes water from baths, showers, sinks, washing machines, and dishwashers. The average household generates between 66 and 192 gallons of wastewater daily. Businesses also contribute large amounts of wastes, which some firms treat with their own wastewater treatment system. Among business-produced wastes are those from nonhazardous, light industrial, sludge, mining, and agricultural uses.

Most treatment plants have primary treatment (the physical removal of floatable and settleable solids) and secondary treatment (the biological removal of dissolved solids). An increasing number of facilities also employ tertiary, or advanced, treatment to remove nutrients such as nitrogen and phosporous and toxic chemicals or metals. In a *combined sewage system,* water from storm drains is added to the wastewater stream.

MANAGEMENT

Subtitle D of the Resource Conservation and Recovery Act regulates wastewater treatment. The governing body, through its long-range capital planning process, decides the amount of sewage-treatment capacity to allocate to residential, commercial, and industrial customers. Small local units, with one or a few major industries, should not overcommit too much capacity to one or a few plants, especially to those that pose expensive toxicity-treatment issues.

As with water rates, generally accepted accounting principles require that sewer revenues cover the expense of the system. Sewerage use, except that by large industrial users, is not metered. The accepted rule of thumb therefore is to assume that the amount of sewage treated directly equals the amount of water consumed. In other words, if a customer consumed 10,000 gallons of water in a month, the sewerage rate is charged against an assumed 10,000 gallons treated.

Plant Manuals and Records

Departments keep a record of drawings of as-built conditions, flow schematics, valve tables, the hydraulic profile, and structural and electrical diagrams, which are used to diagnose operating problems, make repairs, and plan for future construction. The drawings are commonly kept in a digital format. Departments also must file the state-compliance reports and correspondence required by the plant's permit. The records must be kept for five years until the permit is renewed. The records and reports should be kept at the plant and at a backup location outside the plant.

The plant should have an operation and maintenance (O&M) manual that details such maintenance requirements as:

- Maintaining equipment according to manufacturers' O&M manuals
- Systematically replacing parts like bearings and pump impellers
- Prominently posting manufacturers' warranty schedules and conditions

- Solving process-control problems like accumulated solids and failed instruments due to hydraulic overload, intermittent heavy loadings, and noxious odors

Plant Plans

The department should prepare three principal plans. First, the *emergency operating plan* (EOP) identifies potential hazards, flowcharts emergency procedures, lists emergency contacts, establishes the chain of command in the event of an emergency, and assesses the plant's vulnerability to a terrorist attack.[1] A sewage spill constitutes an emergency if effluent bypasses the treatment plant. In the event of a spill, the CEO must immediately notify the state and the local units downstream. The local jurisdiction, according to EPA regulations, must contact the news media to notify the public within forty-eight hours of an overflow of 1,000 gallons. In the event of a chemical spill, local and state emergency management personnel are notified.

Second, the *process control system plan* is a statement of the plant's sewage-treatment goals according to the NPDES permit.[2] Finally, the *conservation plan* is a strategy to reduce energy costs and conserve water. Energy costs are a large portion of a plant's operating budget. The plant manager may conduct an energy audit to discover how to reduce peak energy demand. For instance, wastewater reuse reduces costs by using treated wastewater for land irrigation, vehicle washing, industrial processes, toilet flushing, fire protection, and dust control. Energy-efficient toilets and showers lessen costs as well. One leaky toilet adds about 750 gallons of wastewater to the system monthly; a leaky faucet adds about 300 gallons monthly.[3] The conventional toilet uses 5–6 gallons per flush; a low-flush toilet uses 3.5 gallons per flush; an ultra-low-flush toilet uses only 1.0–1.6 gallons per flush. A low-flow showerhead reduces water flow, as do energy efficient, front-loading washing machines.

WASTEWATER TREATMENT

The two principal measures of plant performance focus on the quality of treated water as it returns to the receiving stream. The amount of *biological oxygen demand* (BOD) measures the rate at which microorganisms use oxygen to decompose organic material. A high BOD level reduces the water's oxygen supply, which fish need to survive. *Total suspended solids* (TSS) is a measure of the suspended solids present in wastewater. A high TSS level restricts the sunlight in water and coats the water, likewise killing aquatic life.

Figure 10.1   **Wastewater Treatment Plant**

Source: Used by permission from the town of Cary, NC.

There are four wastewater-treatment-plant classifications:

- Class 1 Plant: Treatment by lagoon or sedimentation
- Class 2 Plant: Treatment generally of less than 1 million gallons per day (MGD)
- Class 3 Plant: Treatment generally of 1–5 MGD
- Class 4 Plant: Treatment generally of more than 5 MGD

Federally mandated treatment and discharge levels are based on the type of treatment:

- Primary treatment—60 milligrams per liter (mg/l) BOD and 90 mg/l TSS
- Secondary treatment—30 mg/l BOD and 30 mg/l TSS
- Advanced (tertiary) treatment—5 BOD mg/l, 30 TSS mg/l, and 2 mg/l ammonium

States certify plant operators at four levels. Class 1 and Class 2 certified operators must visit Class 1 and 2 plants daily and maintain a log. The amount of time they spend at the plant depends on its complexity. Class 3 and Class 4 certified operators must work full-time at Class 3 and Class 4 plants, respectively. They cannot do any ancillary tasks like grass cutting. Figure 10.1 is an aerial view of a Class 4 wastewater treatment plant.

The plant's permit specifies the wastewater sampling frequency and records

Table 10.1

Secondary Treatment Water-Quality Standards

Element/Characteristic	Recommended Secondary Standard
Aluminum	0.05 to 0.2 mg/L
Chloride	250 mg/L
Color	15
Copper	1.0 mg/L
Corrosivity	noncorrosive
Fluoride	2.0 mg/L
Foaming Agents	0.5 mg/L
Iron	0.3 mg/L
Manganese	0.05 mg/L
Odor	3
pH	6.5–8.5
Silver	0.10 mg/L
Sulfate	250 mg/L
Total Dissolved Solids	500 mg/L
Zinc	5 mg/L

Source: U.S. Environmental Protection Agency, National Secondary Drinking Water Regulations, Title 40, Volume 19, CITE: 40CFR143.1, revised as of July 1, 2002.

to be kept. State inspectors certify and annually inspect laboratories. At Class 1 and Class 2 plants, a sample is taken weekly. These plants often find that contracting out sampling to a private firm is most cost-effective; however, in-house sampling is usually done at Class 3 and 4 plants because a sample must by taken three times per week.

The NPDES permit specifies the discharge location, the allowable flows, the allowable pollutant concentrations, and the monitoring/reporting requirements.[4] The permit must be renewed every five years. Failure to operate according to the permit's conditions can result in civil and criminal penalties, including imprisonment. The local government's CEO is responsible for reporting a permit violation to the state and for correcting it. Table 10.1 describes the EPA's secondary treatment standards for particular elements.

Pretreatment[5]

Some industries discharge waste to a municipal treatment plant instead of into waterways. These discharges may contain a significant amount of toxic pollutants that negatively affect treatment performance. The EPA thus requires that a treatment plant with a flow of more than five MGD operate an *industrial waste pretreatment program* (IWPP). Industrial plants that discharge more than 25,000 gallons daily must obtain a pretreatment permit.

Figure 10.2   **Primary Treatment Process**

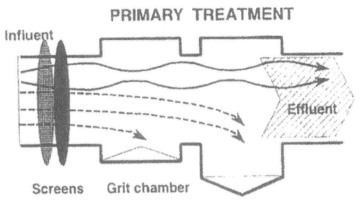

Source: U.S. Environmental Protection Agency, "How Wastewater Treatment Works . . . The Basics," EPA Pamphlet 833-F-98-002, May 1998. Office of Water. Washington, DC.

To create an IWPP, the first step is to identify and classify industrial users. Two treatment options are available. The local unit may require firms to release treated effluent evenly over a twenty-four-hour period or as soon as it is produced. Large departments usually enforce pretreatment program requirements with their own personnel, but small departments are more likely to contract out enforcement.

In the event of a violation, the EPA requires that the firm and local unit agree to a conciliation plan to prevent the problem. Should the firm violate the plan, the government will implement an enforcement action, possibly obtaining an injunction to prevent further discharge. A list of violators must be published at least annually in the area's largest daily newspaper.

Primary Treatment [6]

Figure 10.2 shows the primary treatment process. Primary treatment screens grit and sedimentation. Coarse screening removes solids and trash (such as tree limbs, rags, and rocks) that clog pipes and pumps. Fine screens remove finer materials. Several times a shift, the operator visually checks to ensure that the screening equipment is functioning properly. As appropriate, the debris on the screens is removed and sent to a landfill or incinerator. Mechanically cleaning the screen is more efficient than manual cleaning.[7] A screen must pass a paint-filter-liquids test that measures the amount of water that leaches from the screenings.

Grit includes materials like coffee grounds, cigarette filters, and cinders. If not removed, grit causes problems later in the treatment process, including clogged pipes, mechanical-equipment damage, and waste accumulation in the aeration tanks and digesters. A grit chamber slows down the flow to allow the grit to settle.

Primary treatment separates readily settleable and floatable solids from the wastewater in a *sedimentation* basin. Mechanical flocculation or pre-aeration may precede sedimentation to improve settling performance. The suspended materials are either granular or flocculent. Granular materials (silt and sand) settle constantly and do not change shape or size. The grit chamber should have removed most of these materials earlier. *Flocculent* particles (such as biological growths and organic matter) change size and shape during the settling.

Chemicals are added to form a heavy precipitate to trap finely divided materials, which do not settle. Floatables (grease and scum) are removed with a skimmer to reduce pollutants and protect plant machinery downstream.

Secondary Treatment

Secondary treatment, the minimum treatment level required by the Clean Water Act, converts dissolved and suspended pollutants to a form that can be removed. Secondary treatment, utilizing biological treatment followed by settling, normally removes about 85 percent of the BOD and TSS in wastewater. The three most common secondary treatment methods are activated sludge, trickling filter, and lagoon. Figure 10.3 shows the secondary treatment process.

Activated Sludge

The most common method, activated sludge, was accidentally discovered by engineers in the United Kingdom in 1913. The wastewater enters an aerated tank where previously developed biological floc particles contact the organic matter in the wastewater. The organic matter converts to cell tissue, water, and an oxidized end product (mainly carbon dioxide). The detention time in the aeration tank, between 30 minutes and 36 hours, depends on the type of treatment but typically takes from six to eight hours.[8] The aeration tank's contents, *mixed liquor,* are discharged into a settling tank (a secondary clarifier), which separates the suspended solids from the treated wastewater. Part of the settled material, the *sludge,* returns to the aeration tank to reseed

Figure 10.3 **Secondary Treatment Process**

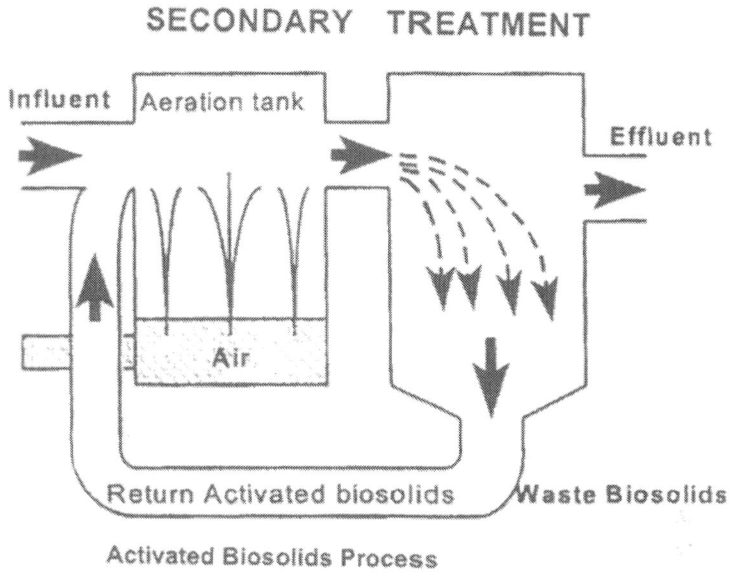

SECONDARY TREATMENT

Activated Biosolids Process

Source: U.S. Environmental Protection Agency, "How Wastewater Treatment Works . . . The Basics," EPA Pamphlet 833-F-98-002. Office of Waste Water. Washington. DC.

the sewage entering the tank. This is *return-activated sludge.* The remaining sludge, *waste-activated sludge,* is further treated prior to its disposal. The most frequent cause of poor sludge removal is improperly mixing the biological solids with incoming waste.[9] Hence, operators need to accurately measure concentration and flows. Operators also need to detect and remedy aeration-tank and clarifier problems.[10]

Table 10.2 indicates the federal allowable pollution concentrations for sewage sludge.

Trickling Filter

A *trickling filter* is a three- to ten-foot-deep bed of coarse media, often plastic or stones, known as the filter media. Used since the late 1880s, a trickling filter emulates the natural purification that occurs when polluted wastewater trickles over a rocky riverbed. From above the bed, a rotating pipe evenly distributes the wastewater (aeration), which then trickles through the media. The microorganisms in the wastewater attach themselves to the bed, which is covered with bacteria that break down the organic waste and remove pollutants from the water.

Table 10.2

Allowable Pollution Concentrations: Sewage Sludge

Pollutant	Monthly Average Concentration (milligrams/kilogram)[a]
Arsenic	41
Cadmium	39
Copper	1,500
Lead	300
Mercury	17
Nickel	420
Selenium	100
Zinc	2,800

Source: Code of Federal Regulations, Protection of Environment, 40 § 503.13 1999, Table 3, 756.

[a]Dry weight basis.

In vogue since the 1980s, a *rotating biological contractor* consists of plastic discs mounted on a long, horizontal, rotating shaft. A biological slime grows on the media. The filter discs rotate in the settled wastewater and then emerge into the atmosphere, where the microorganisms are exposed to oxygen that consumes the organic materials in the wastewater.

Lagoon[11]

Land treatment and stabilization lagoons treat wastewater naturally. Lagoons are a slow, relatively inexpensive process used principally by small governments (for example, less than 20,000 population). Though most lagoons are lined with impervious clay, a synthetic-lined lagoon is preferable because it leaks less. As wastewater enters the lagoon, heavy solids settle near the inlet, where anaerobic bacteria stabilize the organic matter. Next, materials undergo sedimentation and anaerobic decomposition in a primary pond. Secondary treatment, reducing BOD and suspended solids through oxidization, occurs in both the primary and a secondary pond. The wastewater may be purified further in a third pond. The residual sludge is then sprayed on nearby land (the *land-application method*).

Among the factors affecting natural land treatment are the soil structure, soil permeability, the cover crop, weather conditions, and the soil infiltrative capacity. Similar to the land-application method, the *constructed-wetlands method,* used in warmer coastal climates, releases treated wastewater into a natural wetland or a constructed natural area before its release into a sound or river.

Tertiary Treatment[12]

Secondary treatment, when coupled with disinfection, usually removes over 85 percent of conventional pollutants, biological oxygen demand (BOD), and total suspended solids (TSS), and nearly all pathogens. Nevertheless, some pollutants (such as nitrogen, phosphorus, and heavy metals) may require further treatment. For instance, phosphorous can be treated by adding chemical coagulants; nitrogen, by adding chlorine.

Disinfection

After primary and secondary treatment, wastewater is usually disinfected. Indeed, even after tertiary treatment, regulatory agencies may require disinfection to reduce the risk of disease from intestinal bacteria, viruses, and parasites. *Chlorination,* though the most common disinfection method, can have a lasting, toxic effect on aquatic life. Two alternatives are *ultraviolet (UV) irradiation* and *ozonation.* UV irradiation kills bacteria and viruses by destroying their genetic material. UV light can severely damage eyes and exposed skin, so operators should wear gloves, full-face shields, long-sleeved shirts, and full-length pants. Ozonation disinfects wastewater without chlorine, eliminating the threat of residual chlorine buildup.

Operations

Operators measure hydraulic, electronic, mechanical, and pneumatic operations with flowmeters, video monitors, gauges, control-panel indicators, and computerized control systems. Such instruments should be well calibrated.[13] Samples are best taken at locations specified by the plant's NPDES permit.[14] Operators should follow best practices for operating submersible lift stations, centrifugal pumps, pneumatic air injectors, and sludge-pumping systems, including:[15]

- Establishing pump-replacement schedules
- Minimizing peak-load electrical costs by phasing the plant back into operation after being off-line
- Recording pump stations' incidence of outages, overflows, and demands not met
- Keeping spare, interchangeable pumps on hand to avoid undue downtime
- Establishing redundant process controls, for example, pumps, starters, and relays

Management of Solids

Wastewater treatment produces five types of *residuals:*

- *Primary Residuals.* Raw primary sludge that has an unpleasant smell and whose pathogens can cause disease when in contact with a cut or abraded skin. If properly removed, they have a TSS concentration between 4 percent and 6 percent.
- *Secondary Residuals.* Produced during secondary treatment, they have a TSS concentration between 0.5 percent and 1.5 percent, if properly treated.
- *Chemical Residuals.* Are produced when chemicals are added to the wastewater stream.
- *Stabilized Residuals.* Stabilized anaerobically in a digester, after which they are applied on land, put in a landfill, or incinerated.
- *Other Residuals.* Left from screenings, they include grit (such as coffee grounds, corn, seeds, and eggshells), scum (for example, fats, oils, grease, and floating debris), and ash.

Sludge used beneficially (for example, sprayed on land as a fertilizer) is called a *biosolid*. In 1993, the EPA permitted more widespread use of sludge.[16] The state must permit the land on which sludge will be sprayed. Before the application, the sludge is stabilized by the methods described below:

- *Dewatering.* Mechanically removing water from the residuals to reduce the drying time. After dewatering, the consistency of the residuals is more a damp solid than a liquid.
- *Thickening.* Reducing the volume of the residuals by extracting water from the slurry. Mechanical collector arms skim and collect floatable solids on the top of a tank.
- *Anaerobic Digestion.* Breaking down organic matter, changing it into methane and carbon dioxide.
- *Aerobic Digestion.* Oxidizing organic matter, turning it into carbon dioxide.
- *Composting.* Adding a bulking agent, building a compost pile, aerobically decomposing the solids.
- *Lime Stabilization.* Adding lime to dewater solids on drying beds.
- *Thermal Treatment.* Evaporating the residuals by heat drying.
- *Drying.* Mechanically air-drying the residuals.
- *Incineration.* After dewatering the residuals, incinerating them.

Performance Measurement

High levels of BOD and TSS harm water quality. Treatment performance is therefore principally measured by the percentage of BOD and TSS removed annually. Most high-performance cities report BOD and TSS removal percentages well above 90 percent.[17] Other performance measures include:

Treatment

- The number of days in compliance with coliform (contaminants in drinking water) regulations
- The number of months in compliance with allowable sewage-sludge requirements for arsenic, cadmium, copper, lead, mercury, nickel, selenium, and zinc

COLLECTION-SYSTEM MAINTENANCE[18]

Collection-system infrastructure include drains, manholes, lift stations, flushing stations, cleanouts, pumps, and four types of pipes. A *sanitary sewer* carries waste in pipes made of cement, bituminized fiber, cast-iron, ductile iron, clay, concrete, or polyvinyl chloride (PVC). A *force main* carries waste in pipes made of pressure-ductile iron, steel, or PVC. A *storm drain* carries surface runoff water and underground seepage in pipes made of cement, steel, aluminum, clay, or concrete. Finally, a *combined sewer* carries both wastewater and storm-water runoff.

The location and size of facilities is mapped, often with use of Geographic Information System software. Sewer pipes are designed to maintain the flow of sewage at a rate of two or three feet per second. In order to avoid waste settling, though, a bigger pipe may be needed to carry sewage over a flat terrain.

The department head should approve construction plans "for maintenance," assuring the plans can locate and identify

- changes in grade, direction and pipe size,
- terminal end lines,
- major service connections (such as to schools and industries).

Safety[19]

The department should have a safety committee that is representative of the workforce. The safety committee prepares a safety policy, enforced by the departmental safety officer. The safety program should train employees to avoid risks such as

- a trench shoring cave-in,
- an injury in a confined space,
- a fall on manhole steps,
- a volatile-gas explosion,
- infections and infectious diseases,
- strains and ruptures from lifting manhole covers,
- bites from insects, bugs, rodents, and snakes,
- a fire at a lift station.

Most dangerous is the risk of injury in a confined space, such as a manhole.[20] Safe practices include:

- Sweeping the area clean around a manhole before entering it
- Lifting the manhole cover with a hook, not manually
- Ventilating the area with a blower
- Ventilating the line by opening the manholes upstream and downstream
- Operating an explosive detector while in the sewer
- Wearing a hard hat, steel-toed shoes, long-sleeve coveralls, and a safety harness
- Continuously monitoring the lifeline connected to someone in a manhole

OSHA offers a useful forty-hour confined-space training course and an eight-hour refresher course.

Chemical handling is also especially risky. Chemical suppliers provide Materials Safety Data Sheets (MSDS), which detail a chemical's characteristics, its possible hazards, first-aid procedures, and environmental concerns. The MSDS should be prominently posted at the treatment plant.

Pipe Installation

An inspector should visit the site prior to installation to compare the contract's specifications to the field conditions. The inspector ensures that the surrounding structures, utility lines, roads, power lines, rock outcrops, streams, and other features have been accurately located and identified. The inspector closely surveys the installation, checking the size and type of pipe and its condition.

A trench more than five feet deep must be supported or sloped back to avoid a cave-in. Typically, the metal trench box is moved down as the excavation deepens. Ladders should be placed in a trench over four feet deep. Pipe and equipment should be lowered, not dropped, into the trench. Work should begin at the lower end of the trench, inserting the spigot end of the pipe joint into

Figure 10.4   **Sewer Line Installation**

Source: U.S. Environmental Protection Agency, "Region 10 Superfund: Boomsnub/ AIRCO. Boomsnub 2001 Removal." Available at http://www.epa.gov/.

the bell of the previous joint. The ends of the pipe should be covered daily to prevent flooding and silting in the pipeline. The trench bottom should be smooth to structurally support the pipe because pipe in a trench bed with an incorrect slope and elevation leaks and breaks.

The inspector determines whether the removed material can be used to backfill the pipe. An excessive amount of rock will break a pipe. Typically, rocks over six inches in diameter are not suitable for backfill. Mud-laden soil that cannot be compacted to the required density should also be rejected. The inspector should test whether the compaction density standard has been met. Figure 10.4 shows a sewer line being installed.

Inspection and Maintenance

Crews should inspect pipelines regularly for faulty sealing and infiltration and inflow (I/I). There are four principal inspection methods: closed-circuit television (CCTV), cameras, visual, and lamping. CCTV, the most efficient and most often used method,[21] is recommended for sewer lines with a diameter between four and forty-eight inches.[22] In a large sewer (over 1,000 linear feet

Figure 10.5   **Typical Infiltration and Inflow Entry Points**

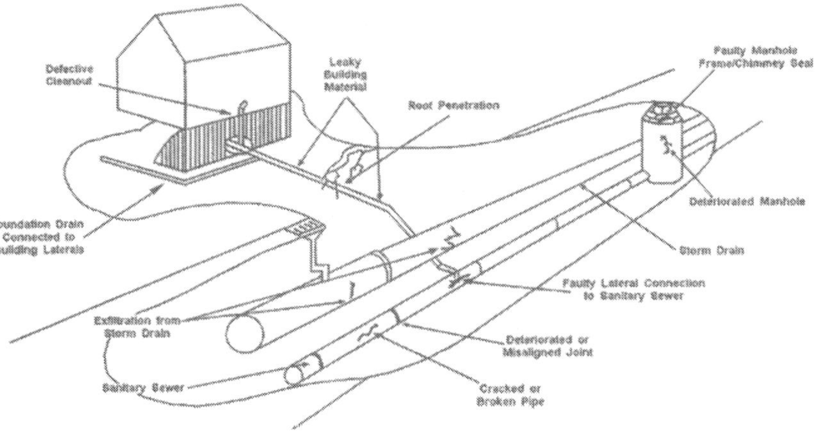

Source: U.S. Environmental Protection Agnecy, "Sewer System Infrastructure Analysis and Rehabilitation." EPA/625/6-91/030. Office of Water. Washington, DC.

apart), a camera inspection is usually preferred. A raft-mounted film camera and strobe light are used to photograph the condition of pipe. In a *visual inspection,* inspectors examine for sunken areas, areas with water ponds, and deteriorated manholes. In a large sewer line, a walk-through visual inspection can be made. Finally, *lamping,* the least expensive and least effective method, uses a flashlight to look at the pipe's interior.

Crews should clean lines of roots, grease, and solids by water pressure, mechanical devices (such as a hand rod, power rod, or bucket line), or with chemicals. An on-call emergency crew should handle emergency situations such as a sewer-gas explosion, a pump-station failure, a collapsed sewer, or a rescue. The public should be encouraged to report problems such as sewer backups and unusual odors.

Infiltration and Inflow [23]

Infiltration occurs when groundwater enters the distribution system through defective pipes, pipe joints, connections, or manholes. *Inflow* is storm water that enters the system from roof gutter drains, cellar drains, storm- and sanitary-sewer cross connections, street washing, and hydrant tests. In some systems, especially old ones with combined sanitary and storm-drain sewers, the problem of inflow is substantial. A heavy rainfall can overload the hydraulic and treatment capacity, spilling effluent into a lake or river. Figure 10.5 shows typical entry points of inflow and infiltration.

Inspectors should examine manholes, pipes, and collapsed sewer sections to pinpoint I/I locations. Inspection should be made at least twenty-four hours after a rainfall to eliminate the rainfall's effect.[24] Conversely, an inflow inspection should be made when it is raining and between midnight and six AM to minimize the effect of wastewater flows.[25] Inspection methods include:[26]

- *Visual*. Visually inspect sunken areas over a sewer, water ponds, and damaged manholes.
- *Lamping*. Shine a flashlight between two adjacent manholes to ascertain whether the line is open.
- *Smoke*. Over a centrally located manhole, force nontoxic smoke through a sewer line. Visually inspect for smoke around the tested area, especially smoke emitting from pavement cracks. Notify property owners and the fire department of an upcoming test. Figure 10.6 is a sample notification letter.
- *Dye*. Detect inflow in storm drains, storm sewers, and on private property in particular. After stopping both ends of a storm-drain section, put dyed water in the middle and monitor downstream for evidence of the dyed water.
- *Television*. Detect infiltration from faulty service connections, manhole rims, and joints with a television camera.

Infiltrated grease, debris, and roots cause sewers to back up in homes. The governing board usually requires customers to maintain and repair the sewer line between their house and the right-of-way or easement.

Odor Control

Some systems have persistent odor problems caused by long septic travel lines, excess discharges, and treatment-plant and pump-station conditions. The most common smell, hydrogen sulfide, is that of a rotten egg. To control odors, their source must first be identified. To control an odor problem at the plant, operators can add odor-masking agents and chemicals. They should also schedule foul-odor-producing work at the plant for the middle of the day when the fewest people are at home. If plant odors prove too offensive, a more permanent solution (for example, installing air scrubbers or filter systems or redesigning the plant) may be necessary.

Fats, Oils, and Grease (FOG)

The United States is the ultimate "fast-food nation," generating massive amounts of FOG, which blocks sewer lines and causes overflows. Recommended FOG-prevention measures include:

Figure 10.6   **Sample Letter to the Public**

Dear Resident:

The sewage treatment facility will test for leaks in the sanitary-sewer system in your neighborhood on Wednesday, April 5. We will blow non-toxic smoke into the system to detect leaks that allow stormwater and other surface waters to enter the system. Stopping such leaks conserves the capacity of the wastewater treatment facility. The smoke will leave no residual stains nor affect plants and animals. The smoke does have a distinctive, but not unpleasant, odor, which lasts for only a few minutes. The smoke normally does not enter a home unless:

- The vents connected to your building's sewer lateral are defective or improperly installed.
- The traps under sinks, tubs, basins, showers, and floor drains are defective, improperly installed, or missing.
- The pipes, connections, and seals of your building's sewer system are damaged, defective, have missing plugs, or were improperly installed.

If smoke traces enter your building, there may also be an unpleasant and potentially health-hazardous odor. In such instance, please contact us (888-123-4567), so we can assist to locate the source of smoke. However, correction of any pipe or sewer defects on your private property is your responsibility. To prepare for the test, we ask that prior to April 5 that you please pour water down **ALL** drains in your home or building.

Sincerely,

Superintendent

- Educating citizens to deposit FOG and food waste in a trash receptacle, not down a drain
- Adopting a Sewer Use Ordinance (SUO), requiring restaurants to install a grease trap that limits grease to a specified level (such as 150–200 milligrams per liter)
- Inspecting restaurant food traps and penalizing SUO violators
- Encouraging restaurants to dry-wipe pots, pans, and food-preparation surfaces before washing them

Performance Measurement

Among the collection-system performance measures are:

Failures

- Stoppages per 100 miles of sewer line
- Backups per 1,000 service connections
- Percent of I/I

Emergency Response

- Percent of responses to working-hour emergencies within x amount of time
- Percent of responses to non-working-hour emergencies within x amount of time
- Response time to pump-station trouble alarms

Maintenance

- Number of sewer lines cleaned in x amount of time
- Amount of pipe inspected in x amount of time
- Number of worker-hours per main- and service-line repair
- Number of catch basins cleaned in x amount of time
- Number of manholes repaired in x amount of time

Service

- Number of complaints responded to within x amount of time
- Number of sewer connections made within x amount of time

STORM WATER MANAGEMENT

The EPA requires that local governments obtain an NPDES permit to discharge stormwater to surface water.[27] The EPA specifically requires:

- *Public Participation.*[28] Encouraging the public to reduce its use of fertilizers and pesticides, plant indigenous species, and apply integrated pest management.
- *Illicit Discharge.* Inspecting for the release of contaminated substances.
- *Construction Site Runoff.* Controlling erosion and sediment.
- *New Development Runoff.* Creating nondevelopment buffer zones along water bodies, using porous pavement, and adopting restrictive zoning in environmentally sensitive areas.

Figure 10.7   **Elements of an Urban Drainage System**

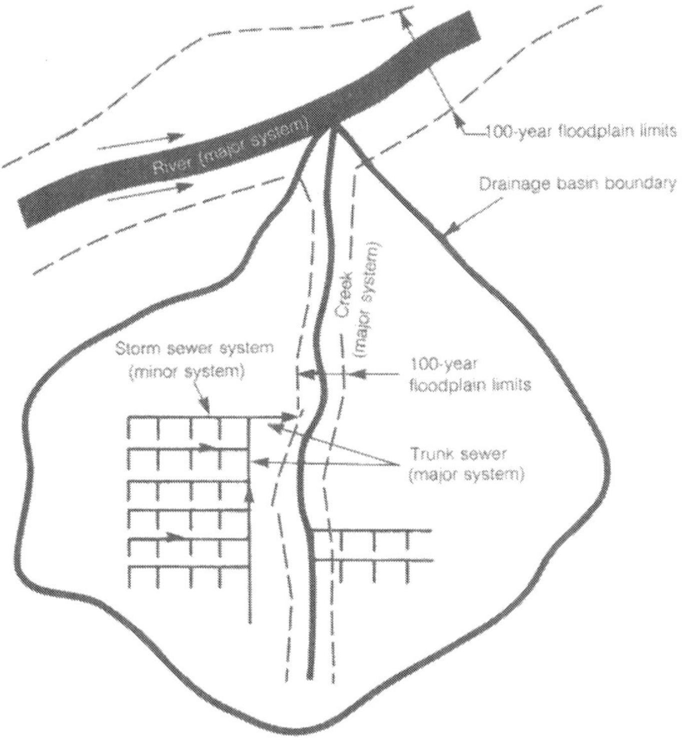

Source: Sam Cristofano and William Foster, *Management of Local Public Works* (Washington, D.C.: The International City Management Association, 1986), p. 240. Reprinted with permission of the International City/County Management Association, Washington, D.C. All rights reserved.

Figure 10.7 shows the elements of an urban drainage system.

The publication *An Internet Guide to Financing Stormwater Management* (accessed at http://stormwaterfinance.urbancenter.iupui.edu) is a helpful guide to locating funding. Among the sources are each state's Clean Water State Revolving Fund, Clean Water Act section 319(h) funds, and other grants (see www.lgean.org/documents/stormwatercontacts.pdf).

NOTES

1. For a further discussion of the EOP, refer to Water Environment Federation (WEF), *Operation of Municipal Wastewater Treatment Plants* (Alexandria, VA: WEF, 1996), 41–46.
2. For further explanation, see ibid., 46–50.

3. National Small Flows Clearinghouse, *Inflow/Infiltration: A Guide for Decision Makers* (Morganton: West Virginia University, n.d.), 4.

4. For further discussion of permit requirements, see Water Environment Federation (WEF), *Operation of Municipal Wastewater Treatment Plants* (Alexandria, VA: WEF, 1996), 6–9.

5. For further explanation, see ibid., 56–77.

6. For more explanation, see ibid., 509–534.

7. Ibid., 511.

8. Ibid., 588.

9. Ibid., 635.

10. For more explanation, see ibid., 748.

11. For more explanation, see ibid., 793–849.

12. For more information, see ibid., 851–886.

13. For more explanation, see ibid., 143–189.

14. For more explanation, see ibid., 475–508.

15. For more explanation, see ibid., 192–258.

16. Elizabeth Royte, *Garbage Land* (New York: Little, Brown, 2005), 211.

17. David Ammons, *Municipal Benchmarks,* 2nd ed. (Thousand Oaks, CA: Sage Publications, 2001), 454.

18. For a comprehensive discussion of collection-system management, see WEF, *Wastewater Collection Systems Management,* 2nd ed. (Alexandria, VA: WEF, 1994).

19. For a discussion of plant safety measures, see WEF, *Operation of Municipal Wastewater Treatment Plants,* 79–113.

20. National Small Flows Clearinghouse, *Inflow/Infiltration: A Guide for Decision Makers,* 19.

21. U.S. Environmental Protection Agency (EPA), *Collection Systems O&M Fact Sheet: Sewer Cleaning and Inspection* (Washington, DC: EPA, 1999).

22. Ibid.

23. For a discussion of whether to conduct an I/I analysis with a consultant or in-house staff, see Sharon Rollins, *Managing Infiltration Inflow in Wastewater Collection Systems* (Knoxville, TN: The Municipal Technical Advisory Service, 2006).

24. Ibid., 9.

25. Ibid., 10.

26. For a more complete discussion of the methods, see ibid., 10–18.

27. Waivers are permitted for small systems. See Wyatt Green, *Stormwater Management* (Washington, DC: International City/County Management Association, 2001).

28. For a complete discussion of best practices, see http://cfpub.epa.gov/npdes/stormwater/menuofbmps/index.cfm.

For Further Reading

National Small Flows Clearinghouse. *Inflow/Infiltration: A Guide for Decision Makers.* Morganton, WV: West Virginia University, n.d.

Water Environment Federation. *Operation of Municipal Wastewater Treatment Plants,* 2nd ed. Vols. 1–3. Alexandria, VA: WEF, 1995.

———. *Wastewater Collection Systems Management.* Alexandria, VA: 1994.

11

Street Maintenance and Construction

HISTORY

The Pre-Automotive Era (Roman Days to 1895)[1]

The first paved street linked the Circus Maximus to the Aventine in Rome in 174 BC. The Romans eventually constructed the world's first superhighway system, stretching across most of Europe. The interconnected system, which facilitated communications and trade, chiefly explains the Romans' 500-year hegemonic rule. After Rome's fall, warring barbarian tribes shut the system down, ending the trade network and plunging Europe into the Dark Ages.

In the United States during colonial times, streets generally followed the European gridiron pattern. Free men, indentured men, or slaves performed roadwork, called "statute labor." A master of two or more slaves or servants could delegate one to work in his stead. After the Revolutionary War, road traffic increased, especially in and around large cities, and "voluntary" labor could not keep up with needed roadwork. Towns and states therefore permitted private turnpike companies to build toll roads. The first, built in 1785, ran from Alexandria to the Potomac River. The sixty-two-mile-long Philadelphia and Lancaster Turnpike, opened in 1795, had thirteen toll stations, charging stages and coaches 2.5 cents per mile; four-horse freight wagons paid 5 cents per mile. By the 1850s, thousands of turnpike companies were in the toll-road business.

Early roads were comprised of gravel or pounded stone, but the prevalent material became macadam around 1820. Invented by John McAdam, macadam consisted of densely packed, angular broken stones that protected the base soil from abrasion and wetting. Pine or oak planks, 8 to 16 feet long and 3 to 4 inches thick, called sleepers or stringers, began to be used as road material in 1846. In 1887, asphalt was applied.

The "good-roads movement," launched by bicyclists in 1891, catalyzed road funding by state and local governments. In 1891, New Jersey adopted the first state-aid road plan, requiring that towns adopt a highway plan as a condition of state aid.

The Automotive Era (1895 to the Present)

In 1895, the Duryea Motor Company sold the first gasoline-driven automobile. In 1906, vanadium-alloy steel enabled Henry Ford to build the considerably lighter, smaller, and cheaper ($350) Model T, which revolutionized car production. From 1906 to 1915, the number of cars manufactured multiplied from 25,000 to 969,930. To farmers' consternation, increased traffic stirred up dust clouds on unpaved country roads. It also damaged macadam and gravel-paved roads. Therefore, in 1909, Wayne County, Michigan, paved streets with more durable concrete.

From 1904 to 1914, the number of state highway departments increased from nine to thirty-three, which then created the American Association of State Highway Officials. In 1916, the Federal Aid Road Act required state highway departments to prepare plans, specifications, and cost estimates for federally funded projects. The federal government annually allocated funds to states based on their number of rural post-road miles (1/3), population (1/3), and land area (1/3). In 1919, Oregon enacted a gasoline tax to pay for road maintenance and construction.

Choked by traffic in the 1930s, Los Angeles built a freeway system in 1940. In 1944, at President Roosevelt's urging, Congress enacted the Federal-Aid Highway Act, designating a National Interstate Highway System and increasing federal spending from $25 million to $2.5 billion annually. Figure 11.1 shows the present Interstate System. In 1964, Congress enacted the Urban Mass Transportation Act to fund mass transportation, and in 1991, it enacted the Intermodal Surface Transportation Efficiency Act, further increasing mass transit funding and creating metropolitan planning organizations, which prioritize federally funded projects in local jurisdictions.

MANAGEMENT

Road workers, observed daily by motorists and pedestrians, are among local governments' most highly visible ambassadors. Idle workers leave a bad impression. Yet motivating maintenance and construction workers can be difficult because much of the work is highly repetitive and unchallenging.

Roads are classified according to their use. The Institute of Traffic Engi-

Figure 11.1   **The Interstate Highway System**

NATIONAL SYSTEM OF INTERSTATE AND DEFENSE HIGHWAYS

Source: U.S. Bureau of Public Roads, General location of national system of interstate highways, including all additional routes at urban areas designated in September, 1955 (Washington, DC: GPO, 1955). Also known as "The Yellow Book."

neers, the American Public Works Association (APWA), and the International City/County Management Association (ICMA) have each developed road-classification systems. The ICMA system specifies five road types:

- Limited Access Road—An expressway.
- Arterial Road—Provides direct, relatively high speed service for longer trips and large traffic volumes; mobility is emphasized and access limited.
- Collector Road—Links arterial roads and local roads.
- Local Road—Provides direct access to individual homes, businesses, and farms.
- Rural Road— Located in a low-traffic area and has no curbs, gutters, or sidewalks.

Some states require that local units utilize the state's road-classification system as a condition of receiving state road funds.

ROAD MAINTENANCE[2]

A governing board faces the issue of how much to spend on road maintenance versus construction. A road's condition deteriorates by about 40 percent dur-

Figure 11.2   **Pavement Life Cycle**

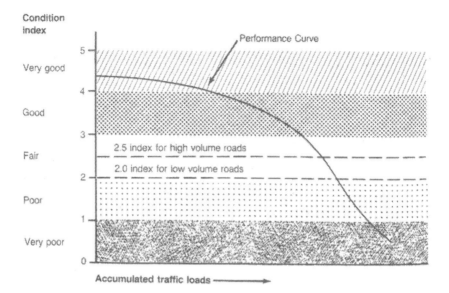

ing the first 60 percent of its life, but by 40 percent more during the next 15 percent.[3] Without adequate maintenance, the deterioration process accelerates even faster. Figure 11.2 graphically depicts how poorly maintained roads can deteriorate. To prevent rapid deterioration, the department should prepare an asset-management plan that prescribes each street's required maintenance level based on its age and condition.

Maintenance work can be done by government employees (*force account*) or by a private firm under contract. Force-account work gives the department flexibility to respond more quickly to an emergency and to shift maintenance priorities. Privatized work, though, may be more cost-effective, especially with regard to specialized, infrequently performed functions like bridge painting and repair, pavement marking, and pavement sealing. To select a firm, the bid specification should be based on desired performance outcomes such as

- the number and size of potholes filled per lane mile,
- the height of grass mowed,
- the depth of debris, if any, left next to a swept curb,
- the reflectivity of signs and striping.

Work Program

Departments should prepare an annual work program for scheduling purposes. The work program estimates the number of full-time-equivalent and temporary positions required to complete the annual maintenance program. The APWA recommends that about 80 percent of work be scheduled, leaving unscheduled time to respond to weather variations and changed work-program priorities.[4]

A large department may utilize a job-order-cost (JOC) system to schedule work. A JOC charges the cost of time, equipment, and materials on a daily basis to both jobs (for example, patching Main Street) and types of work (such as street repair, pavement marking). A JOC system reports work efficiency (for example, the cost per street sign installed or cost per crack sealed) and the cost of particular jobs (such as the cost to repave Elm Street).

To schedule work and evaluate performance, a department may establish work standards. A work standard specifies the method, the number and type of personnel, the materials, and the equipment that should be used to complete particular maintenance tasks such as asphalt repair, asphalt repaving, concrete-pavement repair, curb repair, and sidewalk repair. The standard also specifies the average amount of time that should be taken to complete the task.

Safety and Training

Road maintenance and construction can be highly dangerous. The Manual on Uniform Traffic Control Devices, published by the National Safety Council, recommends how to control work-zone traffic, erect signs, mark pavement, and the like. OSHA regulates particular practices like excavation, trenching, vehicle operation, and heavy-equipment operation. State or OSHA inspectors enforce OSHA regulations and can levy fines for noncompliance. Inspectors may make a random inspection or may inspect based on a complaint by a street-department employee or concerned citizen. Figure 11.3 shows how a work zone should be designed to accommodate pedestrians safely while work is in progress.

The Technology Transfer Program (TTP), funded by the Federal Highway Administration, run by state Departments of Transportation, offers training in

- asphalt-pavement maintenance,
- concrete construction and maintenance,
- soils fundamentals,
- unpaved-roads maintenance,
- vegetation management,

Figure 11.3   **Accommodating Pedestrians in a Work Zone**

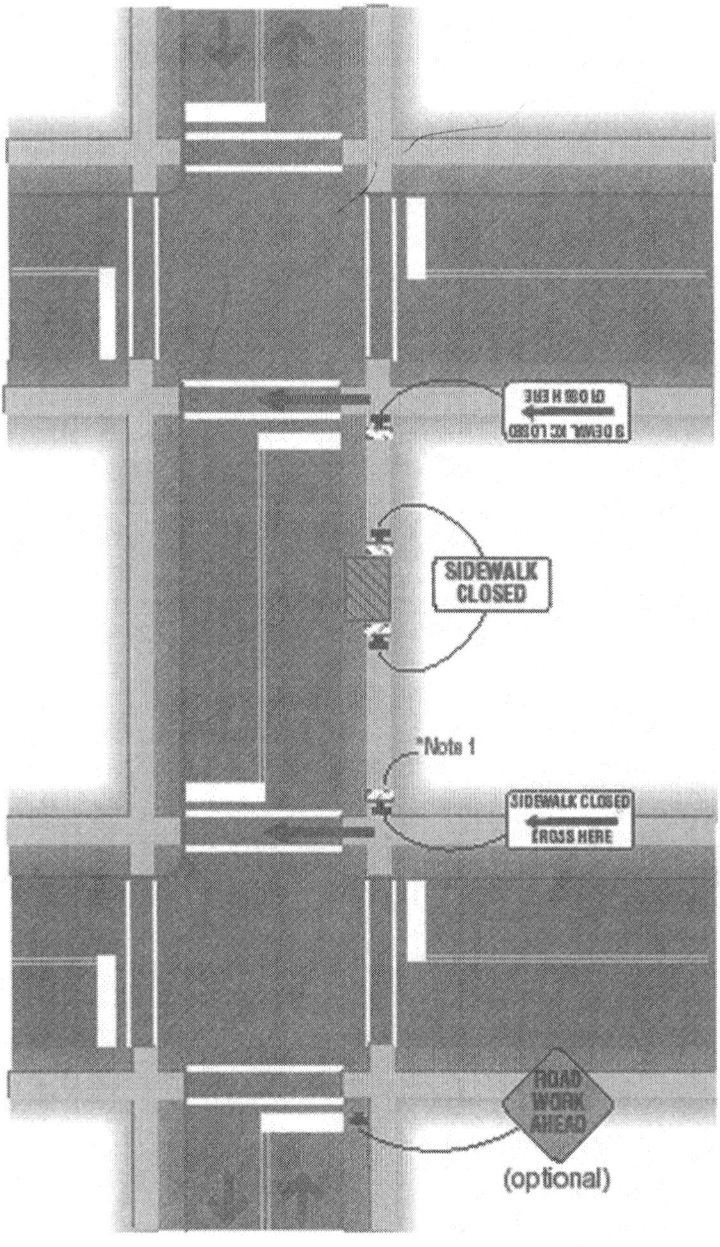

Source: Office of Safety, Federal Highway Administration, U.S. Department of Transportation. Available at http://safety.fhwa.dot.gov/wz/docs/wzpedest.pdf.

- storm-water-drainage design,
- storm-water detention and basin design,
- work-zone traffic control,
- flagger operations,
- maintenance/repair of utility cuts (cuts in road for cable, telephone, and power lines),
- asphalt-pavement technology and inspection,
- asphalt-parking-lot design,
- Geographic Information Systems (GIS),
- writing skills, presentation skills, and communicating with the public and the media.

TTP staff also may provide consulting assistance to local jurisdictions in pavement and bridge management, traffic engineering, GIS, road maintenance and construction, vehicle routing, and public transportation planning.

The National Institute for Certification in Engineering Technologies certifies personnel in asphalt and concrete inspection, bridge-safety inspection, highway design, and road construction and maintenance. Other assisting agencies include:

- The APWA (Local Transportation Assistance Program)
- State certification programs in concrete and asphalt application
- The National Highway Institute
- The National Association of County Engineers
- The National Institute for the Certification of Engineering Technicians
- The Institute of Transportation Engineers

Road-Condition Inventory

The Governmental Accounting Standards Board requires that local governments maintain an inventory of their assets, including roads. Departments should record streets' value, location, and condition, drainage systems, sidewalks, signs, signals, pipes, culverts, and drainage systems. Among the specific data kept on each road are its

- location,
- length, width, and lanes,
- classification,
- average daily car and truck usage,
- shoulder type and width,
- surface type,
- curb and gutter.

The department should periodically assess each road's condition. Small local units with few staff may engage the services of the state transportation department to conduct the assessment. Raters can either visually or mechanically evaluate road conditions. A visual evaluation is based on raters' visual observations of road conditions. The mechanical method more accurately measures road roughness with a measuring device placed under a car. The most common pavement-assessment method, the present-serviceability rating, ranks roads on a scale from 0 (very poor) to 5 (very good). Ideally, an inventory should be updated every two to four years.

The department should also track the condition of street signs and signals. A local government can be held liable for an accident caused by a missing sign or an inoperable signal light. Liability cannot not be assigned, however, if the department maintains an up-to-date inventory and repairs defective conditions when identified.

Asphalt Maintenance

Asphalt maintenance includes sealing cracks, patching potholes, seal coating, and overlays.

Crack Sealing

An early sign of distress, a crack, indicates that the pavement is leaking. A nonworking crack does not move. A working crack, which moves vertically and/or horizontally, is best treated with a rubberized asphalt seal applied when temperatures are moderate in the spring or fall and the crack is partially open.[5] The most critical steps are crack preparation and material application.[6] The crack should be clean and dry. Routing opens small cracks to provide a reservoir for the sealant and produces uniform edges for better adhesion.[7] The types of cracks include:

- *Reflection.* Underlying crack in the original pavement.
- *Edge.* Along the pavement edge, caused by poor structural support.
- *Longitudinal.* Along a joint as pavement ages.
- *Transverse.* Parallel to a joint, caused by thermal stresses, poor subgrade support, or heavy loadings.
- *Block.* In a large block, due to age and shrinking asphalt.
- *Slippage.* Crescent-shaped, due to breaking caused by heavy traffic.
- *Alligator.* Small interconnected cracks resembling an alligator's hide. Normally due to base or subbase failure. May need more extensive repair than other cracks to rebuild the pavement structure.
- *Meander.* A wandering crack.

Asphalt Patching

Asphalt patching includes base repair, trench patching, and pothole patching. A base repair is a deep patch made to an alligator crack or a large subbase failure. A trench patch is the restoration of utility trenches including drainage facilities. An unsealed crack can deteriorate into a pothole, which is a bowl-shaped hole in the pavement resulting from deterioration caused by moisture and traffic. Moisture from rain or snow works its way into road surfaces and the materials underneath. Traffic, particularly from heavy vehicles, stresses the road surface. The process intensifies during periods of freezing and thawing that expand and contract road surfaces.

Cold mix is applied during winter months usually as a temporary solution. The Strategic Highway Research Program has found that a bituminous hot-mix patch (which is laid and rolled while hot) lasts the longest.[8] The repair cost of a road in fair condition is about one-fourth of repairing a road in poor condition.[9] Patching a pothole entails

- controlling the traffic zone,
- marking the area to be patched, extending at least one foot outside the distressed area,[10]
- cutting away the weak, deteriorated area,
- cleaning up loose dust and/or water,
- tacking the area (spraying or brushing a thin asphalt coating on the vertical side of the hole),
- compacting the hole with hot-mix asphalt,
- applying an edge seal to waterproof the joint,
- cleaning up the site.

Figure 11.4 shows a crew filling a pothole.

Seal Coating

Aging asphalt dries (oxidizes) in the sun, becoming a brittle, grayish surface. A seal coat, less expensive than an asphalt patch, rejuvenates and waterproofs pavement for five to ten years.[11] A *chip seal* is a liquid asphalt mixture covered by a layer of uniform-sized aggregate chips of crushed gravel. Before the application, the surface is cleaned of dust and debris. A distributor then sprays an even layer of hot-asphalt emulsion at a calibrated angle and height. Following the sprayer, a pneumatic rubber-tire roller compacts the mixture. Chip sealing is done at a temperature of at least 60° F under clear (no possibility of rain) conditions. The expected life of a chip seal is from five to seven years.[12]

Figure 11.4   **Pothole Repair**

Source: U.S. Department of Transportation, Public Works.

A *slurry seal* is a mixture of well-graded, fine-aggregate mineral filler (portland cement), asphalt emulsion, and water. A slurry truck applies the liquid slurry. Because a slurry applicator is such a highly specialized piece of equipment, most local units contract out the application. A slurry seal is more rapidly applied than a chip seal and has no loose cover aggregate, making it highly suitable for residential streets in subdivisions. Slurry sealing is done when the temperature is over 50 ºF under clear (no possibility of rain) conditions. The expected service life is five to seven years.[13]

A *novachip seal* is a coat of polymer-modified asphalt emulsion applied before an ultra-thin overlay of graded hot-mix asphalt. A specially designed machine lays down the novachip seal in one pass. The expected life is ten years.[14]

Overlay

After the pavement is prepared, an automated asphalt-paving machine spreads a tack coat of asphalt emulsion. The mix is applied at hot temperatures (300° F). The paver spreads the mix at the proper grade and thickness as the work crew corrects spreading flaws. Traffic is kept away until the temperature cools to 185° F. An asphalt overlay lasts from fifteen to twenty years.[15]

Concrete-Pavement Repair

During concrete paving, operators test the mix periodically to ensure that the recommended water-to-cement mixture ratio is kept. A cement-paved street should not be reopened to traffic until the concrete is sufficiently strong: usually about ten days during warm weather and fifteen days in the spring and the fall. Crews should follow recommended procedures with respect to

- patching spills and joints,
- resealing joints,
- slabjacking (raise sunken slab by pumping grout under it),
- diamond grinding (reduce slab thickness by 3/16" to 1/4" to increase concrete strength),
- partial-depth patching,
- full-depth patching,
- thin-bonded portland cement concrete resurfacing,
- asphalt-concrete resurfacing,
- utility-cuts repair.[16]

Unpaved-Surface Repair

Local units leave some roads unpaved due to budgetary constraints. An unpaved surface is usually covered with a gravel aggregate that forms a crust when exposed to water. Conditions that require maintenance include ruts, corrugations, soft spots, and holes. Crews should follow recommended procedures regarding

- smoothing and preserving the crust,
- reshaping,
- adjusting the blend of aggregates,
- blading dry and loose surface material caused by long periods of dry weather,
- dust prevention,
- base stabilization,
- portland cement,
- lime stabilization.[17]

Drainage-Facility Maintenance

Drainage facilities include storm sewers, culverts, catch basins, underdrains, and ditches. Standing water and frost heaves in the winter damage roads. Standing water softens the road base; frozen water expands the road. Indeed, the life of an improperly drained road is reduced by about one-third.[18] Recommended drainage practices include:

- Designing the road crown (cross slope) to be slightly steeper than the road surface so that water flows away from the road
- Inspecting drainage facilities quarterly and after major storms to assess drainage flow
- Routinely cutting vegetation away from road shoulders
- Maintaining curbs to ensure water flow
- Sealing joints along the curb and around inlets and catch basins
- Properly installing drainage facilities (such as drains, pipes, inlets)[19]

States require local jurisdictions to prepare a storm-water-management plan, some provisions of which include:

- An inventory of the natural and man-made features that influence runoff over a hundred-year period
- The location of floodplains
- Warnings to be given to the public and steps to be taken in an emergency
- Flood-insurance requirements
- Restrictions on water and sewer facilities in floodplains
- Excess-runoff detention, retention, and land-treatment requirements
- Flood-control and drainage-construction methods
- Procedures for installing erosion-control devices

The department should follow practices that reduce runoff, including:

- Limiting development
- Increasing filtration
- Storing precipitation and runoff and then slowly releasing it
- Installing flood-control devices
- Limiting erosion and sedimentation[20]

Bridge Maintenance

Most bridges are owned and maintained by the state. In the event a local unit is responsible for the maintenance, it usually contracts the work out to a private firm or the state department of transportation (DOT). Bridge-maintenance activities include:

- Cleaning bearing-abutment areas and piers near the bridge
- Repairing the foundation and shotcrete (concrete or mortar) substructure
- Lubricating and repairing bearings
- Maintaining and repairing the superstructure
- Cleaning the seal joints on the bridge deck
- Repairing pre-stressed concrete, sidewalks, and curbs[21]

Maintenance of Traffic-Control and Safety Devices

Signs should be inspected at least biannually, overhead supports at least annually. Signs should be routinely cleaned and cleared of obstructions, roads periodically restriped, and burnt-out streetlights replaced. Departments can reduce the incidence of sign vandalism by using durable, vandal-resistant signs that are strategically placed and marked for identification if stolen.

Snow and Ice Control

Local governments should prepare a snow-and-ice-control plan, designating snow-removal routes, snow-removal priorities, and a contingency scenario for a long-lasting storm. The preparation and implementation of the plan should be coordinated with the state DOT. Some plans set a goal for the service level desired after a snowfall, which is ideally "bare pavement."[22] The plan establishes shift schedules, communication procedures, equipment assignments, and salt-application methods.[23]

Street Cleaning

Among recommended street-cleaning practices are the following:[24]

- Designing dead-end streets to include a turning circle
- Designing the flushing routes to be on a downhill grade as far as possible
- Prohibiting contractors from depositing construction dirt on streets
- Sweeping and flushing streets when traffic is minimal
- Alerting the public to street cleaning times and routes
- Operating street-cleaning vehicles slowly

Freeway Maintenance

Freeway maintenance differs from conventional maintenance activities since freeways are less accessible to workers and have heavier traffic loads that move at higher speeds. Maintenance crews should therefore use a preplanned route to reach a work site and when at the site, be alert to moving traffic.

Performance Measurement

Common maintenance-and-repair performance measures include:

- Percent of potholes patched within x amount of time
- Percent of utility cuts patched within x amount of time
- Square feet of asphalt or concrete repaired per labor hour
- Percent of responses to emergencies within x amount of time during working and nonworking hours
- Percent of overall centerline miles and crosswalks restriped annually
- Percent of malfunctioning signals repaired within x amount of time
- Percent of signs repaired within x amount time

ROAD CONSTRUCTION

States require that local units prepare a transportation plan as a condition of state aid. Small units may plan only for state roads that run through their boundaries as required. Large local units, though, usually prepare a comprehensive transportation plan with a twenty-year planning horizon for both state and local roads.

Road Location and Design

Road locations affect land-use patterns. To site a new road or expand an existing one, the local staff often conducts an *origin-and-destination* (O&D) study to ascertain where traffic comes from and where it wants to go. The O&D analysis factors in existing and future road locations.

After locating a road, a large local unit typically designs the road with its own engineering staff. Small units, by contrast, usually engage the services of a consulting engineer. In either case, the design team and maintenance staff should work closely together.

Work Inspection

Bid notices for contract work should be widely circulated to potential bidders in order to get the most competitive price. Inspectors should regularly monitor contractors' work because substandard work causes excess maintenance and excessive repair costs. For example, a street that should be repair-free for

Figure 11.5   **Road Paving**

Source: U.S. Department of Transportation, Public Works.

fifteen years may need repair after only five years if improperly constructed. The department may assign its own inspector or engage the services of the consulting engineer. In evaluating work, the inspector should refer to the construction plan's specifications. The inspector should take core samples to test the thickness of the base, test the compaction rate, and examine the subbase conditions. Figure 11.5 shows a road being paved.

There are four types of inspections, depending on the type of work being performed: one-time, critical-point, spot, and continuous. The inspector should be authorized to reject or suspend substandard work and should record construction activities, measurements, materials used, conversations with contractors, laboratory tests, and visits by state and federal officials. The contractor should follow OSHA guidelines to ensure safety in the work zone.

Performance Bond

To insure against faulty work, local units should require contractors to purchase a *performance bond,* which is typically in effect for one year after a project's completion. The local jurisdiction may seek a longer protection period because substandard work may not be revealed for several years. However, the longer the time period, the higher the insurance premium the contractor must pay, which will be included in the bid price. The contract for an especially time-sensitive project might include a financial penalty for past-due work and perhaps a financial incentive for work completed ahead of schedule.

Utility Cuts

Utilities make cuts in roads to lay gas, electric, cable, and telephone lines. The public-utility companies should be viewed as partners who have input in the planning and installation of underground utilities. Large-sized local units typically may form an inter-utility coordinating committee, representing private utilities and affected city departments.

More deeply laid sanitary-sewer and storm drains should be installed before shallower telephone, power, gas, and cable lines. Utility companies should obtain a permit to cut city streets. Some jurisdictions even require that the water-and-sewer department obtain a permit before making a utility cut. Inspectors should carefully inspect utility cuts made by utility companies because a poorly patched cut can drop a pavement by as much as three to four inches, causing a pothole.

NOTES

1. The early history draws heavily on Ellis Armstrong, ed., *History of Public Works in the United States: 1776–1976* (Washington, DC: The American Public Works Association [APWA], 1977).

2. Road maintenance is highly technical. For more information consult APWA's *Street and Highway Maintenance Manual* (Chicago: APWA, 1985).

3. James M. Banovetz, Drew Anderson Dolan, and John W. Swain, eds., *Managing Small Cities and Counties: A Practical Guide* (Washington, DC: ICMA, 1994), 109.

4. APWA, *Street and Highway Maintenance Manual,* 150.

5. Governor's Center for Local Government Services, *Public Works Manual,* 19. Available at http://www.newpa.com/default.aspx?id=20.

6. Ibid., 20.

7. Ibid.

8. Ibid., 21.

9. Richard Wolters, *Repair of Potholes with Hot Mix Asphalt* (Minnesota Asphalt Pavement Association, 2003). Available at http://www.asphaltisbest.com/PDFs/potholerepair.pdf.

10. Ibid.

11. Ibid., 22.

12. Ibid., 23.

13. Ibid., 24.

14. Ibid., 25.

15. Ibid., 27.

16. For a thorough discussion of these procedures see APWA, *Street and Highway Maintenance Manual,* 69–116.

17. Ibid., 121–128.

18. *Public Works Manual,* 18.

19. For a more detailed discussion of drainage facility maintenance, see APWA, *Street and Highway Maintenance Manual,* 135–152.

20. *Public Works Manual,* 35–42.

21. For a thorough discussion of bridge maintenance, see APWA, *Street and Highway Maintenance Manual,* 153–237.

22. *Public Works Manual,* 29.

23. For a thorough discussion of snow and ice control, see APWA, *Street and Highway Maintenance Manual,* 317–362.

24. These practices and others are described in APWA, *Street Cleaning Practice* (Chicago: APWA, 1978).

FOR FURTHER READING

APWA. *Street and Highway Maintenance Manual.* Chicago: APWA, 1985.
———. *Street Cleaning Practice.* Chicago: APWA, 1978.
Governor's Center for Local Government Services. *Public Works Manual.* Available at http://www.newpa.com/default.aspx?id=20.

12

Solid-Waste Collection and Disposal

HISTORY

The Pre-Disposal Era (Colonial Days to 1937)

The book of Deuteronomy (23:13–14) admonishes soldiers to make a latrine outside camp and carry a trowel "lest God see them as unclean." Before water and sewer pipes existed, excreta and other waste were flushed into a backyard cesspool or sealed vault tank. At night, scavengers collected and disposed of the euphemistically called "night soil" at farms, dumps, or in rivers. Trash and rubbish, burned in stoves, was collected by "dustmen," who sorted it for use as manure or bricks. Garbage was simply put out in the street to be eaten by roving bands of dogs, rats, and especially pigs.

In 1792, the amazing Mr. Benjamin Franklin established a rudimentary waste-disposal system by having his household servants deposit waste in the Delaware River.[1] As the U.S. population increased from 31 million to 91 million between 1860 and 1914, garbage disposal became a chronic problem, especially in urban areas. Animal waste, especially that of horses, compounded the problem. For instance, in Chicago in 1914, 82,000 horses, cows, and mules produced about 600,000 pounds of waste.[2] Private collectors burned trash and garbage in incinerators or deposited it in waterways or open dumps, which bred disease-bearing flies, rats, and mosquitoes.

The Sanitary-Landfill Era (1937 to the Present)

In 1937, Fresno, California, built a sanitary landfill, covering waste daily with soil to reduce odors and vermin.[3] In World War II, the U.S. Army disposed of its waste at sanitary landfills located on military bases. After the war, in 1945, about one hundred localities had sanitary landfills. Fifteen years later the number of sanitary landfills had leaped to about 1,400.[4] Nonetheless,

163

open burning at dumps persisted. Accordingly, Congress enacted the Solid Waste Disposal Act in 1965, prohibiting open burning and funding sanitary-landfill creation.

Between 1960 and 2002, the amount of packaged and canned foods in the nation's waste stream nearly tripled to 369 million tons.[5] To transport the added waste, trucks' carrying capacity increased with compaction trucks in the 1950s, sideloader trucks in the 1970s, and now one-person loaders.

In 1976, Congress enacted the Resource Conservation and Recovery Act to regulate solid and hazardous-waste disposal and underground chemical and petroleum storage. In 1989, the EPA mandated that landfills be lined to prevent contaminants from leaching into the soil. A lined landfill is far more costly to create; therefore, their number dramatically decreased from 7,900 in 1989 to 2,314 in 2000. Meanwhile, "not in my backyard" (NIMBY) activists flexed their political muscles. Finding a site for landfills became considerably more problematic for some local jurisdictions, causing them to redouble their recycling efforts and to export waste to other localities and states.

MANAGEMENT

The Bureau of Labor Statistics classifies garbage collection as "high-hazard" work, as dangerous as logging or mining. Indeed, collection workers are about three times more likely than firefighters and police officers to be killed on duty.[6] The injury rate is equally high. Workers risk injury from sharp-edged containers, heavy lifting, loading machinery, and hazardous wastes like fuels, batteries, pesticides, solvents, herbicides, and swimming-pool chemicals. The department should therefore train workers in lifting, materials-handling, and driving. Collectors should wear the protective equipment specified by the OSHA Standard, Personal Protective Equipment, including gloves, high-visibility vests, safety shoes, and lift belts to prevent back injuries. During hot weather, workers should be given free beverages to replace their electrolytes. The Solid Waste Association of America offers training in collection and landfill operations and certifies workers in landfill, waste-collection, waste-transfer-station, and recycling management.

COLLECTION

There are four service-delivery options:

- Residents and businesses choose a private hauler.
- The local government contacts with a single private hauler to serve both residents and businesses.

- The local government serves single-family residences and apartments, but contracts out commercial and industrial service.
- The local government serves all customers.

Small-sized jurisdictions in particular often find it more cost-effective to contract out collection service because they are less able than large agencies to maintain, repair, and replace collection trucks. If the service is privatized, the department should monitor contractor performance to ensure service quality. Citizens should be encouraged to report complaints to the private hauler and the local unit.

The type of collection and frequency vary. Most jurisdictions collect waste at the curb, but some collect at the back door. The EPA recommends that food wastes be collected at least weekly and bulky wastes at least every three months. Other than garbage, other wastes that may be collected include yard wastes, leafy items, bulk goods, and hazardous materials.

The financing method has both economic and political implications. If financed by the general fund, the service cost is partially funded by the property tax, which is deductible from the federal income tax. However, a user fee, though not tax deductible, may be politically advantageous to governing-board members desiring a lower property-tax rate. A user fee is more regressive than the property tax; that is, lower-income residents pay a higher percentage of their income than if the service were funded by the property tax.

Balancing Routes

The optimal crew size depends on the collection method, the collection routes, and the cost of labor and equipment. To reduce collection costs, local governments may decrease collection frequency, purchase automated one-person packers, or require that materials be taken to the curb and be presorted.

The amount of waste collected by each crew should be equally balanced. To balance routes, an analyst may ride in collection trucks, recording

- the routes taken,
- the number and type (for example, household, apartment, condominium) of dwellings,
- the amount of waste collected,
- the collection times.

The routes should minimize the number of left-hand turns to reduce the risk of accidents from turning into oncoming traffic. A software route-balancing system can account precisely for block configurations, waste-generation rates,

Figure 12.1 **Routed Collection Area**

Source: A Guide for the Selection and Design of Solid Waste Management Systems.
Stillwater, OK: Center for Local Government Technology, 1975. Prepared through a
research grant (D1–41031) by the National Science Foundation.

distances to the disposal and transfer-station sites, topography, and loading
times. When a local unit's collection stops are added to, or subtracted from,
a collection route, crews' workload should be rebalanced accordingly. Figure
12.1 is an example of a routed area.

Safety

The EPA's "Guidelines for the Storage and Collection of Residential, Commercial, and Industrial Wastes" (CFR 40, Part 243) recommend that the weight of a manually lifted trash container not exceed seventy-five pounds and that single-use plastic and paper disposal bags meet the National Sanitation Foundation Standards Nos. 31 and 32. For safety purposes, the department may prohibit collectors from lifting difficult-to-handle containers like large cardboard boxes and fifty-five-gallon drums.

Scavenging should be prohibited, and collectors should wear clothing that meets the OSHA Standard, *Personnel Protective Equipment.* Collection vehicles should be enclosed or provided with a suitable cover. Collection equipment should meet the American National Institute Standard, *Safety Standard for Refuse Equipment.*

Transfer Stations

The collection system may establish transfer stations at which waste is transferred to larger tractor-trailers. To be economical, the transfer station should be located about ten to fifteen miles from the landfill.[7] There are three types of transfer stations:

- Small (less than 100 tons/day)
- Medium (100 to 500 tons/day)
- Large (more than 500 tons/day)

There are three types of large transfer stations:

- A *direct-discharge station* has two operating floors. At the upper level, waste is dumped down into a compactor or open-top container located on the lower floor.
- A *platform* or *pit station* temporarily stores refuse at peak collection times.
- A *compaction station* compacts waste before it is transferred.

EPA requirements regulate the design and operation of a transfer station.[8]

Performance Measurement

Among the solid-waste-collection performance measures are:

- The percentage of collections made on schedule
- The number of missed collections per scheduled stops

- The number of complaints per 1,000 households, per population, and per collections
- The number of tons collected per household
- The frequency and severity of work-related accidents

SOLID-WASTE DISPOSAL

There are four types of landfills. The most common and most heavily regulated, a sanitary landfill, must have a liner, a system to collect liquid that leaches through the landfill, a groundwater-monitoring well, a gas-monitoring system, cover material, and a plan for landfill closure and post-closure. Less regulated, a construction-and-demolition landfill disposes of only construction and demolition wastes. Finally, an industrial-waste and inert-debris landfill, usually run by a private firm, disposes of specialized industry wastes.

At the sanitary landfill site might be located a facility to recycle electronic items (such as televisions and CD players), computer equipment including toner and cartridges, office equipment, pesticide containers, cardboard and chipboard, lead-acid batteries, motor oil, telephone books, tires, and white goods (for example, refrigerators, washers, and dryers). Also at the site may be a hazardous material collection center for items like batteries, cooking oil, fluorescent lightbulbs, photographic chemicals, pesticides, solvents and thinners, antifreeze, motor oil, and so forth.

Landfill Location and Design[9]

Locating a landfill is often highly contentious. Though few doubt the need for a landfill, those living near a proposed site may shrilly cry out: "Not in my backyard!!" Sensitive to their constituents, local elected officials may support them with NIMTO ("Not in my term of office") or NIMEY ("Not in my election year"). Not all local jurisdictions, though, are opposed to landfills. Indeed, some economically struggling communities, usually rural, avidly seek a landfill, whose tipping fees provide a much-needed source of revenue. Some jurisdictions export their waste across state lines as well. In 2002, local governments in thirty-two states imported garbage from other states.[10]

To site a landfill, the governing board may appoint a steering committee to be a liaison with the community. Subtitle D of the RCRA specifies the procedures to locate, design, monitor, close, and post-close a landfill site. The steps taken to construct a landfill include:

- Reviewing state and federal regulations
- Making a preliminary drilling and a soils investigation

- Selecting a preliminary site
- Holding public hearings
- Acquiring the land
- Designing the site
- Constructing the landfill

The site-design engineer must follow Subtitle D and state requirements, taking into consideration

- the availability of space,
- road access to the site,
- the supply of fill dirt,
- the land's topography.

In particular, a site's topography may influence landfill location and design. The topography affects drainage patterns, groundwater contours, site accessibility, and the method of working the site. Generally, one acre, filled to a depth of six feet annually, is needed to serve a population of 10,000, though less space with greater compaction and deeper fills may also be used.[11] The site should be connected to highways and arterial roads, but not to residential streets. The roads to the landfill should be able to accommodate all types of fully loaded trucks during any type of weather. A soil analysis should be made to ensure that an adequate amount of fill dirt is available. The site design should enable each landfill cell to be sealed daily with six inches of compacted dirt and with twenty-four inches of dirt at the landfill's closing.

The liner, about as stiff as a roofing shingle, is spread on two feet of compacted clay to prevent water penetration. Atop the liner is a grid of pipes designed to collect toxic juices produced by decomposing garbage. The pipes drain off the liquid to prevent standing water on the liner. Too much water can causes breaches in the liner that cause leaking. Located around the landfill are monitoring wells to detect leaks from the landfill into the groundwater. Figure 12.2 shows a typical landfill.

Equipment

Types of mechanized equipment for landfills include dozers, compactors, backhoes, track loaders, water trucks, scrapers, motor graders, and wheel loaders. When purchasing equipment, the department head can consult *Solid Waste Technologies, American City and County Waste News, Waste Age,* and other periodicals. A fiscal analysis should be made to determine the most cost-effective acquisition method: buy, rent, or lease.

Figure 12.2   **Typical Landfill**

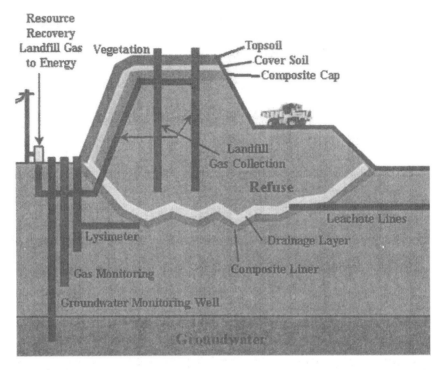

Source: Greg Hill, "A Demonstration Project Designed to Remove Contaminated Sediment and Generate Information for an Assessment of Large-Scale Dredging and Disposal from the Lower Fox River," Wisconsin Department of Natural Resources, August 1998. Available at http://dnr.wi.gov/org/water/wm/foxriver/sites/smu5657.html. Used by permission of Wisconsin Department of Natural Resources.

Operations

Landfill operations include: screening prohibited waste, building the landfill cell, eliminating rodents and insects, minimizing foul odors, testing for *leachate* and gas emissions, and closing the site.

Screening Prohibited Waste

Personnel at the gate should be on the lookout for suspicious wastes and notify authorities when a prohibited waste is detected. Screeners should perform a paint filter liquid test on suspicious liquids and can require haulers to provide a manifest of their hauled materials.

Cell Building

The basic building block of a landfill operation is a *cell* (see Figure 12.3 next page). Solid waste is spread and compacted in thin layers one to two feet thick within a confined area. The way a cell is built depends on the type of garbage, equipment type, access roads, and weather conditions. Cells can be built

- from the bottom,
- from the top,
- in horizontal lifts,
- in sloping lifts.

At the end of day, the area is covered with a thin continuous layer of compacted soil. The compacted waste and soil constitutes a cell whose height ranges from eight to ten feet. A series of cells, all the same height, constitute a *lift*. Cells are normally built with a slope steeper than 3:1.[12] The working area must be wide enough to prevent trucks from having to queue up to unload.

The spotter directs vehicles to a landfill area based on the type of garbage carried. The compactor operator compacts the garbage to build the cell. The scraper operator, keying on the compactor operator, scrapes covering soil over the dumped garbage. The compactor operator should be in charge of cell construction. The scraper operator should never place cover soil without prior approval from the compactor operator. Generally, hard-to-manage garbage should be placed near the base of the cell and easy-to-handle garbage near the outside or top of the cell.[13] State and federal regulations require that a minimum of six inches of cover material be placed on exposed refuse by the end of each operating day.[14]

Most landfill cells are rectangular, with their sides sloped as steeply as practicable. The operator compacts the settled soil and smoothly shapes the working area. Figure 12.3 shows how a cell is built. The finished cell should be a smoothly graded surface because a smooth surface takes less soil to cover than a rough surface.[15] Scavenging should be prohibited.

Vector and Odor Control

Landfills attract insects, birds, and rodents. Insecticides and pesticides reduce the number of insects and rodents. A rat burrow should be treated. Though more difficult to control, birds cause less harm than rodents.

At some landfills, controlling foul odors is a continuous challenge. The National Solid Waste Management Association has written a helpful publication, *Managing Solid Waste Facilities to Prevent Odor*.[16] Recommended odor-control methods include:[17]

- Quickly covering the area being worked on (the working face)
- Covering wet wallboard waste daily

Figure 12.3   **Building a Cell**

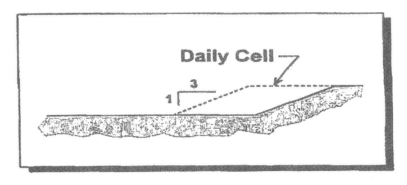

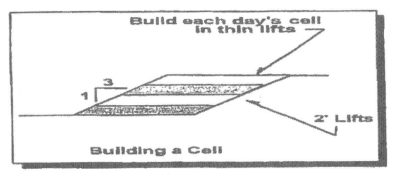

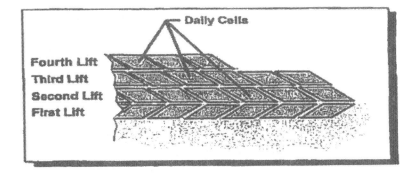

Source: Neal Bolton, *The Handbook of Landfill Operations* (Bozeman, MT: Blue Ridge Solid Waste Consulting, 1995). Used by permission.

- Resolving, if possible, citizens' complaints about odors
- Using odor-neutralizing chemicals
- Reducing odors at transfer operations

Leachate and Gas Testing

If waste materials in a landfill are deprived of oxygen, they liquefy into an acid-water solution called leachate, which may dissolve the toxic materials in the solids as it flows through the landfill. Leached toxic materials can be highly hazardous. If leachate is found outside the landfill's liner, the liner has failed, which is surprisingly commonplace. Indeed, experts note that even the best plastic liner eventually leaks, if only a little.[18] Liners should therefore be regularly tested for leaks.

Methane gas may also be emitted from the landfill and can cause fires and explosions. If gas migration is suspected, a test for the presence of methane should be made.

Landfill Closing

State laws and Subtitle D regulate how to close a landfill, dictating the type and amount of buffer cover material, its depth, its final layer, and inspection and reporting requirements. The EPA requires that local governments monitor a site for thirty years after its closure.

Other Disposal Methods

In addition to landfill disposal, solid waste can be disposed of by incineration, *pyrolysis* (chemical change through heating), shredding, and pulverizing. Incineration converts waste to organic-free residues, reduces the waste volume, provides heat-convertible energy, and produces a residue that may contain valuable metals. An incinerator plant typically has a storage pit, cranes with buckets or grapples to transfer wastes to a hopper, and a combustion chamber. A controlled air supply regulates furnace temperatures and air-pollution-control devices. There are five types of incinerators:

1. *Large with Heat Recovery.* Incinerates up to one hundred tons per day, converting the heat generated to usable steam.
2. *Large with No Heat Recovery.* Incinerates up to one hundred tons per day but does not convert heat to steam.
3. *Large with Cogeneration.* Incinerates up to one hundred tons per day, converting the heat generated to steam, and the steam to electricity.
4. *Modular, with Heat Recovery.* Incinerates one to three tons per day in a prefabricated incinerator equipped with boilers.
5. *Modular, with No Heat Recovery.* An ignition system and burners incinerate waste but do not use the resulting heat.

Pyrolysis, an alternative to incineration, heats some solid wastes (not to the point of combustion), converting them to a low-sulfur, gaseous liquid for use as fuel. For instance, discarded tires can be converted through heat to fuel oil, combustible gas, or carbon. Finally, waste can be shredded or pulverized to reduce its volume prior to its disposal at a landfill.

Records and Performance Measurement

The department must keep the required Subtitle D administrative and operational records. Even if the state does not require it, the department should still operate a scale and record the number of tons and types of materials disposed.

Among landfill-operations performance measures are

- the number of days that the landfill meets environmental standards (leachate, groundwater, surface water, noxious gas),
- the number of days that the incinerator meets emissions standards,
- the number of citizen complaints,
- the severity and frequency of accidents at the landfill.

WASTE REDUCTION

A comprehensive waste-reduction program has four components:

- A disposal-diversion ordinance (DDO)
- A material recovery facility (MRF)
- A source-reduction program
- A recycling program

A DDO mandates that products like aluminum and corrugated cardboard be diverted from the waste stream. Waste haulers caught with banned material must pay an extra disposal fee. The DDO may also require that specified waste products (such as paper, cans, plastic products) be separated before their collection.

An MRF is a transfer station that consolidates recycled products for sale. The MRF separates materials by commodity type, often baling and compressing them. Closer to the collection trucks than a landfill, an MRF can reduce the cost of hauling.

Source reduction and recycling programs need engaged, committed citizens to be successful. Departments should inform the public about effective methods through radio and TV ads, mass mailings (with a water or sewer bill), a Web site, school presentations, and programs like "Recycle Guys," a charming cast of characters who inform children about the value of a clean environment. Among the ways citizens can reduce waste at its sources are:

- *Grasscycling.* Leaving nutrient-rich grass clippings on the lawn.
- *Xeriscaping.* Growing native plants and grasses that need less water.
- *Reducing Junk Mail.* Removing one's name from national mailing lists that generate excess paper.
- *Enviro-Shopping.* Buying recyclable products, such as cloth napkins, rechargeable batteries, and refillable containers.
- *Reducing Toxic Substances.* Purchasing nontoxic inks and less toxic cleaners like baking soda and vinegar.
- *Composting Yard and Kitchen Wastes.* Composted remains produce an earthy, dark, crumbly substance that enriches soil for houseplants and gardens.

Some states mandate that local units operate a recycling program; others simply recommend it. Features of a recycling program can include:

- A waste-exchange center
- A swap shop at which items are dropped off for others to use
- A paint-exchange center at which citizens drop off unwanted paint
- A pallet-exchange program
- A Pay-as-You-Throw (also known as unit pricing or variable-rate pricing) program that charges residents per bag or per can of waste they generate to motivate more recycling and source-waste reduction

Performance Measurement

Among the waste-reduction performance measures are

- the percentage of total waste recycled,
- the percentage of households that recycle,
- the number of waste-reduction programs that citizens adopt.

NOTES

1. Ellis Armstrong, ed., *History of Public Works in the United States: 1776–1976* (Washington, DC: The American Public Works Association, 1977), 434.

2. Ibid., 434.

3. Elizabeth Royte, *Garbage Land* (New York: Little, Brown, 2005), 51.

4. H. Lanier Hickman Jr. and Richard W. Eldredge, "A Brief History of Solid Waste Management in the US, 1950–2000," *MSW Management* (July/August 2000).

5. Ibid.

6. Royte, *Garbage Land,* 32.

7. Environmental Protection Agency (EPA). *Decision Makers Guide to Solid Waste Management,* Vol. II (Washington, DC: EPA, August 1995), chapter 1.

8. Ibid., pp. 4–18 to 4–30.

9. For a detailed description of landfill siting, design, and operations, see Neal Bolton, *The Handbook of Landfill Operations* (Bozeman, MT: Blue Ridge Solid Waste Consulting, 1995).

10. Royte, *Garbage Land,* 52.

11. Salavatore Lucido, "Landfill Management," *MIS Report* 22, no. 10 (Washington, DC: International City/County Management Association, 1990).

12. Bolton, *Handbook of Landfill Operations,* 151.

13. Ibid., 174.

14. Ibid., 206.

15. Ibid., 204.

16. The National Solid Wastes Management Association, *Managing Solid Waste Facilities to Prevent Odor.* Available through NSWMA at http://www.nswma.org; click on "Publications & Research" and then on "Research Bulletins" under the heading "Online Articles"; scroll down until you reach the article. Also available at the following URL: http://wastec.isproductions.net/webmodules/webarticles/articlefiles/478-OdorReport.pdf.

17. Ibid.

18. Royte, *Garbage Land,* 57.

FOR FURTHER READING

Bolton, Neal. *The Handbook of Landfill Operations.* Bozeman, MT: Blue Ridge Solid Waste Consulting, 1995.

Environmental Protection Agency (EPA). *Decision Makers Guide to Solid Waste Management,* Vol. II (Washington, DC: EPA, August 1995), chapter 1. Available at http://www.epa.gov/epawaste/inforesources/pubs/municipal_sw.htm.

Royte, Elizabeth. *Garbage Land.* New York: Little, Brown, 2005.

13

Forestry

HISTORY

By 600 BC, Babylon was beautified by its Hanging Gardens. By the twelfth century, trees lined the outsides of cathedrals. In the early 1800s, Europeans built public parks, a movement that reached the United States in the mid-1800s. In 1857, Frederick Law Olmsted, the father of park design, became the superintendent of New York City's Central Park. Olmsted also designed the gardens and grounds of the Biltmore estate in North Carolina. The gardens, designed in an English-manor style, are located close to the mansion but still afford a majestic view of the surrounding forests and mountains. On the estate's grounds, Olmsted, with the assistance of Gifford Pinchot, designed a 250-acre recreation area within over 100,000 reforested acres. A forestry school was established near the Biltmore estate. Eugene, Oregon, instituted a tree-planting and maintenance program in 1963. Today most large cities have an urban forestry program, usually located in the roadway-appearance section of the street department. Urban foresters prune and remove trees from public rights-of-way and clear nuisance vegetation from roadsides.

MANAGEMENT

Urban forestry is a specialized, technical profession, so the local unit should hire an arborist trained in forestry, horticulture, or a closely related field. A tree commission, appointed by the governing board, may oversee forestry operations. The governing board may adopt a Tree Ordinance, whose provisions typically include:[1]

- *Private-Landowner Regulation.* Protects trees during building construction and regulates tree removal and replanting.

- *Public-Land Regulation.* Protects trees when the local government plants, replants, or removes trees.
- *Arboricultural Specification.* Specifies the type of trees than can be planted.
- *Buffer Requirement.* Specifies the noise, visual, and water buffers to be placed around trees.
- *Penalty.* Specifies the penalties for ordinance violations.

Trees should not be abused, mutilated, or "topped," except in an emergency. Topping, removing all of a tree's branches, is detrimental to its health and aesthetically displeasing.

PLANTING AND MAINTENANCE

As part of the roadway-appearance program, an urban forester may be called upon to sweep curbs and gutters, remove litter and dead animals, mow and control weeds, and clean up illegal dumpsites and city-owned vacant lots. Cities and counties responsible for interstate highway maintenance may contract out mowing services to free up crews to remove hanging limbs and fallen trees and maintain plant beds, greenways, and rights-of-way. Some power companies prune trees whose branches would harm operations should they fall during a major storm. For instance, the Oncor Group, a large utility company in Texas, prunes trees, clears, mows, removes trees from rights-of-way, and sprays herbicides.

Site and Tree Selection

The type of tree planted depends on its intended use such as screening an unpleasant site, providing shade, reducing noise levels, or enhancing the aesthetic look. Soil condition is the most important factor in a tree's growth and survival. Soil characteristics include:[2]

- Texture, which influences its fertility.
- Compaction, which is a major cause of tree decline in urban areas.
- Moisture, which is affected by precipitation patterns and soil texture.
- Nutrients and pH, which affect fertility.
- Temperature, which affects root growth.
- Contamination, which can kill the roots.
- Salt, which binds with nutrients to block their adsorption.

The site location of a tree affects its health and level of maintenance. For example, a tree on a downtown sidewalk normally needs more maintenance that one in a park. A site traveled by vehicles and pedestrians should not have prickly foliage or soft messy berries. Trees need to be sufficiently away from buildings to allow for proper crown and root development. Other siting factors to consider include:

- Utility lines
- Existing vegetation
- Community preferences about trees
- Maintenance requirements

Types of urban planting sites include:

- *Street Lawn.* The space between the curb and the sidewalk, which should be at least three feet wide.[3]
- *Tree or Planting Pit.* Small areas of soil within a sidewalk, parking lot, or other paved area.
- *Roadway.* The median or side of roads.
- *Planter.* Placed at sites impossible to plant because of poor or no soil or underground utilities.

Tree Planting

Fall and spring are the best times to plant trees because moderate weather and water are more available to support root growth. Fall is usually recommended, as time is allowed for root growth before the summer hot weather. The tree should be inspected at the nursery to ensure it meets the minimum standard, the *American Standard for Nursery Stock,* set by the American Nursery and Landscape Association. To prepare the planting site, competing vegetation is removed with herbicides, tilling, plastic sheeting, hand weeding, or stripping the sod. The soil is loosened to encourage root growth. To reduce the amount of soil settling, the bottom of the planting area should not be disturbed.[4] The tree should be picked up from the bottom of the container, rootball cage, or rootball, not by the trunk, which would pull the trunk away from the roots.[5] The rootball is removed just before planting to prevent the soil from drying. Dead, diseased, twisted, or broken roots are cut away.

The care given to a tree after its planting is critical to its survival in an urban setting. The entire planting area should be watered within two hours of planting.[6] The amount of watering thereafter depends on the weather and type of tree. Two to four inches of mulch will reduce evaporation, regulate soil temperature, and reduce competition from turfgrass. However, keep the mulch away from the bark of the tree to prevent disease and insect problems.

A newly planted tree should not be fertilized, because that could cause new crown growth, which would increase the demand for water and nutrients that cannot be met by the tree's roots.[7]

Some trees need protection when planted. Among the protective devices are:

- *Tree Shelter.* A translucent plastic tube that fits around the tree trunk below the lowest branch.
- *Tree Wrap and Guard.* A paper, plastic, or burlap wrap that shields young trees with thin bark (for example, a red maple) from being scalded by the sun.
- *Protective Grate.* A grate, usually near a sidewalk or road, to protect the soil from being compacted.
- *Stake.* Stakes around a tree to protect from damage by string trimmers and lawn mowers.

Some cities aggressively replace trees that have been lost. An example is the NeighborWoods program run by the city of Raleigh, North Carolina. The staff identifies areas within the city's right-of-way most in need of trees. Clear-cut developments have first priority. The staff plants a flag where trees are needed and puts a hanger on the doorknob detailing contact information, planting instructions, and the trees suitable for the location. The program has over forty species from which to select. The city delivers the trees at no charge, but citizens must plant and water the trees for two years. The city has found that persons who plant their own tree usually take more responsibility for its care. The city supplies volunteers to plant trees for those who have identified themselves as too elderly or disabled to tend the tree. The city then checks each tree annually to ensure its care. Almost all the trees are purchased with funds donated by citizens on their water bills.

Tree Maintenance

Localities may adopt a tree maintenance plan that includes an inventory of trees including their species, location, size, and condition. The plan also specifies tree maintenance standards with respect to watering, pruning, fertilizing, disease and pest control, and removal.

Watering a tree the first two years after its planting is essential.[8] Pruning, except for spring flowering trees (such as magnolias and dogwood), should be done in the winter. Removing branches is easier then, as the tree is more visible and growth the lowest. Fertilizing a tree under distress (for example, root damaged, newly planted, or diseased) is not recommended because the tree usually cannot support

Table 13.1

Tree Management Pruning Standard

Standard	Procedure
Pruning Objectives	6.1 Pruning objectives shall be established prior to beginning any pruning operation.
	6.1.1 Objectives should include, but are not limited to: one of more of the following: risk reduction, manage health, clearance, structural improvement/correction, view improvement/creation, aesthetic improvement.
	6.1.2 Established objectives should be specified in writing.
	6.1.3 To obtain the defined objective, the growth, cycles, structure, species, and the extent of pruning to be performed shall be considered.
	6.1.4 Not more than 25% of the foliage should be removed within an annual growing season. The percentage of distribution of foliage to be removed shall be adjusted according to the plant's species, age, health and site.
	6.1.7 Topping and leaving a branch looking like a lion's tailing shall be considered unacceptable pruning practices for trees.
Pruning Methods (Types)	7.1 One of more of the following methods (types) shall be specified to achieve the objective.
	7.2 Clean. Cleaning shall consist of pruning to remove one or more of the following non-beneficial parts: dead, diseased, and/or broken branches.
	7.3 Raise. Raising shall consist of pruning to provide vertical clearance.
	7.4 Thin. Thinning shall consist of selective pruning to density of live branches.
	7.5.1 Thinning should result in an even distribution of branches throughout the crown.

Source: This material is reproduced from ANSI A300 Part I (Pruning) 2008 with permission of the Tree Care Industry Association. No part of this material may be copied or reproduced in any form, electronic retrieval system, or otherwise made available on the Internet, a public network, by satellite, or otherwise without the prior consent of the Tree Care Industry Association.

the increased growth caused by the fertilization.[9] Fertilizer should be applied according to the manufacturer's instructions. To prevent damage from disease and pests, trees should be inspected regularly. Finally, when removing a tree, care should be taken to not damage the site, nearby trees, or nearby infrastructure.

Tree work can be extremely dangerous. The tree pruning standard, approved by the American National Standard Institute (ANSI), and published by the American Tree Care Industry Association, is shown in Table 13.1.

When pruning, trimming, repairing, or removing trees and cutting brush, ANSI Standard Z133.1–2006 requires operators to

- Wear protective equipment.
- Avoid electrical hazards and work ten feet farther from energized conductors.
- If working less than ten feet from energized conductors, the worker must be certified to do so and must have permission from, or be working on behalf of, the utility.
- Remove and trim trees according to specified practices.

OSHA Standard 29 (CFR 1910.266) specifies how to log trees and how much training is needed to trim trees. The state typically regulates spraying chemicals on nuisance weeds. An operator must be state-licensed to apply, handle, store, and dispose of chemicals. The landscaping and plantings along the public right-of-way, quite conspicuous to citizens, should be regularly mowed and cleared of litter and nuisance vegetation.

Major-Storm Cleanup

Local governments should have a comprehensive weather-emergency plan to respond to natural disasters like hurricanes, tornadoes, floods, and major snowstorms. The tree department coordinates with the public electric companies to remove trees and limbs downed on power lines. After a major storm, crews may spend days, weeks, or even months chipping limbs and grinding stumps. The debris can be mountainous, making its disposal challenging. Debris and yard waste can be given or sold to citizens at a minimal cost. Recyclable chipped or ground debris can be used as mulch on public flower beds and plants. A one- to three-inch layer of mulch on a bed reduces weed growth and holds in moisture during hot, dry summer months.

NOTES

1. For more information on how to prepare a tree ordinance, refer to the Web site http://www.isa-arbor.com/related/resources/ordinance.aspx.
2. Urban Forestry South, "Site and Tree Selection" unit, in *The Urban Forestry Manual* (Athens, GA: U.S. Department of Agriculture, Forest Service, Southern Center for Urban Forest Research & Information, 2004), 4.
3. Ibid., 9.
4. Urban Forestry South, "Tree Planting" unit, in *The Urban Forestry Manual,* 13.
5. Ibid., 14.
6. Ibid., 17.

7. Ibid., 18.

8. Urban Forestry South, "Tree Maintenance," in *The Urban Forestry Manual,* 15.

9. Ibid., 24.

FOR FURTHER READING

Urban Forestry South. "Resources." Available at http://www.urbanforestrysouth.org/resources.

U.S. Department of Agriculture, Forest Service, Southern Center for Urban Forest Research & Information. *The Urban Forestry Manual* (Athens, GA: U.S. Department of Agriculture, 2004). Available at http://www.urbanforestrysouth.org/resources/collections/urban-forestry-manual.

Part III

Leisure Services

14

Library

The Private Library Era (Colonial Days to 1893)

Early public writings were exceedingly practical. The first recorded book, the Egyptian Book of the Dead, written about 4500 BC, gave explicit directions about how to prepare for one's death and afterlife. In 2100 BC, the Sumerians publicly recorded financial accounts, purchases, receipts for goods and slaves, and official correspondence. The first fictional novel, *Tale of the Shipwrecked Sailor,* written about 2000 BC, became an "Oprah" book-of-the-millennium bestseller, read for over 1,000 years. By 47 BC, the great library of Alexandria contained about 400,000 scrolls, which were tragically destroyed by Caesar's troops. Caesar, perhaps in self-redemption, founded a Roman public library, and by the fourth century, Rome had twenty-eight public libraries.

During the Dark Ages, monks preserved the literary tradition, painstakingly copying classical works. Most books, though, were written by, and the province of, the Catholic Church; however, the Renaissance witnessed a return of public libraries. In 1441, Cosimo de Medici built a public library in Florence. Gutenberg's invention of movable-type printing in 1452 made books far more available to the public.

In the United States, libraries were privately operated or church-owned until Ben Franklin founded a subscription library in 1731. Franklin rounded up fifty "friends of reading," who paid a forty-shilling initiation fee and a ten-shilling annual-membership fee. Open 2:00–3:00 PM on Wednesdays and 12:00–4:00 PM on Saturdays, Franklin's library let any "civil gentlemen" peruse books, but only members could borrow them.

In 1800, Congress appropriated $5,000 to build the Library of Congress, which British troops burned in the War of 1812. The perennially financially strapped Thomas Jefferson came to the rescue and sold his 6,487-volume collection, the largest and finest in the country, to the Library of Congress for $23,940 in 1815.

In 1873, Melville Dewey created the Dewey Decimal Classification System. Books that had been in a fixed location by room, tier, and shelf could now be moved to other locations and were grouped into related fields for ease of search.

The Public-Library Era (1893 to the 1980s)

Andrew Carnegie jump-started library construction. Carnegie believed that everybody could pull themselves up by their bootstraps, as he had done, and that reading was the key to self-improvement. Funding his first library in Fairfield, Iowa, in 1893, Carnegie eventually donated $56 million to build 1,956 libraries in the United States and an additional 553 worldwide. Carnegie did not, though, ascribe to the "free lunch" theory of philanthropy. To get a Carnegie grant, towns had to levy a $2-per-resident charge to fund part of the construction cost and had to fund all of the operating costs.

The Technology Era (1980s to the Present)

Since the 1980s, libraries have heavily embraced technology. Patrons can use automation to reserve books from their homes, renew materials over an automated phone machine, and check out materials. Patrons with a reading disability and travelers can borrow books on tape and discs. Today's libraries, if space permits, abound with computer stations used for myriad purposes, such as researching school assignments. Finally, online systems compile circulation statistics, update borrower-registration records, and send recorded messages telling patrons that a reserved book is available.

In 2003, the Supreme Court upheld the constitutionality of the Children's Internet Protection Act, requiring libraries to use Internet-pornography filters or forfeit federal funds, which amounted to about $1 billion in 2007.

MANAGEMENT

In 2004, there were 9,207 public libraries in the United States run by

- cities (53 percent),
- nonprofits (15 percent),
- library districts (14 percent),
- counties or parishes (10 percent),
- multijurisdictions (3 percent),

- school districts (3 percent),
- city/county governments (1 percent),
- other (1 percent).[2]

Most library systems are small: 83 percent have just one branch,[3] and 29 percent spend less than $50,000 annually.[4] Some libraries therefore outsource services like cataloging and bibliographic referencing. Indeed, some libraries contracted with the Library of Congress for cataloging and processing services as far back as 1913.

Among the services offered by libraries are basic literacy programs, referrals to community-service agencies, consumer information, business and career information, cultural-awareness programs, materials on current topics and titles, learning support to students, government information, general information, information literacy, lifelong learning, local history, and genealogy.[5]

A library's physical condition sends an unmistakable message to the public. A bright, cheerful, and well-maintained facility gives a positive, customer-focused impression, but an unkempt, poorly lighted, cluttered library discourages patronage. The physical conditions of a library should

- meet the Americans with Disabilities Act requirements,[6]
- be cleaned, lighted, well heated and air-conditioned, and have adequate signage,
- include data cables, computer furniture, computers, printers, wires, and specialized equipment (such as scanners, digital projectors, and fax machines).

Figure 14.1 shows the physical layout of a typical public library.

Library Plans

Libraries may adopt three types of plans. Most adopt a *service plan,* often based on Public Library Association (PLA) guidelines, which specifies the level of service to be given to patrons. A *collection plan* is a library's blueprint for the collection and maintenance of print and nonprint materials. Finally, a *technology plan* articulates a library's technology objectives.[7]

Human-Resource Management

Library staff classified as librarians typically have a master's degree in library/information science from a graduate school accredited by the Ameri-

Figure 14.1   **Public Library Layout**

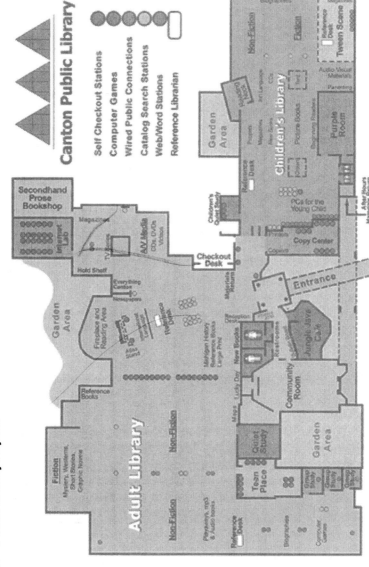

Source: Canton Public Library, Canton, Michigan. Available at http://www.cantonpl.org. Copyright © Canton Public Library. Used by permission.

can Library Association (ALA) and usually belong to the PLA. A librarian in a small library is usually a generalist, serving both adults and children. In contrast, a librarian in a large library (serving a population over 50,000) usually specializes in an area like cataloging, reference services, adult services, children services, or library technology/web design. Because patrons may ask questions of any kind, specialized librarians should be cross-trained in adult and children services and learn the basics of reference services.

Volunteers are a great source of assistance to libraries. They can help with book fairs, special events, and other duties. Library management should therefore routinely recognize volunteers' valuable service by awarding plaques, certificates, or service pins.

COLLECTION MANAGEMENT

All print and electronic media, both circulating and noncirculating, are called the *collection*.[8] Collection usage generally can be grouped into four basic categories:

- *Popular/Recreational*. Current titles and best sellers.
- *Basic*. Standard reference titles and recognized works.
- *Instructional*. Reference materials, access to specialized electronic databases, and specialized technical titles.
- *Research*. Bibliographies, important journals, and research reports.

Library patronage, a primary measure of library effectiveness, is heavily influenced by customer satisfaction,[9] which is much affected by the availability of books and other resources. Libraries measure satisfaction by the results of a customer-service survey and set materials-availability goals, including:

- The number of reference questions answered within x amount of time
- The number of best sellers on the *New York Times* best seller list that are acquired within x amount of time
- Customer travel time to the library
- Returned books back on shelves within x period of time

Large library systems may use a computer program to map patrons' residences and analyze their usage. These data help staff to assess the aspects of the service plan that are working and what can be improved. For instance, after pinpointing the location of low-usage patrons, staff might decide to place a mobile library there.

Customers should be permitted to check out and return books at any library

Table 14.1

Recommended Number of Operating Days/Hours per Week

Population	Excellent	Good	Adequate
Under 500	5 days/24hrs.	5 days/22hrs.	4 days/20hrs.
500–999	5 days/24hrs.	5 days/22hrs.	4 days/20hrs.
1,000–2,499	6 days/35 hrs.	6 days/24hrs.	5 days/20hrs.
2,500–4,999	6 days/46 hrs.	6 days/35hrs.	5 days/29hrs.
5,000–9,999	7 days/55 hrs.	6 days/46hrs.	5 days/41hrs.
10,000–24,999	7 days/65 hrs.	6 days/55hrs.	6 days/51hrs.
25,000–49,999	7 days/65 hrs.	6 days/61hrs.	6 days/57hrs.
50,000 and above	7 days/68 hrs.	6 days/65hrs.	6 days/61hrs.

Source: Excerpted from State Library of Iowa, *In Service to Iowa: Public Library Measures of Quality,* 4th ed. (Des Moines: State Library of Iowa, 2004). Used by permission.

branch. Libraries can reduce book-waiting time by purchasing another copy for every *x* number of reserves placed on a title. However, reducing waiting time for interlibrary-loan materials is more problematic because the requesting library cannot control the other library's operations.

The three most common measures of availability are:

- The percentage of successfully found title searches (the title-fill rate)
- The percentage of successfully found subject searches (the subject-fill rate)
- The percentage of browsers who left satisfied (the browser-fill rate)[10]

Staff Size

From 1921 to 1956, the ALA arbitrarily recommended that governments minimally spend $1 per capita for libraries; [11] however, it now recommends that each library establish its own funding criterion.[12] In the 1950s, based on the population served, the PLA also recommended specific staffing levels, collection sizes and quality, patron-travel time, collection-maintenance standards, and facility standards.[13] In the late 1980s, though, the PLA discontinued these standards, recognizing that they were not empirically grounded. Nonetheless, some state library associations still recommend performance standards, but only as a general guide. Large libraries may find some or all of the standards too low; small libraries may find some or all too stringent. Table 14.1 shows the staffing norms recommended by the State Library of Iowa.

The PLA workbook, *Staffing for Results: A Guide to Working Smarter,* is an excellent guide to determine a library's appropriate staffing level.[14] The workbook explains how to calculate the amount of available work hours, establish standard service times, and record the time spent with the public and on demand-driven tasks.[15]

Materials Acquisition

Staff acquire materials, basing their decisions on past usage and feedback from the public, the library board, Friends of the Library (if such a group exists), businesses, governments, and other stakeholders. A community's demographics may also factor into acquisition decisions. For instance, a community with more senior citizens should acquire relatively more large-print books; a library serving more school-age children relatively more children's materials.

A selection team usually makes acquisition decisions. Large libraries typically get input from their specialists in specific areas (for example, science, children's materials, or materials in Spanish) and from each branch library. The selection team may select reference materials or delegate their selection to a committee of reference specialists. To determine what books to select, the selection team should read book reviews in publications like *Kirkus Reviews, Library Journal, Publishers Weekly,* and the *Baker and Taylor Forecast.* Reviews in *Booklist* and *Choice,* which come out subsequent to publication, are less useful. Though also ex post facto, the *New York Times* Best Sellers List is the gold standard for gauging reader interest.

As reader demand for a book increases, the selection team should increase the number of copies and then discard copies as reader interest subsides. If reader interest is initially overestimated, the selection team may try to stimulate readership with a catchy display.

A general benchmark for gauging reader demand is the size of the reading population served. Table 14.2 indicates the number of books recommended by the State Library of Iowa, based on population size. Likewise, a local unit's population may be used to estimate the number of periodicals to circulate. Table 14.3 shows the State Library of Iowa's periodical-holdings benchmarks.

Among the materials-acquisition-processing measures are

- the percentage books available within x days of ordering,
- the percentage of *New York Times* best sellers added to the collection within x days of their receipt,
- the percentage of new materials cataloged within x days of their receipt,
- the percentage of periodicals processed within x hours.

Table 14.2

Recommended Number of Books

Population	Excellent	Good	Adequate
0–499	7,000	6,000	5,000
500–999	9,747	6,651	5,521
1,000–2,499	14,570	9,747	7,541
2,500–4,999	25,679	14,200	11,476
5,000–9,999	41,998	25,679	21,425
10,000–24,999	60,555	41,998	31,314
25,000–49,999	106,998	60,555	45,605
50,000 and above	204,520	106,998	91,068

Source: Excerpted from State Library of Iowa, *In Service to Iowa: Public Library Measures of Quality*, 4th ed. (Des Moines: State Library of Iowa, 2004). Used by permission.

Table 14.3

Recommended Number of Periodicals

Population	Excellent	Good	Adequate
0–499	24	16	10
500–999	36	24	17
1,000–2,499	58	36	23
2,500–4,999	85	58	41
5,000–9,999	119	85	69
10,000–24,999	180	119	94
25,000–49,999	289	180	131
50,000 and above	408	289	249

Source: Excerpted from State Library of Iowa, *In Service to Iowa: Public Library Measures of Quality*, 4th ed. (Des Moines: State Library of Iowa, 2004). Used by permission.

Materials Removal

Libraries have two types of collections: the heavily used core collection and the rarely used inactive collection. Rarely used books should be systematically "weeded" from the collection because they take up space and cost customers time when looking for books. One easy weeding criterion is a book's physical condition. In particular, frequently read children's books tend to deteriorate quickly. A commonly used weeding methodology, used particularly by small- and medium-sized libraries, is CREW: Continuous Review, Evaluation, and Weeding. The CREW method recommends criteria to weed books, children's materials, the reference collection, nonprint media, and computers.[16] The CREW method weeds materials based on the mnemonic MUSTIE:[17]

- M = Misleading and/or factually inaccurate
- U = Ugly
- S = Superseded
- T = Trivial
- I = Irrelevant
- E = Elsewhere

The availability of space is a weeding factor. Librarians working in tight quarters (such as in a small branch library) have space constraints. Nonetheless, some books, like the classics, must remain in circulation regardless of their use. Though demand for underused books may be promoted by a special display, such books are often better discarded, because library usage increases when outdated materials are weeded.

To make removal decisions based on usage, a cutoff usage date is set. A common approach is the *Slote method*—staff dot the spines of books when books are checked out and returned. Those books that have not been checked out by the time a percentage (for example, 95%) of the collection has circulated are removed.[18]

A disposal record should be made of each material selected for weeding. The disposal options include:

- *Bind.* Bind the book and return to the collection.
- *Mend.* Mend the book and return to the collection.
- *Discard.* Pull the shelf list and catalog cards, remove copy information from the database, remove bar code, tear off the book pockets. Store for an annual book sale, donate to another library, or box for a garbage pickup or the pulp dealer.
- *Replace.* Replace with a new copy, new edition, or a better title on the subject.
- *Recycle.* Recycle newspapers, periodicals, and other recyclables.

Performance Evaluation

Collection-access performance measures include:

- The average amount of time a patron spends waiting to check out materials
- The percentage of returned items checked in accurately
- The percentage of returned materials reshelved accurately within x amount of time

Table 14.4

Annual Library-Performance Standards

Category	Excellent	Good	Adequate
% of Expenditures Allocated to Collection	14	12	10
% New Books Added to Collection	6	4.5	3
Items Circulated per Capita	14.0	8.0–13.9	N/A
% Of Collection Withdrawn	6	4.5	3
% of Payroll Spent on Staff Development	1	0.75	0.5
Total Annual Circulation of all Materials including Renewals by Population			
Under 2,500 population	1	0.8	0.5
2,500 population and above	3	2	1

Source: Excerpted from State Library of Iowa, *In Service to Iowa: Public Library Measures of Quality*, 4th ed. (Des Moines: State Library of Iowa, 2004). Used by permission.

• The number of end-of-year overdue materials as a percentage of the annual circulation
• The percentage of items lost from the collection
• The number of computer terminals in the library
• The number and kinds of databases available
• The extent of Internet access and bandwidth
• The availability of films, DVDs, and videos

The National Center for Education Statistics annually surveys public libraries to gather circulation data. For instance, in 2004, the average number of circulation transactions per capita nationwide was 7.1, ranging from 14.8 transactions in Ohio to 0.25 transactions in Hawaii.[19] In 2004, the average number of public-use Internet terminals per 5,000 population was 3.01 nationwide, ranging from South Dakota (6.82 terminals) to California (1.89 terminals).[20] Table 14.4 shows selected library-performance standards reported by the State Library of Iowa.

TECHNOLOGY

Online circulation systems compile circulation statistics and update borrower-registration records. The Telecommunications Act of 1996 requires that libraries adopt a technology plan in order to obtain federal funding.[21] In most states, the state library agency approves the plan. Some grantors and foundations, like the Gates Library Foundation, are more likely to fund a library system with a long-range plan.[22] Libraries typically form a technology team to prepare the plan, whose provisions usually include:

- An assessment of the staff's technological skills
- The library's technology-service objectives
- The available technological options
- The number of terminals, user locations, and licensing restrictions
- How to authenticate users
- Training requirements
- Future hardware and software needs and their estimated cost

The library system may hire a consultant to prepare the more technical aspects of the plan. In that case, library staff should prepare a request for proposals (RFP) from consultants. To solicit proposals, the staff can place the RFP on the *Library Hotline,* Pupblib, and an interlibrary listserv.[23]

NOTES

1. For a more detailed history of libraries, see "Libraries" at http://www.libraries.gr/nonmembers/en/main.htm.

2. National Center for Education Statistics, Institute of Education Sciences, U.S. Department of Education, *Public Libraries in the United States: Fiscal Year 2004* (Washington, DC: U.S. Department of Education, 2006), 5.

3. Ibid.

4. Ibid., 7.

5. For a more in-depth discussion of these services, see Diane Mayo and Sandra Nelson, *Wired for the Future* (Chicago: American Library Association, 1999), 23.

6. To see the Americans with Disabilities Act guidelines, see "ADA Accessibility Guidelines for Buildings and Facilities," at http://www.access-board.gov/adaag/html/adaag.htm.

7. Mayo and Nelson, *Wired for the Future,* xiv.

8. Sandra Nelson, Ellen Altman, and Diane Mayo, *Managing for Results* (Chicago: American Library Association, 2000), 112.

9. An excellent book that focuses on customer service is the American Library Association's *Give 'em What They Want!* (Chicago: American Library Association, 1992).

10. Nelson et al., *Managing for Results,* 130.

11. F.N. Withers, *Standards for Library Service: An International Survey* (Paris: UNESCO Press, 1974), 320.

12. Nelson et al., *Managing for Results,* 49.

13. For a comprehensive discussion of library standards and library measures in general, see David Ammons, *Municipal Benchmarks,* 2nd ed. (Thousand Oaks, CA: Sage Publications, 2001), 212.

14. Diane Mayo and Jeanne Goodrich, *Staffing for Results: A Guide to Working Smarter* (Chicago: American Library Association, 2002).

15. Ibid.

16. For more explicit CREW procedures, see the Texas State Library and Archives Commission's "Background and Process—The Cycle of Service: Where CREW Fits In." Available at http://www.tsl.state.tx.us/ld/pubs/crew/background.html.

17. For an explanation of the method, see Belinda Boon, *The CREW Method: Expanded Guidelines for Collection and Evaluation and Weeding in Small and Medium-Sized Libraries* (Austin: Texas State University, 1995).

18. For further explanation of the Slote Method and other weeding procedures, see Overbooked.org, "Weeding the Fiction Collection: Should I Dump Peyton Place?" Available at http://www.overbooked.org/ra/weeding.html.

19. Op. cit., *Public Libraries in the United States: Fiscal Year 2004*, A-4.

20. Ibid., A-5.

21. Mayo and Nelson, *Wired for the Future*, xv.

22. For a detailed discussion of technology planning, see ibid. and *Managing for Results*, 232–298.

23. Mayo and Nelson, *Wired for the Future*, 7.

For Further Reading

American Library Association (ALA). *Give 'em What They Want!* Chicago: ALA, 1992.

Mayo, Diane, and Jeanne Goodrich. *Staffing for Results: A Guide to Working Smarter.* Chicago: ALA, 2002.

Mayo, Diane, and Sandra Nelson. *Wired for the Future.* Chicago: ALA, 1999.

Nelson, Sandra; Ellen Altman; and Diane Mayo. *Managing for Results.* Chicago: ALA, 2000.

15

Parks and Recreation

History[1]

The Passive-Recreation Era (Colonial Days to 1821)

Parks date to about 1000 BC, when the Sumerians built the Hanging Gardens of Babylon as an assembly place and hunting grounds. In the United States during the colonial era, planners provided for open space. William Penn included five open squares in his design of Philadelphia in 1682; James Oglethorpe designated twenty-three squares in Savannah, Georgia; the Boston Common was bought and dedicated for park use in 1728; and Pierre Charles L'Enfant provided for park space in his design of Washington, DC, in 1791.

The Active-Recreation Era (1821 to the Present)

In 1821, the Latin School held outdoor recreation classes in Salem, Massachusetts. In 1886, a teacher, Marie Zakrzewska, created a sand garden, later known as a playground, equipped with gym bars. Taking note that working people seldom used passive-design parks, George Parker, superintendent of parks in Hartford, designed an active park with sports fields in 1900. Meanwhile, states enacted legislation that permitted city parks departments to jointly use school grounds and buildings.[2]

In 1858, the father of landscape architecture, Frederick Law Olmsted, built Central Park, principally as a haven for residents jammed into New York's crowded tenements. The park was a bucolic, rural setting with meadows, lawns, native trees, and low buildings (see Figure 15.1). Active sports, like baseball and football, were not permitted, as they were thought to mar the rustic, relaxing setting. Olmsted went on to design parks in Philadelphia, Baltimore, Washington, and San Francisco with the same passive-recreation approach.

In 1904, Los Angeles created a municipal parks-and-recreation depart-

Figure 15.1   **Park Setting**

Source: National Park Service, U.S. Department of the Interior. Available at http://www.nps.gov/gree/supportyourpark/index.htm.

ment. By the 1920s, about half the states allowed cities to operate and fund recreation programs.[3] By the 1930s, year-round recreation programs were widespread. The public patronized parks even more after World War II, when the workweek shortened, leaving more time for recreation.

In 1967, five organizations—the American Institute of Park Executives, the National Recreation Association, the National Conference on State Parks, the American Association of Zoological Parks, and the American Recreation Society—merged to form the National Recreation and Park Association (NRPA). In 1975, Congress passed the Education for All Handicapped Children Act, which guaranteed equal opportunity for disabled youth and increased therapeutic-recreation services.

In recent years, recreational interests have diversified. Larger departments in particular offer varied recreational opportunities, such as ropes courses, climbing walls, skate boarding, dog parks, and disc golf.

MANAGEMENT

Some department heads have an undergraduate or master's degree in recreation and park administration. However, small departments with a limited budget may be headed by someone with no educational background in parks-and-recreation management. She or he must learn on-the-job, and the NRPA offers a wide array of assistance, including:

- Two monthly magazines: *Parks and Recreation* and the *Journal of Leisure Research*
- The Park and Recreational Professional Certification Program
- A clearinghouse of current, research-based publications
- The Internet-based NRPAnet used for research and collaboration

In addition, the National Therapeutic Certification Board certifies therapeutic-recreation professionals.

Volunteers and Alternative Labor

Most departments rely heavily on volunteers to coach teams, run scoreboards, maintain facilities and fields, mentor youth, partner with the disabled, work at special events, and the like. Volunteers are drawn from the retirement community, parents, service clubs (for example, Keystone, Interact), civic clubs (such as Lions, Rotary, Kiwanis), colleges (sororities and fraternities), organizations with a specific interest (a runners club, for example), women's groups, and college sports teams. Volunteers should be certified when required. For instance, the National Youth Coaches Association and the American Sports Education Program certify coaches.

Other sources of alternative labor include:

- Workers performing required community service, who require careful supervision
- Prison labor, especially for site clean-up, who also require careful supervision
- Employment-program trainees
- High school students considering a parks-and-recreation career
- Landscape-design students willing to design a park area for college credit

The department should formally recognize volunteers' contributions with a congratulatory dinner, plaques, or some other type of recognition.

Parks-and-Recreation Board

States permit the local jurisdiction's governing body to delegate some or all of its authority to three types of parks-and-recreation boards:

1. *Independent Board.* Has the power to levy taxes and adopt a budget.
2. *Semi-Independent Board.* With staff, prepares the annual operating budgeting for approval by the local governing board.
3. *Advisory Board.* Advisory only, serves as a sounding board for the local governing board.

The semi-independent board is the most common arrangement. Under this model, local governing and parks-and-recreation boards should create a shared vision, formulating common goals, policies, and procedures. The department head should orient new board members about departmental programs and objectives, encouraging them to volunteer and attend departmental events and activities.

User Fees and Funding

Recreation departments recover part of departmental expenses with user fees. Some governing boards adopt a *user-fee policy,* which specifies the percentage of the cost of each program (for example, swimming pools, adult league activities, and so forth) to be recovered by a user fee. The amount of the fee reflects the relative benefit that the individual and community as a whole receive from the program. For instance, adults who receive the full benefit from participating in a softball league should be charged 100 percent of the program's costs. On the other hand, young boys participating in a Little League baseball program may be judged to receive only 40 percent of the benefit and the community at large 60 percent, in which case the fee would cover 40 percent of the program's cost.

The governing board may also set rates that recognize that low-income participants are less able to pay than those with higher incomes. Among ways to adjust for those with low incomes are to

- use a sliding-rate scale based on different income levels,
- sponsor children below a certain income level,
- allow children to volunteer in return for free entrance,
- issue passes to lower-income people,
- establish a scholarship program.

Residents typically pay a lower rate for fee-supported recreation programs than nonresidents, who do not pay local property taxes. However, if the local unit receives federal construction funds, nonresidents can only be charged 50 percent more than residents' cost.

Some departments creatively fund program costs, including:

- Soliciting corporations to sponsor programs
- Engaging community groups to adopt and maintain a park
- Creating an IRS-recognized 501-C-3 entity, to which citizens can make a tax-deductible donation
- Building a facility with private-sector financial support

Some communities levy an *impact fee* on developers to defray part of the cost of serving a newly developed area. The impact fee relieves the cost of providing parks, water, sewer, roads, and schools. Another method to relieve the cost of growth, an *exaction,* requires a developer to set aside land in a development for a park. Finally, states fund park acquisition, as do these federal agencies:

- *Health and Human Services.* Funds public-housing playgrounds and senior-citizens and community centers.
- *National Parks Service.* Uses monies from the Land and Water Conservation Fund to acquire parkland and develop recreational facilities.
- *Education.* Funds learning centers that complement school academics.
- *Transportation.* Funds bike trails, walking trails, acquisition of scenic easements, and recreational use of abandoned railroad corridors.

Facilities Planning and Design

The comprehensive parks-and-recreation master plan is a blueprint for the future. Large departments typically hire a consultant to prepare the plan that forecasts facilities and programs needed over the next ten- to fifteen-year period. In preparing the plan, departments typically seek widespread community input, often with the assistance of a citizen advisory board. Shaping the plan are the forecasted population, community demographics, citizens' preferences, and funding availability. Historically, some departments used NRPA-suggested per-capita standards (such as x number of parks per 1,000 persons) to forecast capital facilities. However, in 1995, the NRPA dropped these rigid standards, advising each community to project its needs based on its unique characteristics. The plan should provide for the preservation of open space and protection of historic resources.

In designing a new park, planners consider safety, access for the disabled, after-school access, maintenance requirements, and energy costs. Planners may also propose to construct and operate a facility jointly with another city, the county government, or the school system.

To save on the land acquisition costs, citizens should be encouraged to donate land to the community in their wills. Other cost-saving measures include using:

- A restored landfill
- A floodplain area donated by a developer
- Land in buffer areas along streams
- Greenways
- Land along sewer lines and abandoned rail corridors

RECREATION SERVICES[4]

Unfortunately, we are becoming a sedentary society. Obesity, even among youth, has reached epidemic proportion. A daunting challenge for a recreation department is to lure the public away from the electronic umbilical cord tying them to televisions, computers, cell phones, iPods, and VCRs. An attractive lure may be a nontraditional recreational opportunity like a skate park, scuba diving, camping, bike trails, dancing, a ropes course, a dogs course, community festivals, a disc-golf field, a climbing wall, or an adventure program.

Safety

Safety is of high concern to a recreation department. Unsafe facilities and activities can cause injury, death, and legal liability. Safety should be a primary concern of all employees—full-time, part-time, contract, volunteers, maintenance, and clerical. The department head should designate a safety officer to coordinate safety training and hold safety meetings. Two areas of special concern are playgrounds and swimming pools.

Playground Safety

The NRPA operates a program that certifies employees in playground safety. It also has prepared helpful playground-safety publications, including:

- The Playground Inspection Probes and Gauges Kit
- Best Practices in Youth Development in Public Park and Recreation Settings
- Public Recreation in High Risk Environments: Programs that Work

Recommended design features for playground swings, slides, seesaws, and merry-go-rounds, are shown in Table 15.1.

Other helpful instructional materials include:

- Standard Consumers Safety Performance Specifications for Playground Equipment for Public Use (F 1487–95) (American Society of Testing and Materials)

Table 15.1

Playground Equipment Design Features

Swings	Replace metal and wooden seats with soft seats. Set swings away from other equipment to avoid children being hit. Have a maximum of two swings per bay on a swing set, at least 24 inches apart. Use full bucket seats for toddlers.
Slides	Be well anchored and have firm handrails. Have good traction on their steps. Install a bar at the top of the slide so that children must sit down before they slide.
Seesaws	Use spring-loaded seesaws. Avoid adjustable seesaws with chains. Put a tire or some other buffer under the seat to avoid hitting the ground.
Merry-go-rounds	Keep the rotating platform level and free of sharp edges. Provide clearance to avoid crushing limbs.

Source: Excerpted from Diane Hurms, "How to Improve Public Playgrounds," *Public Management,* April 2004, 33.

- The Handbook for Public Playground Safety (U.S. Consumer Product Safety Division)
- Playground Equipment Standards (International Playground Equipment Manufacturers Association)

OSHA requires that playgrounds be inspected daily and equipment periodically. Staff should investigate and resolve citizens' complaints about recreational and park facilities.

Swimming-Pool Safety

The aquatics program, like playgrounds, has a high risk of injury. Certified lifeguards should be ever vigilant. Helpful NRPA aquatics-program training materials include:

- *The Aquatic Facility Operator Manual*
- *Renting Personal Watercraft Successfully*
- *Better Beaches*
- *Encyclopedia of Aquatic Codes and Standards*
- *Boating Fundamentals: A Manual for Safe Boating*

Special Populations

Departments must follow the Americans with Disabilities Act (ADA) (1991) by making facilities accessible to the disabled. The National Institute on Recreation Inclusion, run by the NRPA, provides assistance in creating inclusive facilities and recreational programs. Departments should remove physical barriers (for example, install a swimming pool lift), inform the disabled about recreational opportunities, place the disabled on advisory committees, train staff to serve the disabled, and transport the disabled to programs.[5] The NRPA offers the training course, *Sports and Recreation for the Disabled,* as well as these therapeutic-recreation materials:

- The Best of Therapeutic Recreation Journal: Aging
- The Best of Therapeutic Recreation Journal: Assessment
- The Best of Outdoor Adventure Programming in Therapeutic Recreation
- The Best of Therapeutic Recreation Journal: Leisure Services
- Guidelines for the Administration of Therapeutic Recreation Services
- Preparing for a Career in Therapeutic Recreation
- Standards of Practice for Paraprofessionals in Therapeutic Recreation
- Impacting Public Policy: An Advocacy Manual for Therapeutic Recreation
- ADA Self-Evaluation Handbook and Checklist

Older Adults

As the baby boomers born after World War II move into retirement, departments are finding an increasing demand from them for recreational activities. Indeed, some large departments operate facilities dedicated for use by senior citizens. Departments of all sizes should offer programming for seniors. Moreover, seniors make excellent volunteers, sharing their wisdom and time with others.

Performance Measurement

Among the recreation-performance measures are:

Facilities

- Number of park acres per 1,000 residents
- Number of facilities (for example, baseball fields, tennis courts, nature trails, playgrounds, and recreation centers) per x amount of population

Swimming

- Percent of times that the pool water meets required chemical and physical standards
- Number of lifeguards as a percent of the number of pool-area visitors

General Participation

- Percent of eligible youth participating in programs (for example, baseball, soccer, swimming)
- Percent of population participating in specialty classes (such as cooking, scuba, ballroom dancing)
- Percent of disabled population participating in programs designated for them

Consumer Satisfaction

- Percent of youth and adults satisfied with programs and facilities

BUILDINGS AND GROUNDS MAINTENANCE[6]

In all but a temperate climate, parks maintenance is seasonal in nature. Temporary workers are hired to maintain parks and facilities during the busy summer months. Much maintenance work, like operating a mechanical mower is dangerous. Employees should thus follow the OSHA standard for mowing and temps should receive the same amount of training as their full-time counterparts.

Spraying chemicals can be dangerous as well. Toxic sprays pose more of a risk on a breezy day. Chemical handlers should be certified and follow the OSHA spraying standard. A hazardous-material warning sign should be posted outside an area being sprayed. Both the EPA and the state cooperative extension agency offer chemical-application training.

Work Planning

Departments may prepare a work plan for each maintenance task, specifying the method, crew size, type of equipment, and quantity and quality of work to be accomplished. Some departments provide maintenance workers with a photo of the desired maintenance outcome (for example, the mowed grass, trimmed hedge, planted flower bed). Sometimes weather conditions force workers inside; therefore, the maintenance plan should schedule indoor maintenance activities (such as sign repair and painting) during inclement weather and the winter months.

Building Maintenance

The department should maintain a current inventory of its grounds, facilities, and equipment that details their condition, age, and amount of usage. The cleanliness of a facility should be the responsibility of the entire staff, not just the maintenance workers. The department may establish building-maintenance standards, specifying the amount of time that should be taken to perform particular tasks (such as wax a floor, clean a bathroom, replace lightbulbs). A preventive-maintenance program schedules parts replacement, cleaning, routine inspections, maintenance, and alarm testing.

Departments should educate the public not to litter. The *Clean and Beautiful Program* is designed for this purpose. Other recommended building-maintenance practices include:

- Conveniently locating trash receptors
- Promptly replacing burnt-out lamps
- Regularly cleaning light fixtures
- Painting and replacing signs

Grounds Maintenance

The work plan profiles the physical conditions in each park and at each facility, including the type of terrain (for example, banked turf, shrub bed, flower bed, hedge), plot boundaries, plot conditions, conditions of site objects (such as signs, hydrants, picnic tables, benches, and so forth), and a geographic description of the area (for example, acres of turf, acres of shrub beds, yards of banked turf, yards of hedges). The NRPA recommends six maintenance levels, depending on the type of site:

1. *State-of-the-Art Maintenance.* In a high visibility, high-use area, such as a public square or government's grounds.
2. *High-Level Maintenance.* In typical-use areas like a playground, ball field, park, or recreation center.
3. *Moderate-Level Maintenance.* In low-visitation venues.
4. *Moderate Low-Level Maintenance.* In still lower-visitation venues.
5. *Minimum-Level Maintenance.* In areas unaffordable to maintain.

6. *Natural-Area Maintenance.* In natural areas that require no or slight (such as biannual) maintenance.

The NRPA also recommends maintenance outcomes for areas like flower beds, baseball/softball fields, shrubs, soccer and football fields, and turf, examples of which are shown below:[7]

- *Turf and Grass.* Grow grass to its normal length before cutting; cut turf at a length of 1-1/4 to 1-1/2 inches; aerate turf annually; measure soil content with a hydrometer; reduce thatching with vertical mowing, a power rake, aeration, and a top dressing.
- *Ball Fields.* Design and maintain fields according to NRPA standards.
- *Plants.* Select appropriate plants for particular parks and recreation areas.

If the department manages a golf course, specialized training is necessary. Helpful resources include the *Grounds Maintenance* magazine, Grounds Maintenance Society booklets on subjects like turf maintenance and chemical usage, and golf-course maintenance and design assistance from the American Golf Foundation.

Performance Measurement

Among grounds-maintenance performance measures are:

Mowing

- Percent of grass not exceeding x amount of inches
- Percent of areas not covered by x percent of weeds
- Amount of park area mowed per work hour

Flowers

- Percent of flower areas that are weed-free

Trees

- Percent of trees with no sucker growth or injuries
- Percent of area with no leaves on the ground

Repairs

- Percent of work orders completed within the standard time

Safety

- Frequency and severity of accidents
- Percent of facilities inspected on schedule
- Percent of safety-related repairs made within the standard time
- Percent of vandalism calls responded to within the standard time

NOTES

1. For an excellent history of parks and recreation, see Ellis Armstrong, ed., *History of Public Works in the United States: 1775–1976* (Washington, DC: The American Public Works Association, 1977).

2. Ibid., 561.

3. Ibid., 562.

4. For an excellent discussion of recreation services, see Richard G. Kraus and Joseph E. Curtis, *Creative Management in Recreation, Parks, and Leisure Services,* 6th ed. (New York: McGraw-Hill, 2000).

5. For a description of departments that have implemented inclusive recreation programs, see Evilina Moulder, "Focus on Inclusion: Parks and Recreation Departments Welcome All," *Public Management* (Washington, DC: International City/County Management Association, August 2003).

6. Two excellent guides to grounds management are: NRPA, *Operational Guidelines for Grounds Management* (Ashburn, VA: NRPA, 2001) and Robert Sternloff and Rodger Warren, *Parks and Recreation Management,* 3rd ed. (Scottsdale, AZ: Publishing Horizons, 1993).

7. See NRPA, *Operational Guidelines for Grounds Management.*

FOR FURTHER READING

Kraus, Richard, and Joseph Curtis. *Creative Management in Recreation, Parks and Leisure Services,* 6th ed. New York: McGraw-Hill, 2001.

National Recreation and Park Association (NRPA). *Operational Guidelines for Grounds Management.* Ashburn, VA: NRPA, 2001.

Sternloff, Rodger, and Rodger Warren. *Parks and Recreation Management,* 3rd ed. Scottsdale, AZ: Publishing Horizons, 1993.

Part IV

Support Services

16

Public Equipment

Technological advancements in vehicles have required more skilled mechanics. Among them have been the automatic transmission (1904), four-wheel drive (1908), the self-starter (1911), hand-operated windshield wipers and rearview mirrors (1916), four-wheel hydraulic brakes (1920), front-wheel drive (1929), V-12 and V-16 engines (1930), air-conditioning (1939), the high-compression engine using high-octane fuel (1948), air suspension (1957), the "four-on-the-floor" gearshift (1963), the diesel car (1968), steering-column ignition locks (1970), catalytic converters (1975), fuel injection (1976), the microcomputer system with digital display (1980), antilock brakes (1985), air bags (1986), and side-impact air bags (1996). Long gone are the days of the "shade tree", do-it-yourself mechanic; mechanics now need thorough knowledge of computerized diagnostics.

To assure that technicians could repair more mechanically complex vehicles, the National Institute for Automotive Service Excellence (ASE), founded in 1972, created a program that certifies mechanics to repair particular vehicles (for example, automobiles and medium/heavy trucks) with particular skills (for example, engine machinist, alternative-fuel technician, and parts specialist). There are two ASE certification levels:

- *Technician*—Must have experience and pass an exam every two years.
- *Master Technician*—Must master additional skills and pass an exam every five years.

MANAGEMENT

Local governments can organize fleet management in five ways:

- A separate garage in each major department (such as fire, public works, water and sewer)

- A single garage to serve all but the fire department, which has its own mechanic(s) because fire apparatus are specialized
- A single garage that serves all departments, including fire
- A single garage does basic work but contracts out specialized work like major accident repair
- All work is contracted out

A centralized operation is more effective than a decentralized because a centralized department has the authority to rotate underutilized vehicles among all departments to achieve optimal usage. A centralized department can also operate a system-wide preventive-maintenance (PM) program with the authority to require departments to adhere to the PM schedule.

The garage should be well designed and equipped because inadequate equipment and shop space adversely affect productivity. The American Public Works Association (APWA) has prepared an excellent facilities guide: *Vehicle Maintenance Facilities: A Planning Guide.*[1]

Policies

The governing board can set three vehicle-usage and -maintenance policies.

Vehicle-Replacement Policy

A vehicle-replacement policy establishes a time or amount of use after which vehicles should be replaced (for example, after five years of use or 75,000 miles). Empirical evidence shows that at the replacement point, replacement is more cost-effective than continuing use. Exceptions should be made, however, for vehicles with records of unusually high or low maintenance-and-repair costs. Vehicles with high costs ("lemons") should be replaced earlier; vehicles with low costs ("cream puffs") should be kept in use after their scheduled replacement date.

Vehicle Take-Home Policy

In some communities, the question of who should take home city-owned vehicles is an oft-discussed, sometimes heated issue. Particular personnel (such as the city manager, police chief, and fire chief), subject to being called back after work, are authorized to take home a car. Some communities also authorize off-duty police officers to take home police cars. Though more police cars must be purchased, more police vehicles on the road are believed to be a crime deterrent.

Travel Policy

Local units adopt a policy to authorize and reimburse travel-related expenses. The policy should require employees to drive a government-owned vehicle rather than their personal car when possible. The policy specifies the per-mile reimbursement rate to employees who must drive their cars on government business.

Contract Out Operations

Local jurisdictions with a small fleet typically contract out the work to a local garage, assigning one person to oversee the contracted work.[2] In North Carolina, counties with less than 150 vehicles usually contract out work.[3] Local units with somewhat larger fleets usually perform basic maintenance work, but usually contract out to a local garage specialized tasks like body work, major accident repair, and maintenance of fire equipment. Finally, large fleets usually perform all the work in-house.

Funding Options

Two funding options are possible:

- A general fund that pays for all costs
- A fleet-management internal-service fund (ISF), to which all departments pay their pro-rata share of the costs of vehicle maintenance, repair, and replacement (depreciation)

With an ISF, each department pays a monthly amount to cover the cost of maintenance, repair, and replacement. The rate is based on a per-mile charge for cars and a per-hour rate for heavy equipment like a motor grader. An ISF has three advantages over the general fund method. First, a centralized ISF allows the equipment manager to switch underused equipment among departments. Second, unexpected repairs are charged to the using department's budget, causing it to take more responsibility over its vehicles and drivers. Third, an ISF permits replacement funds to be set aside each year. Lacking replacement funding, jurisdictions find themselves with many fully depreciated vehicles that have outlived their scheduled useful life and, as such, incur excessive maintenance and repair costs.

Vehicle Purchasing

Fleet managers should prepare specifications with input from departments. Specifications for some equipment and vehicles are highly specialized. In such cases, specification-writing assistance is available from the APWA state chapter, the League of Municipalities, the Association of County Commissioners, or neighboring large local jurisdictions.

There are three financing options: cash, a reserve fund, and debt.[4] Financing from available cash or a reserve fund avoids interest expense. However, local units with insufficient cash or reserves may have to borrow money from a bank with a revolving line of credit or enter into a lease-purchase agreement. Local units sometimes can buy vehicles on state contract. States buy vehicles for themselves and localities at a lower unit cost due to economies of scale.

Some departments purchase vehicles on a *life-cycle-cost* (LCC) basis. LCC determines the overall cost of ownership including:

- The original purchase price
- The vehicle's estimated operating, maintenance, and repair costs over its life
- The vehicle's value when resold

Though the purchase price of one vehicle may be higher than another, its LCC may be less. The LCC method is especially appropriate for purchasing specialized, high operating-cost such as street sweepers, sewer-pipe vacuum trucks, and pipe video-imaging equipment.

When a new vehicle is purchased, the replaced vehicle should be resold or junked; otherwise "fleet creep" occurs. Fleet creep also occurs when a new vehicle is unnecessarily acquired instead of giving more use to an underutilized vehicle.

MAINTENANCE AND REPAIR[5]

Mechanics should adhere to OSHA regulations and the EPA's underground fuel-storage and air-quality emission standards. The fleet manager should set service objectives measuring:

- The percentage of jobs returned for rework
- The turnaround time to make a repair

Many private-sector garages use *The Chilton Guide* or *Mitchell Manual* to set standard times to complete particular repair and maintenance jobs. However, local jurisdictions usually do not use these standards, because some of their vehicles (such as police cars) have been modified. Still, a public fleet manager can establish repair-and-maintenance time standards, but they should only be used as a general performance guide. If a time standard is unrealistically too short, a mechanic may feel pressured to sacrifice quality. The fleet manager should thus set time standards with input from mechanics.

A priority-repair system should be in effect to ensure that a critically needed vehicle (for example, an ambulance, police car, garbage truck) receives higher priority than less critically needed vehicles.

Fleet managers should record maintenance-and-repair work done on each vehicle. These historical costs aid future purchasing decisions. For example, if maintaining a Chevy police cruiser proves to be more costly than maintaining a Ford, specifications may be written to buy the better performing vehicle.

Because the cost of oil is only 2 percent of total maintenance costs, only the highest quality oil should be bought. Automated fuel-dispensing systems summarize fuel usage and mileage, which departments should analyze to identify fuel-inefficient vehicles.

Maintenance Agreement

Local governments often contract out infrequent, specialized maintenance jobs, such as glass replacement, radiator repair, bodywork, framework, front-end alignment, towing, and warranty work. The bid specification should require that the firm be located within a specified distance of the local jurisdiction to minimize transportation costs. However, warranty work on some vehicles (such as an Oshkosh truck, or an Elgin and Tymco sweeper) may only be done at a too distant location. In such a case, the department either does the warranty work itself or contracts it out to another firm; but in either event, requires the manufacturer to pay for the work.

A *total-cost warranty agreement* caps the time that vehicles can be unavailable due to manufacturer's repair work. After the time elapses, the dealer must furnish a replacement vehicle. Such an agreement is especially needed for frequently used heavy equipment such as dozers and pans that excavate dirt.

Preventive Maintenance (PM)

There are three types of PM. A general inspection, similar to an annual physical examination, is a basic check of a vehicle's major systems. For a comprehensive description of best practices, refer to: U.S. Environmental Protection Agency, *Cars and Light Trucks Inspection and Maintenance Best Practices,* available at http://www.epa.gov/oms/im.htm.

In the second type of PM, oil-and-lube, oil is changed, grease fittings are lubricated, and fluids are filled. Mechanics should take a hot oil sample to detect internal engine wear and oil contaminants. The mechanic visually inspects the vehicle for possible problems. For a comprehensive discussion

Figure 16.1   **Vehicle Maintenance**

Source: FedCenter.gov—Federal Facilities Environmental Stewardship & Compliance Assistance Center. Available at http://www.fedcenter.gov/assistance/facilitytour/vehicle/.

of best practices, refer to: U.S. Environmental Protection Agency, *Oil Life Extension: Best Environmental Practices for Fleet Management*, available at http://www.epa.gov/region09/waste11p2/autofleet/oil/pdf.

Finally, the third PM type, a state vehicle inspection, includes (1) a state-required annual emissions and safety test for passenger cars and light trucks and (2) a safety test for large equipment and diesel-operated vehicles.

The fleet manager assigns each vehicle to a PM service schedule, specifying its PM level. The PM schedule should be adjusted based on the amount of fuel consumed, months since the last PM, and number of hours operated. An automated-fuel dispensing system can generate the PM schedule. PM work should be done after a vehicle's assigned work is completed. Clean vehicles make a statement about a local unit's commitment to providing good service (see Figure 16.1).

To reduce equipment abuse, mechanics should record whether repairs were of a normal nature or due to operator misuse, such as not watching fluid levels or being in a preventable accident. The fleet manager should report equipment abuse to the department head for investigation and possible disciplinary action. Among measures that promote safe vehicle usage are:

- *Safe-Driving Program.* Recognize and reward employees who have operated a vehicle for twelve consecutive months without a preventable accident.

- *Accident-Review Board.* Determine and eliminate the causes of preventable accidents.
- *Preventable-Accident Policy.* Discipline employees for causing preventable accidents.
- *Vehicle-Abuse Policy.* Discipline employees for vehicle misuse.
- *Inspection Policy.* Require operators to inspect their vehicles daily by checking tire pressures, lubricant levels, belt conditions, fluid levels, lights, and accessories.
- *Driver-Training Program.* Teach safe driving.

Parts Inventory

Local governments use three types of inventory systems. The least accurate is simply eyeballing stock levels and reordering parts when they appear to be low. A more accurate system requires the parts manager to record purchases and withdrawals manually and to set maximum and minimum replacement-stock levels. Most accurate, *a real-time computerized system* automatically schedules PM, based on usage data, assigns maintenance-and-repair work, tracks in-house and contracted garage work, records the condition of equipment, and orders new parts based on an *economic-order-quantity* formula that calculates optimal reorder times and amounts. A fleet operation with over thirty vehicles is suitable for an automated system.[6]

Performance Measurement

Among the performance measures are:

Maintenance and Repair

- Whether service standards have been met
- Percent of vehicles that are returned for rework
- Percent of service and minor repair jobs completed within x number of days
- Ratio of mechanics to the number of pieces of rolling stock
- Average number of miles between breakdowns
- Percent of PM inspections completed on schedule
- Time taken to perform jobs (for example, tune up, oil change, tire change)

Safety

- Percent of preventable accidents among all occurrences
- Severity and frequency of accidents
- Number of vehicle-abuse cases

NOTES

1. American Public Works Association (APWA), Special Report No. 51 *Vehicle Maintenance Facilities: A Planning Guide* (Chicago: APWA, 1984).

2. Governor's Center for Local Government Services, *Public Works Manual.* Available at http://www.newpa.com/get-local-govsupport/publications/index.aspx.

3. Matthew Michel, Matthew Bronson, and Matthew Roylance, "County Vehicle Services: Preventing Wear, Repairing Tear," *Popular Government* (Winter 2000), 32.

4. For a more detailed discussion of vehicle replacement financing, see Tim Ammon, "Vehicle Replacement Planning 101," *Public Management* (November 2003).

5. For an in-depth discussion of equipment management, see APWA, *Managing Public Equipment* (Chicago: APWA, 1989).

6. *Managing Public Equipment,* 84.

FOR FURTHER READING

American Public Works Association. *Managing Public Equipment.* Chicago: APWA, 1989.

17

Public Buildings and Facilities

History

Buildings are far more complex to maintain now because of technological advancements. Workers expect buildings to be cool in the summer, warm in the winter, safe, well lit, equipped with modern voice-and-data communication systems and accessible to the disabled. Air- conditioning, invented by Willis Carrier in 1902, greatly improved worker productivity, especially in warmer climates. Before central air-conditioning, occupants relied on fans and open windows for ventilation and cooling. Today's buildings usually have sealed windows and are air-fed through a central heating, ventilation, and air-conditioning (HVAC) system (see Figure 17.1).

Management

Local governments maintain a wide variety of facilities, including police and fire stations, city halls and county courthouses, water- and sewage-treatment plants, civic centers, garages and maintenance complexes. These buildings must be cleaned, painted, reroofed, and occasionally redesigned.

The facilities manager should assemble a team with the appropriate mix of skills (HVAC, electrical, plumbing, and so forth). With licensed staff, more work can be done in-house. The facilities manager should prepare a *facilities master plan*, which is a long-range (for example, ten-year) forecast of staffing, space, technology, building-security, and operational needs.[1] The forecast plans for new building sites, code-compliance provisions, space-use standards, e-government capabilities, aesthetics, and image.

Public facilities have very long lives. The utmost care should therefore go into their planning. Working in an ill-designed, poorly heated and air-conditioned building with inadequate space is extremely frustrating and

Figure 17.1   **Federal Building**

Source: U.S. General Services Administration.

counterproductive. In designing a building, the architect should solicit the views of all affected stakeholders, especially the janitorial staff to ensure that they have adequate maintenance space (mechanical rooms, custodial closets). The design should also consider energy costs. Local governments may use *life-cycle costing,* which considers not only the building's construction cost but also its operational costs (such as heating and air-conditioning).

MAINTENANCE

A clean, well-maintained, well-lighted, safe facility sends an unmistakable message to the public and employees. Though sometimes taken for granted, custodial staff are the behind-the-scenes workers who make a facility a welcoming place in which to work. Facilities must comply with the Americans with Disabilities Act,[2] fire codes, building codes (electrical, HVAC, plumbing, and construction), and Occupational Safety and Health Administration requirements. Maintenance problems encountered in older buildings sometimes include lead-based paint, asbestos, underground storage tanks, mold, and pests like termites and bats.

Assets Inventory

Governmental Accounting Standards Board Standard 34 requires a local jurisdiction to depreciate its assets, including its buildings, building improvements, machinery, equipment, vehicles, land, and infrastructure such as roads, bridges, sewer and water systems. The rate of depreciation is based on the equipment's or structure's expected useful life. Other information to be kept on buildings includes:

- Gross square footage
- Date of construction (including dates of additions)
- Type of construction
- Number of floors
- Acquisition date, value, and current replacement value
- Type of HVAC system
- Electrical system's capacity
- Type of roof and date last reroofed

Building information is obtained from a variety of sources, including: "as built" blueprints, electronic computer-aided drawings, and the contractor's turnover documents after construction.

The *facilities-condition index* (FCI) is often used to estimate the physical condition of a facility. The FCI evaluates the percentage of a building that is in poor condition.

- Good condition: 0 to 5 percent FCI
- Fair condition: 5 to 10 percent FCI
- Poor condition: 10 to 30 percent FCI
- Critical condition: Greater than 30 percent FCI[3]

Maintenance

A preventive-maintenance (PM) program prolongs equipment life and reduces equipment breakdowns. Manufacturers recommend PM schedules for HVAC (filter and belt replacement, lubrication), the electrical system, safety and security systems, elevators, and plumbing. A computerized maintenance-management system (CMM) can schedule PM work. If a CMM is unaffordable, PM schedules can be recorded on a spreadsheet or in a database, which provides a pop-up reminder of when service is due.

The facilities manager, with input from custodial staff, may establish repair-

and-maintenance-service standards for routine work like HVAC maintenance and lightbulb replacement. The manager may also track performance on other tasks like hanging a bulletin board or assembling furniture. The facilities manager should regularly inspect work to ensure high quality and customer satisfaction. To reduce costs, computer-chip sensors can automatically regulate thermostats and security systems, turn lights on and off, and even notify the building staff when a rodent is caught in a trap.[4]

The facilities manager should record maintenance-and-repair work performed on each building and its associated systems. A work-order system may be used to assign work. In this system, maintenance staff record the time they work, their travel time, and the supplies and equipment used. Work performed by outside contractors is recorded as well. Governments should contract out infrequent, specialized maintenance work when doing so is cost-effective.

Frequently used supplies should be kept in inventory. These materials include air filters, motor-pulley belts for HVAC equipment, fluorescent-light tubes and compact fluorescent bulbs, light ballasts, toilet and flush valve-repair kits, acoustic-tile ceiling panels, and touch-up paint. Where possible, makes and models materials should be standardized.

Performance Measurement

For a complete, authoritative discussion of facilities-maintenance measures, refer to David Ammons, *Performance Measures and Benchmarks in Local Government Facilities Maintenance*.[5] Among the measures Ammons discusses are:

General Maintenance

- Percent of preventive-maintenance work orders completed within x days of issuance
- Number of facility audits completed
- Percent of HVAC units in compliance with maintenance contract
- Percent of work repairs processed within x number of days
- Percent of high-priority repairs completed within twenty-four hours

Custodial

- Percent of time restroom-cleaning standards that are met
- Percent of time cleaning standards for other rooms that are met

Electrical/HVAC

- Percent of time temperatures in city buildings that are between 66 and 76° F
- Percent of time specified lighting standards that are met

NOTES

1. For a discussion of facilities master planning done by Aurora, Colorado, see Amy Tabor, "Facilities Master Planning," *Public Management* (April 2004): 14–18.

2. The standards can be accessed at http://www.ada.gov/stdspdf.htm.

3. For more discussion of the FCI, refer to Don Briselden and David Cain, "The Facilities Condition Index: A Useful Tool for Capital Asset Planning," *Facilities Manager* 17 (2001): 33–37.

4. "A World of Connections," *The Economist* (April 28–May 4, 2007), 9.

5. David Ammons, Erin S. Norfleet, and Brian T. Coble, *Performance Measures and Benchmarks in Local Government Facilities Maintenance* (Washington, DC: International City/County Management Association and the School of Government, University of North Carolina, 2002).

Glossary

A

activated sludge treatment system Mechanical aerators pump air into a mixture of raw sewage and heavy concentrations of aerobic microorganisms to stimulate bacterial reduction. (*Chapter 10*)

ADA (Americans with Disabilities Act) (*Chapter 15*)

adhesion principle Organic materials and chemicals stick to the surface of an adsorbent through complex physical forces and chemical actions. (*Chapter 9*)

advanced life support (ALS) (*Chapter 4*)

aeration Exposing water to the atmosphere to remove odors and restore depleted oxygen. (*Chapter 9*)

ALA (American Library Association) (*Chapter 14*)

all-paramedic emergency response system Provides a standard level of service, regardless of the type of call. (*Chapter 4*)

ALS (advanced life support) (*Chapter 4*)

American Library Association (ALA) (*Chapter 14*)

American National Standard Institute (ANSI) (*Chapter 13*)

American Public Works Association (APWA) (*Chapter 11 and Chapter 16*)

Americans with Disabilities Act (ADA) (*Chapter 15*)

American Water Works Association (AWWA) (*Chapter 9*)

anaerobic digestion A method of stabilizing sludge from wastewater treatment by breaking down organic matter, changing it into methane and carbon dioxide. (*Chapter 10*)

ANSI (American National Standard Institute) (*Chapter 13*)

apparatus Fire service vehicles. (*Chapter 3*)

APWA (American Public Works Association) (*Chapter 11 and Chapter 16*)

ASE (National Institute for Automotive Service Excellence) (*Chapter 16*)

AWWA (American Water Works Association) (*Chapter 9*)

B

backflow Reverse flow of contaminants in a water system. (*Chapter 9*)

backward shift rotation From evening to day shift. (*Chapter 2*)

backwashing Reversing and increasing the water's flow during treatment to flush accumulated debris and particles out of the filter. (*Chapter 9*)

basic-life-support (BLS) (*Chapter 4*)

biochemical oxygen demand (BOD) Rate at which microorganisms use oxygen to decompose organic material. (*Chapter 10*)

biological filtration Uses microbes to break down substances in water. (*Chapter 9*)

biosolid Sludge used beneficially. (*Chapter 10*)

BLS (basic-life-support) (*Chapter 4*)

BOD (biochemical oxygen demand) Rate at which microorganisms use oxygen to decompose organic material. (*Chapter 10*)

C

CAD (computer-aided-dispatch) (*Chapter 2 and Chapter 3*)

CALEA (Commission on Accreditation for Law Enforcement Agencies, Inc.) Accredits police departments in forty-three states. (*Chapter 2*)

camera inspection Preferred method to examine a large sewer. (*Chapter 10*)

CAO (chief administrative officer) (*Chapter 1*)

capital improvement program (CIP) (*Chapter 8*)

CCU (critical care unit) (*Chapter 4*)

cell The basic building block of a landfill operation. (*Chapter 12*)

Center for Public Safety Excellence (CPSE) Formerly the Commission on Fire Accreditation International. (*Chapter 3*)

CCTV (closed-circuit television) (*Chapter 10*)

central heating, ventilation, and air-conditioning (HVAC) (*Chapter 17*)

Certified Floodplain Manager (CFM) (*Chapter 5*)

CFAI (Commission on Fire Accreditation International) *See* Center for Public Safety Excellence (CPSE)

chief administrative officer (CAO) (*Chapter 1*)

chip seal A liquid asphalt mixture covered by a layer of uniform-sized aggregate chips of crushed gravel. (*Chapter 11*)

chlorination The most common method used for disinfection of wastewater. (*Chapter 10*)

chute time The time from the receipt of an emergency call before the vehicle gets rolling. (*Chapter 4*)

CIP (capital improvement program) (*Chapter 8*)

citizen surveillance Informed citizens team with police to prevent and solve crimes. (*Chapter 2*)

clearance rate The percentage of cases that have been cleared by arrest. (*Chapter 2*)

closed-circuit television (CCTV) (*Chapter 10*)

CMM (computerized maintenance-management system) (*Chapter 17*)

coagulation Water-treatment process in which one or more chemical coagulants are rapidly mixed with water to form particles, called floc. (*Chapter 9*)

collection plan A library's blueprint for the collection and maintenance of print and nonprint materials, both circulating and noncirculating. (*Chapter 14*)

combined sewage system Water from storm drains is added to the wastewater stream. (*Chapter 10*)

Commission on Accreditation for Law Enforcement Agencies, Inc. (CALEA) Accredits police departments in forty-three states. (*Chapter 2*)

Commission on Fire Accreditation International (CFAI) *See* Center for Public Safety Excellence (CPSE)

community-oriented-policing (COP) Officers do not simply react to incidents but partner with the public, other public agencies, and businesses to prevent and solve crimes. (*Chapter 2*)

community-wide survey Asks citizens how satisfied they are with police services in general. (*Chapter 2*)

company fire inspection A routine check of standpipes, sprinkler valves, obstructed exits, and fire extinguishers. (*Chapter 3*)

compaction station A large solid-waste transfer station where wasted is compacted before it is transferred. (*Chapter 12*)

composting A method of stabilizing sludge from wastewater treatment by adding a bulking agent, building a compost pile, aerobically decomposing the solids. (*Chapter 10*)

computer-aided-dispatch (CAD) (*Chapter 2 and Chapter 3*)

computerized maintenance-management system (CMM) (*Chapter 17*)

conciliation plan Required by the EPA in the event of a wastewater pretreatment program violation. (*Chapter 10*)

conservation plan A wastewater-treatment plant's strategy to reduce energy costs and conserve water. (*Chapter 10*)

constructed-wetlands method Releases treated wastewater into a natural wetland or a constructed natural area before its release into a sound or river. (*Chapter 10*)

Continuous Review, Evaluation, and Weeding (CREW) A methodology for weeding a library's collection. (*Chapter 14*)

conventional-filtration plant Uses sedimentation to remove most suspended material from water. (*Chapter 9*)

conviction rates The percentage of cases that led to conviction and the percentage of cases that led to a conviction on the charge first filed. (*Chapter 2*)

COP (community-oriented-policing) Officers do not simply react to incidents but partner with the public, other public agencies, and businesses to prevent and solve crimes. (*Chapter 2*)

CPSE (Center for Public Safety Excellence) Formerly the Commission on Fire Accreditation International. (*Chapter 3*)

CREW (Continuous Review, Evaluation, and Weeding) A methodology for weeding a library's collection. (*Chapter 14*)

critical care unit (CCU) (*Chapter 4*)

D

DDO (disposal-diversion ordinance) A waste-reduction program component that mandates that products like aluminum and corrugated cardboard be diverted from the waste stream. (*Chapter 12*)

declining-block water rate structure Charges the highest rate to residential customers, the next highest to commercial, and the lowest to industrial customers. (*Chapter 9*)

deinstitutionalization Moving patients from hospitals to the community. (*Chapter 7*)

de minimis variance For a minor zoning deviation, such as a lot being a few feet short of a one-acre requirement. (*Chapter 8*)

Department of Agriculture Regulates the inspection of food establishments. (*Chapter 7*)

Department of Health Monitors and enforces health policies, provides training and technical assistance, and allocates federal and state money to agencies statewide. (*Chapter 7*)

Department of Homeland Security (DHS) (*Chapter 3 and Chapter 5*)

Department of Transportation (DOT) (*Chapter 11*)

dewatering A method of stabilizing sludge from wastewater treatment by mechanically removing water from the residuals to reduce the drying time. (*Chapter 10*)

DHS (Department of Homeland Security) (*Chapter 3 and Chapter 5*)

diatomaceous-earth filtration Feeds diatomaceous earth to a water-filtering unit. (*Chapter 9*)

dimensional variance When a property does not quite comply with yard or setback requirements. (*Chapter 8*)

direct-discharge station A large solid-waste transfer station that has two operating floors. (*Chapter 12*)

direct-filtration plant Does not include sedimentation to remove suspended material from water. (*Chapter 9*)

disposal-diversion ordinance (DDO) A waste-reduction program component that mandates that products like aluminum and corrugated cardboard be diverted from the waste stream. (*Chapter 12*)

domestic-violence policy Specifies when to make an arrest and/or to take other actions, such as escorting a victim to a shelter. (*Chapter 2*)

DOT (Department of Transportation) (*Chapter 11*)

dry tap Made in an empty water main. (*Chapter 9*)

drying A method of stabilizing sludge from wastewater treatment by mechanically air-drying the residuals. (*Chapter 10*)

E

economic-order-quantity A formula that calculates optimal reorder times and amounts. (*Chapter 16*)

EIA (environmental-impact assessment) Estimates the environmental impact of a particular project. (*Chapter 8*)

EIS (environmental-impact statement) (*Chapter 8*)

Emergency Management Accreditation Program (EMAP) A voluntary accreditation process for state and local emergency-management programs. (*Chapter 5*)

Emergency Management Plan (EMP) Assigns standard operating guidelines with regard to logistics, media relations, the line of authority, and the recovery plan. (*Chapter 5*)

emergency medical services (EMS) (*Chapter 4*)

emergency medical technician (EMT) (*Chapter 4*)

emergency operating plan (EOP) Identifies potential hazards; flowcharts emergency procedures; lists emergency contacts; establishes the chain of command in the event of an emergency; and assesses a plant's vulnerability to a terrorist attack. (*Chapter 5 and Chapter 10*)

emergency operations center (EOC) (*Chapter 5*)

eminent domain Power to seize land and property for public use. (*Chapter 8*)

EMP (Emergency Management Plan) Assigns standard operating guidelines with regard to logistics, media relations, the line of authority, and the recovery plan. (*Chapter 5*)

EMS (emergency medical services) (*Chapter 4*)

EMT (emergency medical technician) (*Chapter 4*)

enhanced 911 system Identifies the caller's number, name, and location. (*Chapter 3*)

environmental-impact assessment (EIA) Estimates the environmental impact of a particular project. (*Chapter 8*)

environmental-impact statement (EIS) (*Chapter 8*)

Environmental Protection Agency (EPA) (*Chapter 9*)

EOC (emergency operations center) (*Chapter 5*)

EOP (emergency operating plan) Identifies potential hazards; flowcharts emergency procedures; lists emergency contacts; establishes the chain of command in the event of an emergency; and assesses a plant's vulnerability to a terrorist attack. (*Chapter 5 and Chapter 10*)

F

facilities-condition index (FCI) (*Chapter 17*)

facilities master plan A long-range forecast of staffing, space, technology, building-security, and operational needs. (*Chapter 17*)

fats, oils, and grease (FOG) (*Chapter 10*)

FCI (facilities-condition index) (*Chapter 17*)

Federal Emergency Management Agency (FEMA) (*Chapter 5*)

field training officer (FTO) (*Chapter 2*)

flashover stage Occurs when a fire spreads beyond the room of origin. (*Chapter 3*)

floc A gelatinous substance that bonds with silt to remove the solids from water. (*Chapter 9*)

flocculation Gently mixes the water and coagulants to form larger, heavier, more settleable floc. (*Chapter 9 and Chapter 10*)

FOG (fats, oils, and grease) (*Chapter 10*)

force account Maintenance work done by government employees. (*Chapter 11*)

force main Carries waste in pipes made of pressure-ductile iron, steel, or PVC. (*Chapter 10*)

forward shift rotation From day to evening shift. (*Chapter 2*)

free-patrol time Officers are not responding to service calls. (*Chapter 2*)

FTO (field training officer) (*Chapter 2*)

full-scale exercise Completely simulates an entire disaster scenario in conditions as close as possible to an actual event. (*Chapter 5*)

full-time firefighter Paid an annual salary and fringe benefits. (*Chapter 3*)

functional exercise Evaluation of emergency response procedures in a scenario-driven setting. (*Chapter 5*)

G

GAAP (generally accepted accounting principles) *(Chapter 9)*

GAC (granular activated carbon) *(Chapter 9)*

gallons per minute (GPM) *(Chapter 3)*

generally accepted accounting principles (GAAP) *(Chapter 9)*

Geographic Information System (GIS) *(Chapter 2, Chapter 3, Chapter 8, and Chapter 11)*

GPM (gallons per minute) *(Chapter 3)*

granular activated carbon (GAC) Chemical used in adsorption. *(Chapter 9)*

granular materials. Settle constantly and do not change shape or size. *(Chapter 10)*

gravity filter Moves the water through a filter medium by gravity. The three types of gravity filters are slow-sand, rapid-sand, and high-rate. *(Chapter 9)*

grid Water system design that eliminates expensive-to-maintain dead-end lines. *(Chapter 9)*

H

hazards in the United States (HAZUS) A free FEMA program that utilizes GIS software to compute and display a natural disaster's likely effect on prominent buildings, critical facilities, health-care programs, the transportation system, and utilities. *(Chapter 5)*

heavy rescue vehicle Fire service apparatus that is principally used in rescue operations and usually does not carry water or a large ladder. *(Chapter 3)*

hospital time The time it takes for an emergency vehicle to convey the patient to the hospital and be available again for dispatch. *(Chapter 4)*

Humane Society of the United States (HSUS) *(Chapter 6)*

HVAC (central heating, ventilation, and air-conditioning) *(Chapter 17)*

I

IACP (International Association of Chiefs of Police) (*Chapter 2*)

IAFIS (Integrated Automated Fingerprint Identification System) (*Chapter 2*)

IC (incident commander) Sets the overall objectives and strategy for response to an incident. (*Chapter 3 and Chapter 5*)

ICC (International Congress Code) A uniform set of eleven construction codes (such as plumbing, mechanical, electrical). (*Chapter 8*)

ICMA (International City/County Management Association) (*Chapter 3 and Chapter 11*)

ICS (incident command system) (*Chapter 5*)

I/I (infiltration and inflow) Infiltration occurs when groundwater enters the distribution system through defective pipes, pipe joints, connections, or manholes. *Inflow* is storm water that enters the system from roof gutter drains, cellar drains, storm- and sanitary-sewer cross connections, street washing, and hydrant tests. (*Chapter 10*)

IMS (National Service Incident Management System) A consortium consisting of federal, state, and local government fire services. (*Chapter 3*)

incident command system (ICS) (*Chapter 5*)

incident commander (IC) Sets the overall objectives and strategy for response to an incident. (*Chapter 3 and Chapter 5*)

incineration A method of stabilizing sludge from wastewater treatment, after dewatering the residuals. (*Chapter 10*)

incipient The stage in a fire when flames occur in the immediate area of origin. (*Chapter 3*)

inclining-block water rate structure Charges commercial and industrial customers higher rates than residential customers. (*Chapter 9*)

industrial waste pretreatment program (IWPP) (*Chapter 10*)

infiltration and inflow (I/I) Infiltration occurs when groundwater enters the distribution system through defective pipes, pipe joints, connections, or manholes. *Inflow* is storm water that enters the system from roof gutter drains, cellar drains, storm- and sanitary-sewer cross connections, street washing, and hydrant tests. (*Chapter 10*)

Insurance Services Office (ISO) A nonprofit organization that serves property- and casualty-insurance agencies. (*Chapter 3*)

Integrated Automated Fingerprint Identification System (IAFIS) (*Chapter 2*)

internal-service fund (ISF) all funds pay their pro-rata share of the costs of fleet maintenance, repair, and replacement. (*Chapter 16*)

International Association of Chiefs of Police (IACP) (*Chapter 2*)

International Association of Fire Chiefs (IAFC) (*Chapter 3*)

International City/County Management Association (ICMA) (*Chapter 3 and Chapter 11*)

International City Management Association (ICMA) (*Chapter 1*)

International Congress Code (ICC) A uniform set of eleven construction codes (such as plumbing, mechanical, electrical). (*Chapter 8*)

ISF (internal-service fund) All funds pay their pro-rata share of the costs of fleet maintenance, repair, and replacement. (*Chapter 16*)

ISO (Insurance Services Office) A nonprofit organization that serves property- and casualty insurance agencies. (*Chapter 3*)

IWPP (Industrial waste pretreatment program) (*Chapter 10*)

J

job-order-cost system Charges the cost of time, equipment, and materials on a daily basis to both jobs and types of work. (*Chapter 11*)

L

ladder truck A fire service vehicle equipped with an aerial ladder and a tower ladder or platform. (*Chapter 3*)

lamping The least expensive and least effective method of inspecting a sewer pipe; it involves taking a cameral picture of a pipe's interior. (*Chapter 10*)

land-application method A wastewater treatment process in which residual sludge from a lagoon is sprayed on nearby land. (*Chapter 10*)

land-suitability analysis (LSA) Evaluates the suitability of environmentally sensitive sites like sanitary landfills. (*Chapter 8*)

LCC (life-cycle cost) A basis upon which purchasing and design decisions may be made. (*Chapter 16 and Chapter 17*)

leachate An acid-water solution formed by the liquification of waste materials in a landfill. (*Chapter 12*)

life-cycle cost (LCC) A basis upon which purchasing and design decisions may be made. (*Chapter 16 and Chapter 17*)

lift A series of cells, all the same height, in a landfill operation. (*Chapter 12*)

lime stabilization Handling sludge from wastewater treatment by adding lime to dewater solids on drying beds. (*Chapter 10*)

LSA (land-suitability analysis) Evaluates the suitability of environmentally sensitive sites like sanitary landfills. (*Chapter 8*)

M

master's degree in public administration (MPA) (*Chapter 1*)

material recovery facility (MRF) A transfer station that consolidates recycled products for sale. (*Chapter 12*)

Materials Safety Data Sheets (MSDS) Detail a chemical's characteristics, its possible hazards, first-aid procedures, and environmental concerns. (*Chapter 10*)

metropolitan planning organizations (MPOs) Consisting of the mayors and county chairs in an MPO district, they prioritize projects with input from their respective governing boards and CEOs. (*Chapter 8*)

MGD Million gallons per day. (*Chapter 10*)

minipumper A fire service vehicle that is a smaller version of the pumper and typically responds first to lesser emergencies like car, grass, trash, and brush fires. (*Chapter 3*)

mixed liquor The contents of the aeration tank in activated sludge wastewater treatment. (*Chapter 10*)

MO (modus operandi) (*Chapter 2*)

Model Charter Recommends the governmental structure, the selection and powers of local officials, and the method of executing basic functions, including taxing and borrowing power. (*Chapter 1*)

modus operandi (MO) (*Chapter 2*)

MPA (master's degree in public administration) (*Chapter 1*)

MPOs (metropolitan planning organizations) Consisting of the mayors and county chairs in an MPO district, they prioritize projects with input from their respective governing boards and CEOs. (*Chapter 8*)

MRF (material recovery facility) A transfer station that consolidates recycled products for sale. (*Chapter 12*)

MSDS (Materials Safety Data Sheets) Detail a chemical's characteristics, its possible hazards, first-aid procedures, and environmental concerns. (*Chapter 10*)

N

National Academy of Sciences (NAS) (*Chapter 4*)

National Environmental Policy Act (NEPA) Requires state and local governments to prepare an environmental impact statement (EIS) for a federally financed project with a significant environmental impact. (*Chapter 8*)

National Fire Protection Association (NFPA) The international fire-standard setting body. (*Chapter 3*)

National Flood Insurance Program (NFIP) (*Chapter 5*)

National Governors Association (NGA) (*Chapter 5*)

National Highway Traffic Safety Administration (NHTSA) (*Chapter 2*)

National Incident-Based Reporting System (NIBRS) (*Chapter 2*)

National Incident Fire Reporting System (NIFRS) For reporting fire incidence, fire causes, injuries, deaths, and property loss. (*Chapter 3*)

National Incident Management System (NIMS) Unifies the command of multiple jurisdictions at the scene of an emergency. (*Chapter 3 and Chapter 5*)

National Institute for Automotive Service Excellence (ASE) (*Chapter 16*)

National Municipal League (NML) (*Chapter 1*)

National Pollutant Discharge Elimination System (NPDES) (*Chapter 10*)

National Recreation and Park Association (NRPA) (*Chapter 15*)

National Service Incident Management System (IMS) A consortium consisting of federal, state, and local government fire services. (*Chapter 3*)

National Volunteer Organizations Active in Disaster (NVOAD) Includes thirty-four national, fifty-two state, and territorial and local organizations. (*Chapter 5*)

needed fire flow (NFF) The amount of water required to control a fire. (*Chapter 3*)

NEPA (National Environmental Policy Act) Requires state and local governments to prepare an environmental impact statement (EIS) for a federally financed project with a significant environmental impact. (*Chapter 8*)

Nephelometric Turbidity Units (NTU) (*Chapter 9*)

NFF (needed fire flow) The amount of water required to control a fire. (*Chapter 3*)

NFIP (National Flood Insurance Program) (*Chapter 5*)

NFPA (National Fire Protection Association) The international fire-standard setting body. (*Chapter 3*)

NGA (National Governors Association) (*Chapter 5*)

NHTSA (National Highway Traffic Safety Administration) (*Chapter 2*)

NIBRS (National Incident-Based Reporting System) (*Chapter 2*)

NIFRS (National Incident Fire Reporting System For reporting fire incidence, fire causes, injuries, deaths, and property loss. (*Chapter 3*)

NIMS (National Incident Management System) Unifies the command of multiple jurisdictions at the scene of an emergency. (*Chapter 3 and Chapter 5*)

NML (National Municipal League) (*Chapter 1*)

notification time The interval between the first ring of the 911 call and its transfer to the fire dispatcher. (*Chapter 3*)

novachip seal A coat of polymer-modified asphalt emulsion applied before an ultra-thin overlay of graded hot-mix asphalt. (*Chapter 11*)

NPDES (National Pollutant Discharge Elimination System) (*Chapter 10*)

NRPA (National Recreation and Park Association) (*Chapter 15*)

NTU (Nephelometric Turbidity Units) (*Chapter 9*)

NVOAD (National Volunteer Organizations Active in Disaster) Includes thirty-four national, fifty-two state, and territorial and local organizations. (*Chapter 5*)

O

O&M (operation and maintenance) (*Chapter 10*)

origin-and-destination (O&D) study Conducted by a transportation planner to model where drivers originate their trip, their likely destination, and the amount and type of traffic flow. (*Chapter 8 and Chapter 11*)

oxidation Caused by aeration, combines oxygen with undesirable metals (usually iron or manganese) in the water to remove dissolved materials. (*Chapter 9*)

ozonation Disinfects wastewater without chlorine. (*Chapter 10*)

P

PAC (powder activated carbon) Chemical used in adsorption. (*Chapter 9*)

package-treatment plant Filtration system for water that includes a coagulation/flocculation unit, a settling-floc separation tank, and a gravity-pressure filter. (*Chapter 9*)

paid-on-call firefighter Paid only for the time spent responding to a service call. (*Chapter 3*)

partial-scale exercise Evaluates limited emergency response objectives, often combining an in-house simulation with teams deployed to the field. (*Chapter 5*)

PDAs (personal digital assistants) (*Chapter 2*)

performance bond To insure against faulty work. (*Chapter 11*)

personal digital assistants (PDAs) (*Chapter 2*)

PIO (public information officer) Informs the media of the emergency's status, evacuation routes, contact numbers, shelter locations, and streets that are closed. (*Chapter 2 and Chapter 5*)

PLA (Public Library Association) (*Chapter 14*)

platform or pit station A large solid-waste transfer station that temporarily stores refuse at peak collection times. (*Chapter 12*)

PM (preventive maintenance) (*Chapter 16 and Chapter 17*)

polyvinyl chloride (PVC) (*Chapter 10*)

POP (problem-oriented-policing) Focuses on problems (a series of related incidents) not incidents. (*Chapter 2*)

post-traumatic stress disorder (PTSD) (*Chapter 3*)

pounds per square inch (PSI) (*Chapter 3*)

powder activated carbon (PAC) Chemical used in adsorption. (*Chapter 9*)

preventive maintenance (PM) (*Chapter 16 and Chapter 17*)

primary treatment of wastewater Screening grit and other large suspended materials with a cage screen and a grit chamber. (*Chapter 10*)

prime movers Electronic motors and engines to drive water pumps. (*Chapter 9*)

problem-oriented-policing (POP) Focuses on problems (a series of related incidents) not incidents. (*Chapter 2*)

problem-oriented survey Asks citizens to identify the causes of, and solutions to, problems in the neighborhood, such as gangs, speeding traffic, or burglaries. (*Chapter 2*)

process control system plan A statement of a plant's sewage-treatment goals according to the NPDES permit. (*Chapter 10*)

prosecution rate The percentage of arrests accepted by the prosecutor. (*Chapter 2*)

PSI (pounds per square inch) (*Chapter 3*)

PTSD (post-traumatic stress disorder) (*Chapter 3*)

public information officer (PIO) Informs the media of the emergency's status, evacuation routes, contact numbers, shelter locations, and streets that are closed. (*Chapter 2 and Chapter 5*)

Public Library Association (PLA) (*Chapter 14*)

pumper A fire service vehicle outfitted with a pump, hoses and nozzles, a tank for water or other extinguishing agent, and ladders. (*Chapter 3*)

pursuit-driving policy Specifies the conditions under which an officer should drive a police vehicle in pursuit of a fleeing violator. (*Chapter 2*)

PVC (polyvinyl chloride) (*Chapter 10*)

pyrolysis Solid-waste disposal by chemical change through heating; converts wastes to a low-sulfur, gaseous liquid for use as fuel. (*Chapter 12*)

Q

quint apparatus A combined pumper and ladder truck equipped with ground ladders and an aerial device. (*Chapter 3*)

R

rapid-sand plant Pretreats water with iron, alum, sulfate, and other coagulants. (*Chapter 9*)

real-time computerized system A type of inventory system used by local governments. (*Chapter 16*)

record map The final plat (subdivision map) recorded with the register of deeds. (*Chapter 8*)

request for proposals (RFP) (*Chapter 14*)

reserve firefighter Performs non-firefighting functions like fire prevention. (*Chapter 3*)

residuals Produced in wastewater treatment. (*Chapter 10*)

return-activated sludge The settled material that returns to the aeration tank to reseed the sewage entering the tank in activated sludge wastewater treatment. (*Chapter 10*)

RFP (request for proposals) (*Chapter 14*)

Risk, Hazard, and Value Evaluation (RHAVE) Model used to assess fire risk. (*Chapter 3*)

rotating biological contractor Used in wastewater treatment, it consists of plastic discs mounted on a long, horizontal, rotating shaft. (*Chapter 10*)

S

sanitary sewer Carries waste in pipes made of cement, bituminized fiber, cast-iron soil, ductile iron, clay, concrete, or plastic. (*Chapter 10*)

scanning, analysis, response, and assessment methodology (SARA) (*Chapter 2*)

SCBA (self-contained breathing apparatus) (*Chapter 3*)

school resource officers (SROs) Prevent crimes and maintain order in schools. (*Chapter 2*)

scrubbing Action caused by aeration, which turbulently mixes water and air, physically removing the gases into the surrounding air. (*Chapter 9*)

seasonal water rate structure Imposes a higher rate during a resort town's tourist season, because the system must be built to accommodate the peak seasonal demand. (*Chapter 9*)

sedimentation A process that removes settleable solids suspended in water, thus decreasing the filtration load. Plain sedimentation settles heavy sediments by gravity, without adding chemicals. Chemical sedimentation settles heavier sediments by chemical treatment. (*Chapter 9 and Chapter 10*)

self-contained breathing apparatus (SCBA) (*Chapter 3*)

service plan Specifies the level of service to be given to library patrons. (*Chapter 14*)

Sewer Use Ordinance (SUO) (*Chapter 10*)

sketch plan A simple proposal, consisting of a location map, property-line map, and the general layout of a proposed subdivision. (*Chapter 8*)

Slote method In library collection management; to set a cutoff usage date by taking a representative sample of consecutively checked-out items to determine their return and checkout dates. (*Chapter 14*)

sludge The settled material in activated sludge wastewater treatment. (*Chapter 10*)

slurry seal A mixture of well-graded, fine-aggregate mineral filler, asphalt emulsion, and water. (*Chapter 11*)

smart growth Recommends that areas be more densely developed using redevelopment of existing developments (in-fill), land-use controls, and tax policies. (*Chapter 8*)

smoldering The stage in a fire when heat contacts a combustible material. (*Chapter 3*)

SOGs (standard operating guidelines) (*Chapter 5*)

solvability criteria Used to estimate the likelihood of a case being solved. (*Chapter 2*)

spot zoning Occurs when a small area of land or section in an existing neighborhood is placed in a different zone from that of neighboring property. (*Chapter 8*)

SROs (school resource officers) Prevent crimes and maintain order in schools. (*Chapter 2*)

standard operating guidelines (SOGs) (*Chapter 5*)

storm drain Carries surface runoff water and underground seepage in pipes made of cement, steel, aluminum, clay, or concrete. (*Chapter 10*)

stubout A street with a temporary dead end, which will eventually become a through street. (*Chapter 8*)

subdivision plat Shows streets, lot lines, and easements (right of way) for utilities. (*Chapter 8*)

SUO (Sewer Use Ordinance) (*Chapter 10*)

suspect-detection rate The percentage of cases in which a suspect was identified after the initial investigation. (*Chapter 2*)

T

tabletop exercise Tabletop practice by an emergency response unit of a hypothetical scenario featuring situations likely to be faced in a particular emergency. (*Chapter 5*)

technical fire inspection An inspection of an industrial plant conducted by a specially trained inspector. (*Chapter 3*)

technical review committee Reviews the preliminary plat for a major subdivision. (*Chapter 8*)

technology plan Articulates a library's technology objectives. (*Chapter 14*)

Technology Transfer Program (TTP) (*Chapter 11*)

thermal treatment A method of stabilizing sludge from wastewater treatment by evaporating the residuals using heat drying. (*Chapter 10*)

thickening A method of stabilizing sludge from wastewater treatment by reducing the volume of the residuals by extracting water from the slurry. (*Chapter 10*)

TIA (Transportation Impact Analysis) Estimates road capacity and provides for reducing road congestion and establishing safe turning and deceleration lanes. (*Chapter 8*)

tiered emergency response system Distinguishes between a paramedic-level and basic-service-level response. (*Chapter 4*)

TNR (trap, neuter, and release) A program to control feral cats. (*Chapter 6*)

total suspended solids (TSS) Measurement used in wastewater treatment. (*Chapter 10*)

trap, neuter, and release (TNR) A program to control feral cats. (*Chapter 6*)

Transportation Impact Analysis (TIA) Estimates road capacity and provides for reducing road congestion and establishing safe turning and deceleration lanes. (*Chapter 8*)

trickling filter A three- to ten-foot deep bed of coarse media, often plastic or stones, known as the filter media; it is used in wastewater treatment. (*Chapter 10*)

TSS (total suspended solids) Measurement used in wastewater treatment. (*Chapter 10*)

TTP (Technology Transfer Program) (*Chapter 11*)

turbidity Water sediment that interferes with disinfection and causes bad odors, bad taste, and bacterial growth. (*Chapter 9*)

U

ultraviolet (UV) irradiation A method of wastewater disinfection that kills bacteria and viruses by destroying their genetic material. (*Chapter 10*)

unaccounted-for water The difference between water produced (metered at the treatment facility) and metered use (water sales plus non-revenue-producing metered use). (*Chapter 9*)

uniform water rate structure A minimum monthly charge and a flat charge per 1,000 gallons to residential, commercial, and industrial customers. (*Chapter 9*)

unstable water Corrodes or scales pipelines and plumbing fixtures. (*Chapter 9*)

U.S. Fire Administration (USFA) (*Chapter 3*)

use variation When a property would otherwise be valueless or when it is near another property to which a variance has been granted. (*Chapter 8*)

user-fee policy specifies the percentage of each recreation program's costs to be recovered by a fee. (*Chapter 15*)

UV (ultraviolet) (*Chapter 10*)

V

variable shift Assigns some officers to a fixed shift and other officers to a variable shift. (*Chapter 2*)

vested-rights provision In the subdivision ordinance; allows the developer time to complete a subdivision under pre-amendment conditions. (*Chapter 8*)

volunteer firefighter Receives no compensation, other than perhaps a stipend for out-of-pocket expenses or time spent in training. (*Chapter 3*)

W

waste-activated sludge The sludge that remains in the settling tank during activated sludge wastewater treatment. (*Chapter 10*)

water hammer Erratic changes in water pressure. (*Chapter 9*)

wet tap Made in a water main under pressure. (*Chapter 9*)

Index

D

E

About the Author

Charles K. Coe (PhD) is professor of Public Administration in the Department of Public Administration, North Carolina State University. He is the author of *Public and Nonprofit Financial Management* (Management Concepts, 2007), *Purchasing and Inventory Management Handbook* (Sheshunoff Information Services, 1998), and *Public Financial Management* (Prentice-Hall, 1989), as well as numerous journal articles and handbooks. He has fourteen year's experience serving six years as Budget Officer of Grand Rapids, Michigan and eight years as a consultant to local governments while at the Carl Vinson Institute of Government, University of Georgia.

Made in the USA
Lexington, KY
04 August 2017